*Languages of the World*

33

full text research
abstracts of all titles
monthly updates

*LINCOM webshop*
**www.lincom-europa.com**

# Daughters of Esperanto

*Alan Reed Libert*

University of Newcastle

2008
LINCOM EUROPA

Published by LINCOM GmbH 2008.


All correspondence concerning Languages of the World should be addressed to:


LINCOM GmbH
Gmunder Str. 35
D-81379 Muenchen


LINCOM.EUROPA@t-online.de
http://home.t-online.de/home/LINCOM.EUROPA
www.lincom-europa.com

Die Deutsche Bibliothek - CIP Cataloguing-in-Publication-Data

A catalogue record for this publication is available from Die Deutsche Bibliothek (http://www.ddb.de)


Printed in E.C.
Printed on chlorine-free paper

# CONTENTS

# Preface

I have often preserved the incorrect spelling or punctuation of quotations, i.e only sometimes have I corrected errors in punctuation, spelling, and formatting. In examples I do not always show the full morphological analysis of words when this is not relevant to the point being discussed. When I have omitted one or more entire sentences while quoting I have put ellipsis points inside square brackets; when I have omitted one or more words within a sentence I have used only ellipsis points.

Several designers of languages discussed in this book helped me by giving me information on their languages, and I thank them for this. The Interlibrary Services section of the libraries of the University of Newcastle has been of considerable assistance, for which I am indeed grateful. I also thank Shinji Ido, Silvia Ratcheva, and Jia Hongge for proofreading; in addition Hongge provided much appreciated help with formatting. Of course I alone am responsible for any remaining errors or shortcomings in this work.

I dedicate this book to the memory of my friend and former colleague from the University of Newcastle, George M. Horn.

# Abbreviations

ACC – accusative
ADJ – adjective (word class marker for adjectives)
ADV – adverb (word class marker for adverbs)
antepres. – antepresent
art. – article
att. – attributive
C – common gender (masculine or feminine, but not neuter)
cat. - category
CAUS – causative
CN – common gender including neuter
condit./CONDIT – conditional
copret. – copreterite (a tense of Hom-idyomo)
demonst. – demonstrative
DIR – directional (case)
direct. – direction
E-tida – Esperantida
F – feminine
FOC – focus particle
FUT – future
FUTPASSPARTIC – future passive participle
GART – generic article
hypoth./HYPOTH – hypothetic (a mood of Hom-idyomo)
Hom-id. – Hom-idyomo
imm. – immediate
IMPER – imperative
indef. – indefinite
INFIN – infinitive
M – masculine
mann. – manner
Mod. Esp. – Modern Esperanto
MT – my translation (as opposed to one given by the source)
N – neuter
n.d. – no date
neg. – negative
NF – name forming suffix (in Aiola)
NFD – suffix attached to derived names (or derived members of simple derived name combinations) within complex derived names (in Aiola)
NN – word class marker for nouns
NOM – nominative
Nov-Esp. – Nov-Esperanto
particip. – participle
PASSPARTIC – passive participle
pers. – person
PRESPARTIC – present participle
PRESPASSPARTIC – present passive participle
PSTPARTIC – past participle
PL - plural

possess. – possessive
prep. – preposition
pres./PRES – present
pret./PRET – preterite
PROG – progressive
PST – past
Q – question particle
quant. – quantity
RA – relational adjective forming suffix (in Aiola)
rel. – relational
SG – singular
suggest./SUGGEST – suggestive (a mood of Hom-idyomo)
tr. – translation
univ. – universal
Virgor. – Virgoranto
VOC – vocative

I use the asterisk (*) for a form which is to my knowledge unattested, or for a non-existent word.

# 1      Introduction

Esperanto is the most successful artificial language. However, some of those who learned it were not satisfied with it, and changed it in various ways, and other language designers borrowed heavily from it for their languages. This book is about some of the languages which resulted from such processes, i.e. modified or "reformed" versions of Esperanto and languages based at least to some extent on Esperanto. I shall refer to all of these languages as "daughters of Esperanto", although some of them have taken very many components from other languages, and might not be seen as descendants of Esperanto in a strict sense. In general I only describe points on which these languages differ from Esperanto and I do not describe all such features, but I hope that I shall have given an idea of what these languages are like.

The best known and most successful daughter of Esperanto is Ido, and I shall treat it in this book. However, I shall not discuss projects to reform or modify Ido, which could be seen as granddaughters of Esperanto.[1] Most of the present chapter will be devoted to introducing the languages that I shall be dealing with.

## 1.1      Aiola/Ayola

The "Chief Developer of Ayola" (ARG 2008) is Richard W. Stimets, but at least to some extent Ayola is the product of a collaborative effort, namely by the Ayola Research Group (ARG). Ayola (*Aiola* being an earlier version of the name) seems to have been constructed from several sources: ARG (2005:3) says, "In developing Aiola, ARG has borrowed many ideas from previous international languages such as Esperanto, Interlingua and Loglan, and introduced many new ideas of its own. Ayola's vocabulary and some of its grammatical attributes are largely based on those found in the Romance (Latin, Italian, French, Spanish, and Portuguese) and Germanic (English, German) languages". Further, in the "FAQ" part of the Ayolo website (ARG 2008) is the following answer to the question "Is Ayola a revision of any other constructed language, such as Esperanto, Loglan, or Interlingua?":

> It is essentially impossible in creating a constructed language to produce a result that does not share some features in common with previous attempts. The term 'revision' implies a high correlation between the original and the revised version, i.e. a correlation coefficient of 75 -100%. The correlation between Ayola and other previous international languages such as Esperanto, Interlingua, and Loglan is considerably less than this range for the three principal grammatical categories of word endings, prefixes and suffixes, and roots.

However, some people have judged it to be similar to Esperanto. For example, according to Cowan (2004), "Aiola is essentially Esperanto spelled out in Loglan and with a few Loglan ideas in it". The *Langmaker* website page on the language (Henning n.d. a) states, "By the website's own admission, the very first 'version' of **Aiola** appears to have been a modified Esperanto, although it also admits that the language has since moved significantly far away from that language." Thus it might

---

[1] Among the projects of this type mentioned by Monnerot-Dumaine (1960:108) are Ido Novialisat, Ido simpligita, Ido reformita, Dutalingue, Italico, and Ido Avancit.

be like Neo (v. sec. 1.20), a language descended from Esperanto, but one which over time has come to be rather different from its parent. At the time of writing this (July 2008) the grammar of Ayola was not available on the Ayola website and I have used the formerly available grammar ARG (2005) as my main source for the language.[2] This work uses the previous name for the language (*Aiola*) and that is the name which I shall use from now on.

## 1.2    Arlipo

The creator of Arlipo (from Artifika Lingvo por Omni) is Lubor Vitek. He lists (Vitek n.d. a) several features that an international auxiliary language should have, including "[f]acila prononco" ('easy pronunciation'), "[s]impla kaj logika gramatiko" ('simple and logical grammar'), and "[m]axima parencezo kun le monde plej disvastigita naturala lingvi, tak pri vortstoko, tak anke pri gramatiko" ('maximum relatedness with the world's most widespread languages, both concerning the vocabulary, and also concerning the grammar'), though he is aware that "omna artifia lingvo esat kompromiso" ('every artificial language is a compromise') (ibid.). Although Arlipo is "surzbaze di Esperanto, Ido kaj ikva plusa lingvi" ('based on Esperanto, Ido, and some other languages') (ibid.), Vitek has made changes from Esperanto and Ido so that it will have the desired features. Vitek's webpages (the major sources on the language to my knowledge) include a short description of the grammar, a fairly extensive Arlipo-English dictionary, and a text (the "Gospel of Mark").

## 1.3    Atlango

The designer of Atlango is Richard A. Antonius, who says (2008b):

> **ATLANGO** is an international, Euroamerican auxiliary language intended as a lingua franca for citizens of different countries to learn. Atlango is a **highly euphonious** ("angloromaneska") and **easy to learn** language and without any special accented letters like in Esperanto. Atlango can be learned considerably quicker than any other natural language.
> This language turns to be **the real candidate** to become the basis for **a neutral and common language for Europe** but also for North and South America. [...] Atlango is easy to learn and pronounce and much more euphonious than old constructed languages - Esperanto, Ido, Occidental, Novial, Neo and Interlingua. Atlango can be used as a democratic and intermediary language for all people.
> An excellent **bridge language** between different cultures and traditions.

Concerning the sources for the language he says (ibid.) that it is "bazita su-l cefa langoy di Europo kay Amerika, cefa langoy konstruktita kay le lango Latina" ('based on the main languages of Europe and America, main constructed languages and the Latin language'). Atlango has various features in common with Esperanto, including the word class endings for nouns, adjectives, and adverbs, the infinitive suffix -*i*,  the causative suffix -*ig*-, and the prefix *bo*-. Some affixes and words have

---

different spellings in the two languages but the same pronunciation (due to orthographic differences), e.g. Atlango *-ac-* and Esperanto *-aĉ-*, or are phonetically similar, e.g. Atlango *-ily-* and Esperanto *-il-*. I have obtained information on Atlango from the fairly extensive webpages Antonius (2008b) and (2008c). Antonius has made modifications to his language, which he mentions in another webpage (Antonius 2008a).

## 1.4    Baza

Baza (or Inter-esperanto) was designed by Greg Hoover in 2003. Its main difference from Esperanto is that its lexicon is a subset of that of Esperanto (It is thus the same type of language as Basic English.) The web page *Inter-esperanto* (Hoover:n.d.)) states, "When communicating in Baza, one must submit to the discipline of using only the prescribed vocabulary to express communicative intent. In some languages, using many words is a sign of sophistication. In Baza, the reverse is true".

Although Baza, like Esperanto, was apparently created to serve as a means of communication among speakers of different languages, it was also meant to serve two other purposes: it "functions as a simple basic language that can unite the speaking communities of Esperanto, Ido, Mondlango, and other Esperanto derived language systems" (ibid.) and it "can also simple [sic] be a stepping stone language, learned prior to studying traditional Esperanto, Ido, Mo[n]dlango, and other Esperanto-based language systems" (ibid.). I am not aware of any published materials on this language; my information on it comes largely from the above mentioned web page "Inter-esperanto".

## 1.5    The DLT Intermediate Language

The Distributed Language Translation (DLT) project (which A. P. M Witkam started and which was based in Utrecht) used a modified version of Esperanto as the "intermediate language" (Schubert 1992:78) between source and target languages for translation by computers. The DLT Intermediate Language is not very different from Esperanto; Schubert (ibid.:88) says:

> At the end of the prototype phase [of the development of the DLT Intermediate Language], the difference between common Esperanto and DLT's version can be summarized under a single condition; DLT's version is *syntactically* unambiguous. The term *syntax* is meant in a broad sense which covers all grammatical properties on the formal side of the linguistic sign …

Some of the features of this language are not original but come from earlier modified versions of Esperanto, as Schubert (1986) acknowledges. The DLT Intermediate Language changed somewhat over time; I shall treat the version presented in Schubert (1986).[3] Although this may not have been the final version of the language, it has some interesting features.

---

[3] Therefore when I say "the DLT Intermediate Language" I mean this version of it.

## 1.6    Ekselsioro

Ekselsioro was the work of Frederic Greenwood, who was also the designer of the language Ulla. On the title page of Greenwood (1906a) and (1906b) it is claimed that Ekselsioro "can be Telegraphed, Signalled, Codified, Printed, Typed, Spoken, Sung, Written and Easily Read" and that it is "The Last and Best of all attempts hitherto made. Sonorous, Flowing and Musical. Adapted to Travel, Commerce and Science". The following page in Greenwood (1906a), which is a "reklamajo" ('advertisement'), contains the following statements:

> There is no doubt but that the extensive knowledge of languages had made it possible for the author, having all the efforts and assistance of *Previous Language Builders Before Him*, to produce at least *the Best Universal Language Yet Given to the People*, for be it well noted that
> EKSELSIORO IS FOR THE PEOPLE,
> *AS WELL AS FOR THE LEARNED*, being a practical Every Day Language, which the ordinary mind may easily assimilate. *IN SHORT A BREAD WINNER.*

According to Monnerot-Dumaine (1960:169) Ekselsioro is "Esperanto très peu modifié".

## 1.7    La Lingvo Esperantida and Other Languages of René de Saussure

René de Saussure (1868-1943) created several modified versions of Esperanto over the course of about 30 years. Apparently his involvement in the Esperanto movement was due to his brother Ferdinand, one of the major figures in modern linguistics, who had him attend the 2nd Universal Congress of Esperanto (held in 1906 in Geneva). Künzli (2001) says that he "apartenas al tiuj raraj lingvistoj, kiuj kritikis Esperanton el lingscienca vidpunkto por trovi kompromison inter Esperanto kaj Ido".

The languages and versions of languages by de Saussure that are mentioned by Künzli (2001) are: Lingwo Internaciona di Antido 1 (1907), Esperanto de Antido 2 (1910), Lingvo Kosmopolita (1912), Lingvo Internatsia de Antido (1917), "Reformita Esperanto proponita en la broŝura 'Les "tares" de l'espéranto/Die "Mängel" des Esperanto'" (1917), Esperantido de Antido (1919), Esperantido de Antido (1920), Esperantido dialekto de Esperanto, de Antido (1922), Esperantido da Antido (1924), Nov-Esperanto/Idiomo Mondialo (1925-32), Universal Eo (1935), and Esperanto II (1937). According to Monnerot-Dumaine (1960:69) Saussure's "espérantides" are "assez proche de l'Ido, malgré son pseudonym d'Antido". I have information from primary sources for only three of de Saussure's projects (la lingvo Esperantida as described in de Saussure (1919), la lingvo Esperantida as described in de Saussure (1923),[4] and Nov-Esperanto as described in de Saussure 1926[5]), and I shall

---

[4] I shall refer to these as 1919 Esperantida and 1923 Esperantida respectively although the proper name of the language is *la lingvo Esperantida*. In De Saussure (1919:2) is the following "notico" ('note'): "La Akademio decidis, ke la vorto *Esperantido* signas persono (ne lingvo). La lingvo Esperantida estas do la lingva de la Esperantidon, kie la lingvo franca estas la lingvo de la francon" (The [Esperantida] Academy has decided that the word *Esperantido* denotes a person (not a language). The Esperantida

concentrate on these; Kunzli (ibid.) gives very brief information on and samples of 11 of his projects. There is also a website devoted to Nov-Esperanto, whose home page is Selva (2006).

## 1.8    E-speranto

E-speranto is the work of Neville Holmes, who states (Holmes n.d. a):

> E-speranto is an artificial language intended only as a[n] auxiliary language to make cross-cultural communication easier. A side-effect will be to make translation by machine easier. Esperanto has precisely the same objective, but its adherents tend to overlook this ideal, and come to propound its virtues as a literary language in its own right. Whether or not Esperanto is suitable for literary creation is irrelevant, and advertising this virtue does no good to Esperanto's prospects for wider acceptance.

Holmes (ibid.) says that "E-speranto is a dialect of Esperanto". I have obtained my information on E-speranto from Holmes's webpages about it and from Holmes (2008), as well as from personal communications from Holmes. These materials only give limited on the details of the language. Further, there are some differences in the language as described in the webpages and in Holmes (2008); I shall refer to these two version of the language as webpage E-speranto and 2008 E-speranto.

## 1.9    Esperanto sen Fleksio

Esperanto sen Fleksio (EsF) was created by Rick Harrison. He states that it "is a proposed dialect of ... Esperanto" (Harrison 2004) and that it "is an experiment". It "eliminates many of the unnecessary grammatical inflections that cause trouble for people whose native languages (e.g. Chinese, Indonesian, English) have simpler grammars than traditional Esperanto" (ibid.). EsF only involves four changes from Esperanto, one of which is not related to inflection (v. section 2.1). Harrison (ibid.) had some further ideas about modifying Esperanto:

> ... I have noticed a few things about my own style of EsF. Please experiment and see if you develop a similar style.
> · I use *la* less frequently.
> · I feel the need for an optional way to express plural nouns. Not a suffix, but rather a short word that behaves exactly like *tri*, *kvar* etc. and means "more than one."
> · I feel the need for a particle that would allow us to make some "topic, comment" sentences.
> · I feel the need for a way to turn adjectives into stative verbs. Instead of *esti granda* I seem to want to say *grandazi* (or something).

---

language is therefore the language of the Esperantidists, as the French language is the language of the French [people]').
[5] De Sassure wrote several works on Nov-Esperanto, and not all of the details of the language were identical in all of these works; when I refer to Nov-Esperanto, I mean the version of the language presented in de Saussure (1926).

One might note that EsF is not entirely "without inflection": although the past, present, and future tense suffixes have been done away with, as well as most of the participial suffixes, this is not true of the infinitive, conditional, and imperative endings, as we see in the following examples:

(1a)    Ven-u          via      regno.
        come-IMPER    your    kingdom
        'thy kingdom come' (ibid.)

(1b)    ... vi    pov-us          forlas-i          sufero
         you    can-CONDIT    abandon-INFIN    suffering
        '... you could abandon suffering' (ibid., MT)

Two participial endings have also been retained, *-anta* and *-ita*.

## 1.10    Esperloja

Esperloja was apparently designed by Larry Sulky, who says at the beginning of his webpage entitled *Esperanto by Hindsight: A Smug Redesign* (Sulky, n.d.)

> If only Professor Zamenhof had been as enlightened as we all are in the fabulous 21st century! He would have avoided diacritical marks because computer keyboards were not going to like them. [...]
> The fact is, Esperanto was an amazing creation, as shown by the fact that it has survived for about a century. There are just a few things about it that bug me. So I'll correct them here."

To my knowledge the only substantial source on Esperloja is this webpage by Sulky, who is also the creator of a language called Ilomi.

## 1.11    Farlingo

Farlingo is the work of Matvei Farber (and Vladmir Faber?) and, like the DLT Intermediate Language, was designed to be an intermediate language for computer translators. As far as I know, information on this language is only available from internet sources, mainly from the webpages by Matvei and Vladmir Farber. There is a webpage in Russian on grammar and glossaries from Farlingo into several languages, including Arabic, Bulgarian, and Danish, and English. Farlingo drew on a relatively large number of languages for its construction: Henning (n.d. b) gives as "Language sources" for it "Esperanto, English, French, Spain [sic], Italian, Russian, Hebrew, Yiddish.

## 1.12    Hom-Idyomo

The designer of Hom-iyomo was C. Cárdenas, who says of it, "I may confess that Hom-idyomo is not so easy to learn as Esperanto is, but it is incomparably easier to practise, on account of the abundance of words with which it is endowed and which express exactly and separately every one of the ideas of any scholastic man. In the actual state of Esperanto, nobody is able to translate into it, with sufficient clearness, even half of the English dictionary" (Cárdenas 1923:vi). In spite of this admitted difficulty in learning the language, Cárdenas (ibid.) asserts that it "can be learned, easily and completely, by a work of half an hour a day during one year." To my knowledge Cárdenas (1923) does not explicitly acknowledge any debt to Esperanto, and makes the following statement about how he created it (ibid.:vi): "It has been formed by opening simultaneously five national dictionaries and selecting from them each common word, carefully not changing its form but what has been strictly necessary to arrange the whole in groups ruled by Logic and Philosophy. No preference has been given to any of the five languages by sympathy or passion, only for the sake of simplicity and to the good of humanity." However, an examination of Hom-idyomo will reveal many features that it shares with Esperanto, e.g. the prefixes *bo-* and *ge-*, the suffixes *-em*, *-et*, *-il*, and *-in*, and the word class endings for nouns, adjectives, and adverbs. My source for this language is Cárdenas (1923), a long book containing a grammar and dictionaries from Hom-idyomo to English and from English into Hom-idyomo.

## 1.13   Ido

As mentioned above, Ido achieved more popularity than any other attempt to modify Esperanto and is one of the few artificial languages of any type that has had a real community of speakers. The story of Ido has involved a considerable amount of bitterness and some of the facts may be in dispute; what follows is one version of it. In 1901 the Délégation pour l'adoption d'une langue auxiliaire internationale, which was the idea of Louis Couturat and Léopold Leau, was created and in 1907 a committee of it was organized to decide on the best artificial language. The two major candidates were Esperanto and Idiom Neutral. Louis de Beaufront acted as the advocate for the former. Esperanto emerged as the winner, however, not Zamenhof's form of it, but a modified form that had been put forth anonymously ("Ido" was given as the name of its author; it may have been the work of Couturat, who was one of those making the decision, and/or de Beaufront, who, as has already been said, was supposed to have been arguing on behalf of Esperanto.) Zamenhof rejected this outcome, and there were many who supported him and were proponents of the unchanged version of the language, while others became adherents of the modified form of Esperanto, i.e. of Ido, which underwent some more changes. Thus occurred the so-called "Ido schism" and since then relations between the two camps (or at least some of the people in them) have sometimes been quite unfriendly.

As one would expect of a language associated with so much controversy, opinions on it vary. Kellerman (1909:844) considered Ido not as good as Esperanto, with aesthetics being involved with his view: "Esperanto is more musical, for in cutting out the six supersigned letters Ido and its related systems have been forced to reduce the sounds also; thus a so-called 'purification' has resulted in monotony." He also (ibid.) brings up ease of learning or use: "Ido ... with its harsh Anglo-Saxon pronunciation of the letter *j*, and its fixed Franco-English word order would prove troublesome to most Europeans." The prominent linguist Otto Jespersen was a proponent of Ido before he designed the language Novial. His (1918/1921:36-38) views on the relative advantages of Esperanto and Ido were: "... for Esperanto there is only to be said its greater number of adherents ... Everything else tells in favor of Ido. It is not the product of a single person, and for that reason it is free from the caprices, fancies and individual preferences which a single person can with difficulty avoid. [...] Ido has a vocabulary more extensive and worked out more exactly; it has in general a better conscience in all respects."

Collinson (1924) is a defense of Esperanto in response to criticism from proponents of Ido and in turn brings up what he sees as shortcomings of Ido; these will be mentioned in appropriate parts of the present book, but his general view is:

> In important particulars Ido is retrograde, and careful examination of both languages does not lend support to the view that, as a whole, Ido represents an advance upon Esperanto. From the point of view of the International Language movement generally the launching of Ido and the manner of its presentment to the public have been a psychological blunder of the first magnitude. Until something much better than Ido comes their way, Esperantists will not be tempted to desert a language for which they have conceived a real affection and which they have learned to handle with skill, grace, and power.

Talmey (1938:177) judged Ido to be "vastly superior to any previous project", although he thought Ido was an "absurd name" (ibid.).[6] Bodmer (1944:472) says, "In some ways Ido is better [than Esperanto], but it has the same defective foundations as Esperanto. [...] The system of derivative affixes has been pruned of some glaring absurdities, but inflated by a fresh battery based on quasi-logical pre-occupations". Monnerot-Dumaine (1960:105) states that "L'Ido est agréable à parler. Il est plus facile à traduire que l'Esperanto, pour des Européens." Large (1985:137) states, "Anyone seeking the way to an ideal world through a shared language is likely to be attracted by the more successful Esperantist movement; Ido is likely to appeal only to those who believe that a real or supposed linguistic superiority over Esperanto outweighs its numerical insignificance in terms of supporters." An interesting comparison of Esperanto and Ido (and one that is perhaps more objective than some of those made in the past) is that by Barandovská-Frank (1993), who examines Esperanto, Ido, some other artificial languages, and Latin with respect to 36 criteria of several types: "Komunika kapablo" (ibid.:89), for example "Bona akustika diferencigo de sonoj" (ibid.), "Estetika akcepteblo" (ibid.:90), "Rilato al etnaj lingvoj" (ibid.), "Neŭtraleco" (ibid.), "Lerneblo" (ibid.), Teknika uzeblo", Gobbo (2005) looks at the potential of Esperanto, Ido, Interlingua, Latin, and English for use by the European Union and comes to the following view of Ido:

> Ido has discarded the delicate equilibrium of Esperanto grammar in favor of a clearer but narrower direction: occidentalization. Its grammar may prove unsatisfactory to many EU citizens, as well as speakers of Slavic and Germanic languages, except English. However, most speakers of the Romance group (even if it may 'sound bad', especially to Italians) may be satisfied as there is a certain degree of familiarity at first glance, more than with Esperanto.

---

[6] Talmey was involved in the Ido movement, but became disillusioned with it and designed a revised version of Ido. In fact, he had previously been an proponent of Esperanto but "abandoned it ... having convinced myself of its unfitness even for the rôle of the IL [International Language]" (Talmey 1938:177).

It is interesting, given the hostility towards Ido by many adherents of Esperanto, that Jordan (1987:110) believes that Esperanto may owe its current status partly to Ido: "Esperanto might not have succeeded without the Volapük and Ido movements. [...] Ido probably drew reformists out of Esperanto, leaving the movement loyalists it required. Without Volapük to set the stage and Ido to draw away perfectionists, Esperanto might have collapsed."

There is a large amount of material about and/or in Ido, including a *Bibliographio di Ido* (Carlevaro and Haupenthal 1999). I have gotten most of my information about the details of the language from the extensive grammar by de Beaufront (1925/2005).

## 1.14    Intero

Marq Thompson and Jonathan Moore designed Intero, which dates from 2004. Thompson (2007a) describes the origin of the language as follows: "We both speak Esperanto, both agree that Esperanto has flaws, and both agree that Ido did a poor job of reforming Esperanto. Thus, we began discussing the flaws of Esperanto and before long, we were creating (yet another) clone of it. We decided to call it Intero while we worked on it, and the name stuck. Intero gets its name from the Esperanto preposition inter meaning 'between'." By "between" he means "between Esperanto and Ido" (ibid.), but Thompson does not have a positive view of Ido, since he says (ibid.), "Intero seeks to improve Esperanto as Ido failed to do" and "Intero shall not be a disaster similar to Ido." Thompson (ibid.) also states, "Intero shall not deviate from Esperanto any further than is judged necessary" and "Intero shall be no more than a dialect of Esperanto". There is a feature of Intero which is "not a necessary deviation from Esperanto" (ibid.), the indefinite article, but one is not required to use it. To my knowledge material on this language is only available on the internet; my main source for it is Thompson (2007a).

## 1.15    Linguna

Linguna stands out among the languages discussed in this book in the sense that in several ways it is considerably more complicated than Esperanto. Some other daughters of Esperanto add complications to some part of the grammar, but Linguna to my knowledge is the most complex language derived from Esperanto, and after looking at it one might wonder whether its designer, Hans Dieter Wilhelm Goeres, seriously intended it to be used. The following passage (Goeres n.d.) shows that Linguna was seen as a descendant of Esperanto and gives an idea of what Goeres thought about his language (including the surprising assertion about its simplicity):

> Die neutral angelegte Völkerständigungssprache LINGUA ist eine kosmopolitisiche und internationale Sprache, aufgebaut auf neueste linguistische und etymologishche Erkenntnisse. Die Natülichkeit beachtend, als Fortentwicklung von Esperanto und Esperanto Moderna, ist sie logisch, klar und einfach zu erlernen. [...]
> Sie ist dabei weit einfacher als z.B. Englisch oder andere stark verbreitete Sprachen wie Spanisch oder Chinesisch, u.s.w.; einfacher noch als alle Sprachen der Welt.

In writing about Linguna I have made use of some of the large amount of information on it that Goeres has placed on the internet.

## 1.16    Modern Esperanto

Modern Esperanto was designed by Teddy Hagner,[7] who, in his (n.d.) work on his language, calls himself by "the Esperanto translated name Teodoro Lahago, of being a citizen of the city of The Hague" (p. 51)). In Lahago (n.d.) he sometimes refers to his language as "Moderna Esperanto", which is what the name would be in that language, or in Esperanto, which he (e.g. n.d.:15) calls "Old Esperanto".

In Lahago (n.d.:51-54) he provides information about himself, writing in the 3rd person (e.g. that he "was born at The Hague, on May 16, 1929, 9 PM. [sic] summertime" (p. 51)), including his discovery of Esperanto and his thoughts on the prospects for such a language (pp. 53-4):

> During those five years in Europe [in the 1950s], Lahago lived also for about two months in Antwerp, Belgium, to open a bookstore of scientific books, but because of the high rent and not enough capital was evicted from the store. At this place, he got his first contact about Esperanto, by finding one day some leaflet about Esperanto in his mail-box, instead of book-orders, and he remembers the terrible cold and hunger, because of being so broke. In his sorry not being able to fulfill his dreams of a bookstore, Lahago found this leaflet being his heaven to peace of mind [sic] and the future, and started the study of Esperanto in the following years, with the result of Moderna Esperanto now. Creating again many disillusions among old time Esperantists. But time only will tell the truth, if Modern Esperanto was a waste or a creative creation. Growing and changing it will, according the demand of the users of an international language.
>
> Teodoro saw the many possibilities of one international uniform language, instead of the so many languages and dialects in existence now in the world, creating only hate and isolism [sic]. [...]
>
> This is the way Esperanto and may be Moderna Esperanto will spread out and slowly conquer the world of knowledge. An international language promoting unity among nations with the help of the native languages, in this universe. The time is not far off. Already is the seed laid for its great spread, and can you hear the flow of its music through the air, over the land and the seas. Time will only tell and that is indefinite, without no beginning and no end [sic].

Lahago's efforts met with some disapproval; he states (n.d.:19):

> In earlier attempts of my publications of Modern Esperanto I did received [sic] boxes full of mail with all kinds of critics [sic], hateful letters and postcards, and even an attempt of a lawsuit by an attorney out of Washington D.C., because according his statements [sic], was Esperanto a patented invention by its creator Dr. Zamenhof. If Zamenhof still could

---

[7] This name is the English version of his original Dutch name Teddy Hagenaar.

defend himself, he would may be had [sic] approved the new reforms of Modern Esperanto and it fully supported ... [...] That attorney never admitted that he himself was a big parasite and degenerate to live of [sic] the creation of a deceased person, instead of helping to promote the Esperanto movement in a creative and educ[a]tional manner. It is those kind of Esperantists who misuse the name of Esperanto for its promotion, but only give to themselves big titles of being some kind of a delegate. The so called "white collar workers" with an empty head, but just following, to be along [sic], because of not having any other ideals except destroying unconsciously the evolution of progress.

However, he also says that he got letters with positive opinions about his work. Monnerot-Dumaine (1960:183) says that this language is "sans grande originalité".

## 1.17    Mondezo

Medrano (2002) introduces his modified version of Esperanto as follows:[8]

Esperanto is an easy enough language to learn and it is a beautiful language. But, in fact, it could be made even simpler to learn. Attempts like Ido, a reformed Esperanto, have been made in the past, but they were radical and perhaps less aesthetically pleasing than Esperanto. Perhaps, there is room in this big world for a **dialect** of Esperanto that is even easier than Traditional Esperanto. Perhaps, some are looking for **minimalist** change. Mondezo is such a change.

Medrano, more than a dozen other languages, later gave up on Mondezo and "went back to being a patriotic Esperantist" (Medrano 2007).

## 1.18    Mondlango

In the *Questions and Answers* page of the Mondlango website (anon. n.d. c) there is the following answer to the question "Why can't Mondlango be called 'Reformed Esperanto'?" (ibid.):

Mondlango has absorbed many good points from Esperanto, but the differences between them are great in terms of alphabet and grammar. The First Universal Congress of Esperanto adopted "The Manifesto of Esperanto" which stipulated that every Esperantist must conform to the grammar laid down in the book "The Foundation of Esperanto". No Esperantist will ever have the right to modify this book. That is why many Esperantists know of some shortcomings in Esperanto, but they fail to correct them. The tradition of Esperanto doesn't recognize "Reformed Esperanto". If the Constitution of the United States could never have been amended, then Americans could not have abolished slavery. So Mondlango is an independent language, not a "Reformed Esperanto".

---

[8] The text of this webpage (my main source for the language) is in English and Esperanto. Interestingly, there is a webpage, apparently created by a Lucas Larson, which is quite similar, the major difference being that the text is only in English. The URL of that page is <http://mondezo.lucaslarson.net/>.

However, earlier in the same webpage Mondlango is called "a new international language, which inherits the good points of Esperanto and overcomes its defects". Further, (Mifsud n.d. a) states that "Its author/s ... based it on Esperanto". Consider also the remarks of Boyan Lalov (n.d.) in the page "Zamenhof Would Have Approved Mondlango [sic]":

> Mondlango is the logical continuing of the international language Esperanto created by the great linguist Ludwig Zamenhof ... [...] ...the whole range of language and pedagogical discoveries of Zamenhof are preserved in the lexicology and the grammatical structure of Mondlango. [...] ... the changes are so subtle and logical that the millions of Esperanto followers all over the world will appreciate them. They can use and understand Mondlango without effort and without having to learn it in a special way. [...] Yafu and his team are not negating but continuing the deed of Zamenhof. [...] Mondlango appeared at the beginning of the new millennium and it is an honorable heir of Esperanto. [...] Mondlango, carrying the pedagogical and humane spirit of Zamenhof can be reasonably accepted as the New Esperanto.

There is another name for Mondlango, *Ulango,* which comes from *La Universa Lango* 'The Universal Language'. The language "was born in July 2002" (anon. n.d. c), He Yafu being its "major founder" (ibid.). The list of "other founders" (ibid.) includes David Curtis and Oscar Mifsud. In the home page of the Mondlango website (anon. n.d. a) is the statement, "Mondlango is the common possession of the whole human race, therefore the author of Mondlango has resigned all copyrights to Mondlango. Anyone is permitted to copy any of the contents in the Mondlango website freely". My information on Mondlango comes from the pages in the website for the language, which contains grammatical information, texts, and Mondlango-English and English-Mondlango dictionaries.

### 1.19 Mondlingvo

This language is not to be confused with the language Mond-lingvo (or Mondlingvo) designed by Josef Weisbart. The Mondlingvo to be discussed in this book was designed by H. Trischen and presented in a work by him published in 1906. My source for this language is the short chapter on it in Couturat and Leau (1907/1979), who say (p. 87) that it "est, de l'aveu même de son auteur, un Esperanto réformé".

### 1.20 Neo

Neo was created by Arturo Alfandari. The description of it in Monnerot-Dumaine (1960:185) indicates that it underwent changes over time: "D'abord, en 1937, espérantide avec un conjugaison très synthétique comportant une finale pronominale artificielle, et des modes réfléchi, passif, continu, synthétiques. A partir de 1948 le Néo, réformé, s'éloigne de l'Esperanto; certaines racines raccourcies deviennent méconnaissables...". The title of Svendsen's (n.d.) webpage on the language is *Neo – et volapükisert esperanto* ('*Neo – a volapükized Esperanto*'). I shall be describing the version of the language presented in Alfandari (1961). At the beginning of this book (p. 9) Alfandari states, "Cet ouvrage est avant tout un message de paix".

## 1.21    Novesperant

The designer of Novesperant is Michael Cartier. Not much information on it is publicly available: my only substantive sources for it are a short internet web page (Cartier n.d.) and an e-mail message from Cartier. In the latter he says that Novesperant "is an attempt to make Esperanto easier to learn & speak". The only textual material given in Cartier (n.d.) is the following two sentences:

(2a)    mi   ne   pov   trovi   mi   automobil.
        I    not  can   find    my   car
        'I cannot find my car.' (MT)

(2b)    ji   est   en   la    automobileesc.
        it   is    in   the   garage
        "It is in the garage.' (MT)

Cartier (ibid.) says, "Note this is a work in progress, if you would like to contribute ideas, do so".

## 1.22    Olingo

Olingo was created by R. Stewart Jaque. I was uncertain whether to include it in this book. Jaque (1944:24) states that "Olingo is basically Neo-Latin and Anglo-Saxon with roots and words selected from all of the major languages of both the Western and Eastern Hemispheres" and to my knowledge nowhere does he say that his language is a modification of Esperanto or borrows heavily from it. However, an examination of Olingo indicates that it apparently has a debt to Esperanto: the endings for nouns, adjectives, and adverbs are the same in both languages (i.e. -o, -a, and -e respectively) as are a fair number of derivational affixes, including bo-, ge-, -an-, -ej- (-ey- in Olingo orthography), -er-, -et-, -estr-, and -ul-, and the suffix which forms fractions, -on-. In addition, the stress rule is the same in Olingo as in Esperanto and Olingo, like Esperanto, marks yes-no questions with a clause-initial particle, although the particles are partly different in form (Olingo qu, Esperanto ĉu). According to Monnerot-Dumaine (1961:172), Globaqo, the revised version of Olingo designed by Jaque and Goerge Arnsby Jones, "a beaucoup emprunté" from Esperanto.[9] One could thus justify the coverage of Olingo in the present book as it seems to be partly descended from Esperanto.
    Jaque (ibid.:62) made considerable claims for his language:

> Olingo is more than a language … it is an enjoyable recreation and an inspiring lifetime hobby. Its use removes needless linguistic tension and builds healthy, steady nerves. This neutral tongue also offers you the rare opportunity of dynamic, new professions, since Olingo needs teachers,

---

[9] Albani and Buonarroti (1994:297) say that Olingo is "di derivazione esperantista" but (ibid.:168) that Globaqo is "di derivazione esperantista … e idista".

writers, editors and translators throughout the world. Olingo builds for understanding fellowship, racial happiness! It is the ideal medium for bringing about world tolerance and peace.

At the top of this page is the heading "BE SUPREMELY HAPPY IN WORLD SERVICE THE NEW OLINGO WAY". Earlier in this book (p. 23) Jaque says, "World thought at last has wings … unified word speech is now a factual accomplishment! […] Easy to learn, beautiful in form and musical in sound, Olingo … is the world language that all humanitarians have longed for since the dawn of history."[10] Aside from Globaqo, Jaque designed another project, Gloneo, which was also based at least to some extent on Esperanto, but which I have very little information on.

**1.23   Perio**

Perio was presented in a work published in (1904) whose author was given as Mannus Talundberg, but Couturat and Leau (1907/1979:3) say that this "est manifestement un pseudonyme"; in addition, according to them, the editor of the work, M. K. Wasserloos, apparently contributed much to it, since what he was given was far from being a completed text. Carlevaro (n. d.) is of the opinion that "Mannus Talundberg" was in fact Wasserloos. I had doubts about including Perio in this book: Couturat and Leau describe it in the section on *a priori* languages of their (1907/1979) book, and the title of Talundberg's book is *Perio, eine auf Logik und Gedächtniskunst aufgebaute Weltsprache*. However, Monnerot-Dumaine (1960:191) states that it has "[n]ombreuses imitations de l'Esperanto, en particulier le tableau des particules corrèlatives", and there are many features that the two languages have in common including the ending *-o* marking nouns (although in Perio there are some types of nouns which do not have this suffix), the markers of adjectives and derived adverbs (*-a* and *-e* respectively), the accusative suffix *-n*, the pronouns *mi* 'I' and *li* 'he', and the infinitive suffix *-i*. Esperanto is not an *a priori* language, and so Perio may be evidence that, as Monnerot-Dumaine (ibid.:83) says, "Une langue appartenant à une certaine catégorie peut … avoir pris nombreuses caractéristiques à une langue d'une autre catégorie" since "Le Perio ne peut pas être classé, en effet, avec l'Esperanto" (ibid.).[11] I have gotten most of my information on Perio from Couturat and Leau (1907/1979).

**1.24   Perilo**

Perilo was apparently designed by Róbert Horváth. In his webpage describing the language (Horváth n.d.) he calls it "the new simplified Esperanto". This webpage, which is in Slovak and Hungarian, is my main source on the language. It is fairly

---

[10] Apparently not all of Jaque's readers agreed. In the copy of this work from which I made my photocopy (in the University of Minnesota) someone wrote "garbage" beside the paragraph in which these sentences appeared.

[11] However, I did not cover Perio in my (2000) book on *a priori* languages, probably because I thought it was not sufficiently *a priori*. Janton (1993:7) gives Perio as an example of the class of "Mixed languages using both ethnic and nonethnic roots" (ibid.:6) (which in turn for him is a type of a posteriori language), more specifically, as an example of the group of "Schematically derived languages … with both artificial and ethnic roots" (ibid.:6-7).

15

short, and thus not all details on the language may be brought up, but from what is there, Perilo seems only slightly different from Esperanto.

## 1.25    Reformed Esperanto

Within a relatively short time after the first publication on Esperanto ideas about modifying it started to appear. In response to this climate, Zamenhof (unenthusiastically) created a reformed version of Esperanto, details of which were published in six (1894) issues of the journal La *Esperantisto*. Those who subscribed to this journal then were able to vote on whether to accept this reformed Esperanto, either with or without further modifications, or to carry out other modifications, or not to modify the language. The last choice won, and so Zamenhof's Reformed Esperanto did not replace the previous version of the language.[12] According to Couturat and Leau (1903/1979:35) Reformed Esperanto "présente … un mélange déconcertant de qualités et de défauts, d'améliorations sérieuse et de détériorations graves". The judgement of Monnerot-Dumaine (1960:103) is: "Ce projet … comportait d'excellent réformes, mais d'autres étaient facheuse". I have gotten most of my information on Reformed Esperanto from Gacond and Gacond (1967) and Couturat and Leau (1907/1979:28-35).

## 1.26    Romániço

The designer of Romániço is Mike Morales. From the home page of the website on this language (Morales n.d a) one would not conclude that it is derived from Esperanto:

> Romániço is a reconstruction of this lost common tongue [Vulgar Latin], streamlined for use in our own era. Created in 1991 from the source roots of modern French, Italian, Spanish, and the Latin vocabulary of English, it harkens back to the Vulgar Latin that still united the West before it diverged into the modern Romance languages.
> It's also a bridge between other, past constructed languages, spanning the historical gap between the naturalism and recognizability of languages like Interlingua and the uniformity and simplicity of languages like Esperanto — and striking a balance between the two.

However, the section of the *Romániço Frequently Asked Questions* page of this website (Morales n.d. b) entitled "Where did Romániço come from?" indicates that it has its origin in Esperanto:

> Romániço began as an attempt to teach Esperanto to friends, all of whom were native English speakers. Unfortunately, certain features of the language proved to be unsurmountable hurdles for many of them: […] To deal with these and other difficulties, I began introducing various "house rules" to the language. At first, the accusative case was simply ignored. Then, little by little, other minor adjustments were made to make the

---

[12] However, according to Couturat and Leau (1907/1979:34-5) l'Esperanto réformé de 1894 a inspiré les auteurs de *l'Idiom Neutral*". Large (1985:82) says of the latter language, "Although formally based on Volapük, the new project in fact differed quite fundamentally from its ill-fated parent".

language more immediately usable for people who had little time to spend on it, until what began as Esperanto became so different that it needed its own written grammar and dictionary, and was dubbed, at different stages of its development, "Romanico", "Romániço", and "Romániczo", from the Latin *romanice* "in the manner of the Romans", which later became, in English, *romance*.

Further, in the last section of this page, "How is Romániço different from Esperanto?", appears the statement, "Those familiar with Esperanto ... will no doubt notice a good deal of similarity between it and Romániço. Indeed, Romániço, like most planned languages that came after Esperanto, is largely based on that language; it might even be thought of as an Esperanto dialect". In his website on Romániço Morales gives extensive information about his language, including an English-Romániço (Morales 2008a) and a dictionary with equivalents in English (and usually in French and/or and other languages) of Romániço words (Morales 2008b).

## 1.27 Sen:esepera

Sen:esepera was the work of Jefferey Henning. He says (1995a), "I designed *Sen:espera* as a dramatic reform of Esperanto, which I felt was difficult for speakers of non-European languages (especially Asian languages such as Japanese and Chinese) to pronounce. The primary design goal was to reduce the complexity of Esperanto's phonology ... Secondary design goals were to further simplify Esperanto's grammar and vocabulary." Sen:esepera is not meant for actual use: Henning (1995a) stated, "I explicitly am not interested in proposing that *Sen:esepera* ... be adopted as an international language; the creation of this language is purely an intellectual pursuit." He also indicated (ibid.) that the language was a work in progress.

## 1.28 Snifferanto

One might think from its name that Snifferanto was not a serious project, and indeed this was the opinion expressed on the page *Vikipediista diskuto:Yekrats/Arkivo 3* (at URL <http://eo.wikipedia.org/wiki/Vikipediista_ diskuto:Yekrats/Arkivo_3>): "por mi tio estas esperantan 'dialekton', kiun tute ne estos grava". However, the following passage (Aitai 2006): gives the impression that the language may not be an entirely frivolous creation:

> Finna esperantisto kiun oni konas lau la kromnomo Snifi (posedanto de la babilejo Snifejo) kreis novan planlingvon. Li jam longe insistis por radikalaj reformoj de esperanto kaj ecx planis perfortan forigon de la supersignoj de supersignaj literoj de esperanto-literaro en lia babilejo. Mi sugestis al li ne nomi siajn reformojn kiel "plibonigo" de esperanto (cxar tion ne eblas nomi plibonigo) kaj deklari ke ekestas nova lingvo ekzemple sniferanto... Nun li tiel faris kaj fakte oni povas konsideri ke denove estas inventita biciklo. Kiu kaj kial uzu Snifferanton estas neklara, sed tio ne gravas, cxar cxiu persono en libera lando rajtas ne nur krei kantojn aux krucvortenigmojn sed ankaux lingvojn..

Further, an e-mail message to me from the designer of the language, Jarmo Hietala, indicates some serious intent behind it.[13] My main sources for Snifferanto are the webpages *Gramatiko de Snifferanto* (Hietala 2006a) and *Lernolibro de Snifferanto* (Hietala 2006a). According to the former, Snifferanto's "[n]askitztago" ('date of birth') was February 22, 2006. In general, it is quite close to Esperanto, with e.g. the same adjectival, adverbial, tense, plural, and accusative suffixes. The main differences involve the lexicon and forms of words in it and follow from the elimination of letters with diacritics, and will be discussed in Chapter 3. In Hietala (2006a) it is stated, "La gramatiko ne estas finfarita, vekloj eblas" ('The grammar is not finished, changes are possible').[14]

## 1.29   UTL (Universal Translation Language)

Sabarís (2003) introduces this language as follows:

> The Universal Translation Language is an artificial language intended to express any kind of linguistic content in an unambiguous and computer-tractable way. Using this language in combination with the corresponding translation software would make it possible for users to write in languages they don't know. UTL is based on Esperanto, a language which due to its simple and regular grammar is quite friendly to automated analysis and machine translation. In fact, UTL can be described as variant of Esperanto where a few modifications have been introduced to optimize its performance in this regard.

UTL is very close to Esperanto, differing only in allowing foreign words and having some features which reduce ambiguity. My main sources for UTL are the short webpage Sabarís (2003) and the conference paper Sabarís et al. (2001).

## 1.30   Virgoranto

Virgoranto was created by Dorothea Winkelhofer, who introduces her language as follows (Winkelhofer 2007a):

> So jetzt wird es Zeit für meine zweite Plansprache. VIRGORANTO bedeutet soviel wie "jungfräuliches Esperanto". Das heißt ich versuche Esperanto auf seinen grammatischen Kern zu reduzieren. Die Virgoranto Grammatik paßt bequem auf ein DINA-4 Blatt und kann von jedem in circa 15 Minuten beherrscht werden. Damit steht Vigoranto im krassen Gegensatz zu manchen Plansprachen, die allein über Dutzende von Wortbildungssuffixen verfügen.
> [...] Virgoranto ersetzt im Wortschatz viele lateinische und romanische Wörter durch Wörter aus germanischen Sprachen, vor allem Deutsch und Englisch.

---

[13] In this message Hietala states, "The name of the language will be changed then [after he finishes another project]. Snifejo [the chat room] and Snifferanto are just names people have given to chat and language while lacking a better name".

[14] In October 2008 I was informed by Hietala that Snifferanto is now called *Eonido*. There is a website devoted to Eonido at URL <http://www.eonido.org/>, but I have not made use of it for this book..

Oberstes Prinzip von Virgoranto: Nichts komplizierter machen als nötig!

Virgoranto seems to be more different from Esperanto than some of the languages that I am dealing with, but there are some major features which are the same, e.g. the word class endings for nouns, adjectives, and adverbs, the infinitive suffix and the vowels in the present, past, and future tense suffixes (though the consonant is different). My information on this language comes from webpages by Winkelhofer, which include brief grammatical descriptions in German (Winkelhofer 2007a) and in English (Winkelhofer 2007b), and German-Virgoranto-English and Virgoranto-German-English glossaries (Winkelhofer 2008a and b respectively).

## 1.31    Languages Not Discussed

There are some languages which I have very little information on, and so I shall not treat them in this book. These include Esperanto sen Chapeloj (designed by Louis Couturat), Esperantuisho,[15] Latin-Esperanto,[16] Mez-Voio, Nepo, Ortologia Esperanto (created by Magnus Sondahl), the Reform-Esperanto of Hugon, and the Reform-Esperanto of Rodet. In general I do not have much interest in artificial languages which are clearly non-serious in purpose (such as fictional and personal languages). Therefore I shall not be dealing with Texperanto or Matthias Liszt's Esperan; the former apparently was created for humorous purposes.[17] I also shall not discuss Vivling, which in terms of its lexicon has Esperanto as a parent, but has Mandarin as a parent from the point of view of syntax, and draws on propositional logic. Cornelius (2002) says of it: "It started mainly as an exercise to further my vocabulary in my Esperanto studies, as well as to help me understand Mandarin better. However, the more I work on it the more life it seems to have which defines it [sic] from the root languages."

Esperanto has become a native language of some people and this "Native Esperanto" (Bergen 2001:575) shows some changes from the standard language. I shall not discuss this version of Esperanto here as I am concerned with modifications to the language that were consciously made.[18] I shall not describe the version of Esperanto (called eXperanto) used in the second language acquisition research reported on in de Graaff (1997). I also shall not treat Poliespo[19], Riismo,[20] Gregg

---

[15] Esperantuisho was the work of Jaro Zelezny of Czechoslovakia and dates from 1951. Monnerot-Dumaine (1961:170) gives the following sample of the language, which indicates how its creator viewed it: "Esperantuisho ne esas nova lingvo. Ji esas Esperanto sen la defektoy, kiuy montriqis kom qenumento por la universala acepto de Esperanto en la mondo ey ankaw che la UNO ey la UNESCO, kien esis taxata kom «lingvo montresa»."
[16] This language was designed by Giuliano Vanghetti and dates from 1911. Monnerot-Dumaine (1960:178) says of it, "Vocabulaire de base emprunté à l'Interlingua de Peano; grammaire de l'Esperanto".
[17] May (2006) states: "Texperanto is an artificial language invented in 1886 to commemorate the fiftieth anniversary of the Texican Revolution by Dr. Lazarus ("Lou") Zamenhof of the Douglass University Medical School at Port-au-President, Haiti. [...] It became an official language of Texas, along with Spanish, English, French, Haitian Creole, and Cherokee in 2004. ... by 2100, it was the most widely spoken language on Earth, Luna, Mars, and the Asteroid Belt. It went on to become the lingua franca of the Galaxy."
[18] For details about Native Esperanto v. Bergen (2001).
[19] Poliespo ('polysynthetic Esperanto') was designed by N. I. Sequoya and according to Gant (1997) is "based on Cherokee" and contains features taken from Esperanto.

Shorthand for Esperanto,[21] or Signuno, although at least the last three of these were created with a serious communicative purpose in mind.[22]

---

[20] Riismo corrects the supposed sexism of Esperanto with a small number of changes. *Li* and *ŝi* are removed from the language, with the new pronoun *ri* being used instead of them. The suffix *-iĉ-* is required for nouns denoting males, parallel to Esperanto's *-in-* for nouns denoting females; nouns with neither of these suffixes are not specified for sex (i.e. there are no default assumptions about the sex of the entities that they refer to). Thus, for example, *patro* means 'parent' and not 'father', for 'father' one is must use *patriĉo*. To make it very clear that a noun is not specified for sex, one can add the prefix *ge-* to it, e.g. *gepatro* 'parent'. For Riismo v. Grimley Evans et al. (1994).

[21] This did involve some changes to the language; for example the adverbial suffix *-e* was done away with. V. Jackson (1918).

[22] Several projects only came to my attention at a late stage in the writing of this book and there I have not discussed them. These include Esperajo, designed by Dana Nutter.

## 2 Phonetics and Phonology

It should perhaps be noted that (as far as I know) the DLT Intermediate Language and UTL were not designed to be spoken.

### 2.1 Sound Inventories and Orthography

EsF has one orthographic difference from Esperanto: <ŭ> of Esperanto is <w> in EsF, e.g. *law* 'according to' (cf. Esperanto *laŭ*). The same change has been made in Mondezo, but this language diverges in other ways as well: the circumflex of Esperanto has been dropped, and the letters over which they appeared have been made into digraphs by the addition of a following <h> or replaced, in two cases by a digraph and in one case by another letter. Specifically, Esperanto <ĉ> and <ŝ> become <ch> and <sh> respectively in Mondezo, <ĥ> and <ĵ> become <kh> and <zh>, and <ĝ> becomes <j>. In addition, the <j> of Esperanto is changed into <y>. To distinguish between digraphs and sequences of the same two letters that do not make up a digraph, hyphens are inserted between the members of the latter, e.g. *bus-halto* 'bus stop'.

According to Gacond and Gacond (1967) the alphabet of Zamenhof's Reformed Esperanto is: <a, b, c, d, e, f, g, h, i, k, l, m, n, o, p, r, s, t, u, v, z>. Thus all the letters with a circumflex or a breve have been removed. The phonetic value of <z> has been changed to [ts] ([z] is no longer phonemic), while <c> stands for [ʃ]. Possible pronunciations for <h> are [h] and [x] and for <s> are [s] and [z]. The letter <i> stands for [i] and [j], and <u> stands for [u] and [w].[1]

E-speranto's alphabet consists of all of the letters of the English alphabet, as well as <dj>, <hj>, and <zj> in webpage E-speranto and <hy> and <zy> in 2008 E-speranto. None of the publicly available materials on the language gives information on how these diagraphs are to be pronounced,[2] but Holmes (p.c.) indicates that <hj>/<hy> has the same phonetic value as Esperanto <ĥ> and that <zj>/<zy> has the same phonetic value as Esperanto <ĵ>. Holmes (p.c.) also indicates that in 2008 E-speranto <j> has the phonetic value that <dj> has in webpage E-speranto, i.e. presumably [dʒ]. The letters <q> and <x> have the phonetic values [tʃ] and [ʃ] respectively in 2008 E-speranto.[3] The English example words given in Holmes (n.d. c) for the pronunciation of the vowels <i>, <e>, <a>, <u>, and <o> are *pit, pet, putt, put,* and *pot* respectively.[4] In webpage E-speranto the letter <y> does not stand for any sound; it has two functions, both of which involve foreign words (including names):

> The letter *Y/y* is only[5] used to signal a letter or sound imported into
> E-speranto within the name of something specific to a culture, some

---

[1] I do not know whether the phonetic value is always determined by context, i.e. whether one sometimes has a choice between the two pronunciations of these letters.

[2] There is a section "The Consonants" in Holmes (n.d. c), but it consists of nothing but this title; presumably the section was meant to be written at some point.

[3] The letter <x> has the same value in webpage E-speranto; I assume this is also true of <q>.

[4] Holmes is aware of the difficulty in using words from English as guides for pronunciation when there are different accents of English, stating (ibid.), "In comparing sounds … all that can be said is that the English sound used as an example is the closest available to the E-speranto sound".

[5] The occurrence of "only" here is an error, since <y> has another function, brought up in the second paragraph of this quotation.

specific concept or notion that it would be inappropriate to bring into the language. Such words will not be found in a purely E-speranto dictionary, and are not expected to follow E-speranto's rules. Indeed, such words will often be fitted into E-speranto's patterns (for example, of grammatical endings) with great difficulty if at all.

A foreign word or stem must have its first letter in upper case. A hyphen or the letter *Y/y* is used to separate the foreign word from any E-speranto suffixes and endings. If, for emphasis, a word is given in all uppercase letters, the first and last letters of the foreign stem must be followed by a *Y*, unless a hyphen is used to separate foreign from other.

Personal names, since E-speranto can have none of its own, are always foreign, and this will be indicated by the upper case initial letter. When the text is of a kind that includes many uses of personal names, the *y* or hyphen separating the names from E-speranto endings may be left out for aesthetic reasons, but normally they should not be omitted. (Holmes n.d. b)

However, in 2008 E-speranto <y> is a pronounced letter, with the phonetic value [j] (Holmes p.c.); in webpage E-speranto the letter <j> has that value, as it does in Esperanto.

Holmes (ibid.) discusses the possibility of E-speranto being written in other alphabets and in syllabaries:

Esperanto is required to be written only using the Latin alphabet. This is unreasonably restrictive. Provided that equivalent measures can [be] and are taken in another writing system then computed conversion of E-speranto and others should be relatively trivial.
The Latin alphabet is simpler than other major alphabetic systems, such as Greek or Cyrillic, so use of those systems should present few problems.
The world's many syllabic writing systems present problems. The widely used Arab [sic] system, arguably syllabic, would need to be used always with the vowels marked (not the usual practice) and would need extra vowel markings.

Intero has both spelling and pronunciation differences from Esperanto. (Thompson 2007a) states, "Intero words shall be easier to pronounce [than those of Esperanto]".) The way that these differences are presented in Thompson (2007a) may be somewhat difficult to follow; in the table below I describe some of them (as I understand them):

| Esperanto | Intero |
|---|---|
| <c> [ts][6] | <c> [ʃ] |
| <ĉ> [tʃ] | <x> [tʃ] |
| <ĝ> [dʒ] | <j> [ʒ] |
| <ĥ> [x] | <k> [k] |
| <j> [j] | <y> [j] |
| <ĵ> [ʒ] | <j> [ʒ] |
| <sc> [sts] | <c> [ʃ] |
| <ŝ> [ʃ] | <c> [ʃ] |
| <ŭ> [w] | <w> [w] |

Table 2.1: *Some Phonetic and Orthographic Differences between Esperanto and Intero*

Another change is that "An Esperanto *ps-* becomes an Intero *s-*" (ibid.). I assume that this means that a word-initial *p* immediately before *s* is dropped. In various contexts *w* replaces Esperanto *v*; these contexts include: immediately after word-initial *s*, and immediately after *g* and *k*. Also, the sequence *cw* replaces the Esperanto sequence spelled <ŝv> and "An Esperanto *v-* becomes an Intero **w-** when the origin of the word had a 'w' sound" (ibid.). However, Thompson (ibid.) indicates that the latter replacement is at least temporarily optional: "Since I don't have a list of words to which this change applies, I would leave it up to the speaker for now, and accept either the **v-** or the **w-** variants as correct." When *z* occurs immediately after *k* it is replaced by *s*. There are two types of consonant cluster simplification: *k* is deleted when it occurs immediately after a consonant and immediately before *t*, and when it occurs immediately after a consonant and immediately before *c* (which is pronounced [ts] in Esperanto but [ʃ] in Intero, as shown in the table above). Also, two Esperanto words beginning with the sequence *kn-* lose their *k*: *knedi* and *knuto* become *nedi and nuto*, while three such words have a different word substituted for them: *grinti* is used instead of Esperanto *knari*,[7] while Esperanto *knabo* and *knali* are dropped in favor of *infano* and *eksplodigi* respectively. Similarly the *g* in the word-initial sequence *gn-* in the Esperanto words *gnjeso* and *gnuo* is deleted, the Intero words being *neyso* and *nuo*, while in two other words *a* is inserted between the members of this cluster: Intero has *ganomo* and *ganomono* for Esperanto *gnomo* and *gnomono*.

Ido does not have the Esperanto letters involving the circumflex or the breve, and has added four letters to Esperanto, <q>, <w>, <x>, and <y>. The letter <q> must have <u> after it and the two letters together stand for the sequence [kw]; <w> and

---

[6] I shall not distinguish between dental and alveolar consonants, and shall use the IPA symbol for an alveolar consonant for both it and its dental counterpart. In Esperanto and in at least most languages based on it, the difference does not seem to be of significance. For example, Wennergren (2005:24) says that *t* is "denta", and likewise for *d*, *s*, etc., but defines (ibid.:23) *dente* as "la lango kontraŭ la karno tuj malantaŭ la supraj dentoj, aŭ kontraŭ la supraj dentoj mem", which might allow for them to be pronounced as alveolars.

[7] The word *grinti* appears to involve an exception to the rule "An Esperanto c becomes an Intero c" (Thompson 2007a), since the Esperanto cognate is *grinci*, and one would therefore expect the Intero word to be *grinci* (with the two words being pronounced differently, due to the different phonetic values that <c> has in the two languages). Perhaps an error in either the design or the description of the language was made here.

and <y> have the phonetic values [w] and [j] respectively,[8] while <ĵ> stands for [ʒ].[9] One has a choice of phonetic value for <x>, [ks] or [ɡz]. Ido also has two digraphs, <ch> and <sh>, but these are not counted as letters of the Ido alphabet, as they are in some languages. The sequence <sh> is not always pronounced [ʃ]: when one root of a compound word ends in <s> and the following root begins with <h> it is pronounced [sh] and a hyphen is placed between the two letters, e.g. *chas-hundo* 'hunting dog'.

Esperloja has also dropped letters with the circumflex or the breve; <c> is not present in its alphabet either. The letter <x> has been added; it stands for [ʃ]. The phonetic value of <ĵ> is [ʒ] and thus is not the same as in Esperanto. Sulky (n.d.) says, "The sound of Esperanto 'h-circumflex' is not phonemic; it is merged with 'h'". There is freedom with respect to the formation of diphthongs from adjacent vowels in the same word; Sulky (ibid.) states, "Any vowels that can be pronounced as a diphthong, may be". He says later (ibid.) on the pronunciation of diphthongs that "When pairs [of vowels] are pronounced as diphthongs, those beginning with **i-** are pronounced as though they begin with 'y'; [those beginning with] **u-**, as 'w'".

The Perilo alphabet is <a, b, c, cx, d, e, f, g, gx, g, i, j, jx, k, l, m, m, n, o, p, r, s, sx, t, u, v, z>. The letters <cx>, <gx>, <jx>, and <sx> stand for [tʃ], [dʒ], [ʒ], and [ʃ] respectively, thus <x> replaces the < ˆ > of Esperanto, as sometimes happens in Esperanto itself, but note that there is no equivalent of Esperanto <ĥ>. The letter <u> is used instead of <ŭ>, e.g. *au* 'or' (cf. Esperanto *aŭ*), as well as retaining the same (I assume) phonetic value that it has in Esperanto, e.g. in *ludi* 'to play' (cf. Esperanto *ludi*).

The alphabet of Snifferanto is the same as that of English, thus there are no letters with diacritics. Neither the *Gramatiko de Snifferanto* (Hietala 2006a) nor the *Lernolibro de Snifferanto* (Hietala 2006b) gives any instructions on how the letters are to be pronounced; the only such information that I have found is from a cached archive of the Snifferanto chatroom (available at URL <http://www.google. com/search?q=cache:ohvF6A_Mv5UJ:pp.kpnet.fi/jhii/sablo/arkivo.php%3Fmontri%3 D48h+snifferanto+prononco&hl=en&ct=clnk&cd=2&gl=au>), where "Snifi" (i.e. Jarmo Hietala) gives IPA symbols to show the pronunciation of letters and digraphs, although he does not do this for <q> or <y>. The letter <x> is indicated to have the phonetic value [ɡʒ]; perhaps [dʒ] is what is actually meant. The letter <n> is said to have the pronunciations [n] and [ŋ], the latter presumably before velars, as is partly confirmed by the fact that the sequence <ng> is to be pronounced [ŋg]. The sequences <ch> and <sh> are pronounced as in English and the remaining letters have the same pronunciation as they do in Esperanto.

The Mondlango alphabet consists of the same letters as the English alphabet, but <q>, which, according to anon. (n.d. e), represents the sequence [kw],[10] does not

---

[8] The letter <u> also has the phonetic value [w] in some contexts; as we have just seen, this is the case in the sequence <qu>, and it also has this value when immediately after <g> and immediately before a vowel, e.g. in *linguo* 'language'.

[9] De Beaufront (1925/2005:8) says that <ĵ> is pronounced as "*j* en la Franca, o *s* en la vorto Angla *vision. Ma, se on ne povas pronuncar ol tale, on darfas donar a ta konsonanto la sono di *g* en la Angla *gin*, o di *g* en l'Italiana *giardino*" ('*j* in French, or *s* in the English word vision. But, if one cannot pronounce it this way, one may give to this consonant the sound of *g* in the English *gin*, or of *g* in the Italian *giardino*').

[10] This sequence occurs in other words in Mondlango, and is spelled <kw>, e,g, *kwar* 'four'.

occur other than in proper nouns. The letters <c>, <g>, <j>, <x>, and <y> stand for [tʃ], [g], [dʒ],[11] [ʃ], and [j] respectively. It is not entirely clear how all the vowels are to be pronounced, since for at least some of them[12] there is an apparent discrepancy in the table of the Mondlango alphabet in anon. (n.d. e) between the "International Phonetics" symbol given for them and the vowel appearing in the English word which is supposed to illustrate their pronunciation (assuming that "International Phonetics" means a symbol from the International Phonetic Alphabet). This is shown below in (1), which contains part of the relevant lines of the table; for example, the vowel in bit is *not* [i]:

| (1) | Capital | Small | International Phonetics | English |
|---|---|---|---|---|
| | A | a | [a] | a (father) |
| | E | e | [e] | e (bed) |
| | I | I | [i] | i (bit) |
| | O | o | [o] | o (plot) |
| | U | u | [u] | u (put) |

The description of the pronunciation of the vowels as indicated in the first lesson of the Mondlango Course (anon n.d. g) is somewhat different, i.e. some of the illustrative words are different (phonetic symbols are not given there):[13]

(2)     a: like "a" in "father"
        e: like "e" in "bed"
        i: like "i" in "street"
        o: like "o" in "for"
        u: like "oo" in boot

Arlipo uses the same alphabet as English, but <q>, <w>, and <y> are limited to appearing in words from other languages. There are also four digraphs, <ch>, <kh>, <sh>, and <zh> (as in *chefo* 'chief', *khaoso* 'chaos', *shinko* 'ham', and *zhurnalo* 'journal, magazine') "[p]or soni neapearanta [sic] en la origina Latina alfabeta" ('for sounds not appearing in the original Latin alphabet'; Vitek (n.d. b)), which I would guess have the values [tʃ], [x], [ʃ], and [ʒ] respectively.[14] There are two diphthongs, *au* and *eu*. Vitek (ibid.) states that the following types of words are capitalized: "propra nomi di personi, nacii, landi, urbi ktp., anke derivita adjektivi" ('proper names

---

[11] The table of the alphabet in anon. (n.d. e) gives [dz] as the pronunciation of <j>, but one might assume that this was due to the fact that a phonetic font was not used and that [dʒ] was meant, since this table indicates that Mondlango <j> has the same pronunciation as the <j> in English *job*.

[12] I say "at least some of them" since the number of discrepancies here depends on the accent of English and on how one transcribes the accent.

[13] Other illustrative words are given in the following passage from Mifsud (n.d. b), which indicates a strict attitude with respect to pronunciation of the vowels: "it must be stressed that the first thing a new learner (especially if British) must get used to, is how to pronounce the vowels a,e,i,o,u phonetically, using one pure sound only: a = Ah (not ey); e =e(lm), not (k)ey; i = ee(l), not m(y); o = au(tumn), not Oh!; u = (l)oo, not ou. Unless this is done correctly, it is impossibly, repeat, impossible to speak Mondlango propery; or any other phonetic language for that matter!".

[14] Vitek (n.d. a) says, "Aperado di le duj-literi ne esat tre ofta, do tio ne kauzat plulongigado je skriba texto" ('Appearance of the digraphs is not very often, therefore it does not cause lengthening of a written text').

of people, nations, lands, cities, etc., also derived adjectives'). I assume that this means adjectives derived from names of countries, etc. are capitalized.

The alphabet of 1919 Esperantida is the same as that of English; and there are two digraphs, <ch> and <sh>, which have the same pronunciation that they usually do in English. De Saussure (1919:3) allows the use of <ĉ> and <ŝ> rather than these digraphs "[e]n la manskribo k. en literaturan verkon" ('in handwriting and in literary works').[15] The letters <c> and <j> have the phonetic values [ts] and [dʒ] respectively; <w> and <y> are pronounced as in English. De Saussure (ibid.) states, "$q = kv$ (or $kw$)" and "Litero $q$ estas prononcata $kv$ or $kw$ sloprefere; sed la pli prononco estas $kw$" ('The letter $q$ is pronounced $kv$ or $kw$ according to preference, but the more correct pronunciation is $kw$').[16] As for <x>, it "estas prononcata $ks$ or $gz$, slo la pincipo de minima peno" ('is pronounced $ks$ or $gz$, according to the principle of least effort', ibid.). The letter <h> "estas elspirenda" ('is to be breathed out', ibid.). Nov-Esperanto has the two digraphs of Esperantida and an additional one, <kh>, which corresponds to the <ĥ> of Esperanto.

Although de Saussure (1926:5) gives <w> as a letter of the Nov-Esperanto alphabet, its pronunciation being a "kurta $u$" ('short $u$', ibid.), i.e. presumably [w], when writing words in the language in this work he uses <ù> for the "kurta $u$" rather than <w>, e.g. *aùdas* 'hear'.[17] According to de Saussure (ibid.) the Nov-Esperanto letter <j> has the same pronunciation as in English. However, there is an exception to this; on p. 10 he states, "En la sufixo *-aj'* [18] la litero *j* havas la franca sonu, kiel en Esp. *(-aj)*" ('in the suffix *-aj'* the letter *j* has the French sound, as in Esp[eranto] *(-aj)*').

The alphabet of Aiola is <a, b, c, d, dj, dz, e, f, g, h, i, j, k, l, m, n, n, o, p, r, s, t, tc, ts, u, v, w, y, z>. The letters <c> and <j> stand for [ʃ] and [ʒ] respectively. The four diagraphs all represent the sequences of sounds that their individual components stand for, e.g. <tc> has the phonetic value [tʃ]. ARG (2005:5) gives the following English words to show the pronunciation of the vowels: *fa̱ther, café, mari̱ne, o̱bey, rude.*

---

[15] De Saussure (ibid.:67) defends the presence of these digraphs in Esperantida as follows:

> Al la personon, kiun miros, ke mi akceptis *ch, sh*, mi respondas la cio: dur la propaganda periodo estas pli praktika uzi tin digramon; tamor la uzo de la diakritan literon *ĉ, ŝ*, ne estas malpermisita, kay kiam la Ligo de la Populon (or Societo de la Nacion) decidos pri la lingvo internacia, ji tiam povos trudi al omnin printiston la deviga uzo de la signon *ĉ & ŝ*, se ji ne volas akcepti la digramon, kay e tio la Ligo povos fari sen tuchi la Fundamento de la lingvo, kar (tio estas pley grava punkto*) la lingvo Esperantida estas naw eqale bone skribibla per digramon or sen digramon.*
>
> ('To the people who are amazed that I have accepted *ch, sh*, I answer as follows: during the propagandizing period it is more practical to use these digraphs. However, the use of the diacritic letters *ĉ, ŝ* is not forbidden, and when the League of Peoples (or the Society of Nations) makes a decision about the international language, the obligatory of use of the signs *ĉ* and *ŝ* can then be imposed on all printers, if it is not desired to accept the digraphs, and the League can do that without touching the Fundamento of the language, for (it is a very important point) *the Esperantida language can now be written equally well with digraphs or without digraphs.*')

[16] In de Saussure's Reformita Esperanto of 1917 <q> stands for [dʒ], i.e. it is equivalent to Esperanto <ĝ>.

[17] De Saussure (1926:8) seems to indicate that one may use <ù> or <w> for [w].

[18] When discussing points of grammar de Saussure (ibid.) uses the apostrophe to mark morpheme boundaries, but it does not appear in his (ibid.) texts in Nov-Esperanto.

Apparently [ɔ] does not occur in the language; ARG (ibid.) states that the vowels "are articulated in a sharp, clear fashion, regardless of stress".

Another language which has the same alphabet as English is Atlango, but some of the letters are not pronounced as they are in English: <c> and <x> are pronounced [tʃ] and [ʃ] respectively.[19] According to Antonius (2008b) <q> has the sound "k+short u or k+f", while <r> is "like in Spanish – *more vibrating*". The vowels are to be pronounced "Like in italian or spanish [sic]" (Antonius 2008b). Antonius (ibid.) says further about the pronunciation of vowels, "Such forms like **-ia, io,** are also pronounced as iya, iyo. (Fransio, Polonio, Germanio. ['France', 'Poland', 'Germany')" and "The forms **eu, au** -(ne-utrala, a-uto, a-utoro ['neutral', 'car', author']) can also be pronounced as **ew, aw** (newtrala, awto, awtoro)". The sound [ʒ] is represented by the sequence <zh>; [ts] is represented by <ts> or <zz>.[20]

Mondlingvo has kept all of the letters of the Esperanto alphabet, but changed the values of three of them, and has a letter not present in Esperanto, <x>, which stands for [ç]. The letters with changed values are <s>, <c>, and <z>, which in Mondlingvo stand for [z], [s], and [ts] respectively.

The Esperanto letter <r> is meant to be pronounced as a trill. In contrast, Hoover (n.d.) says, "Preferably, the letter 'r' is not rolled in Baza. However, it may be lightly flapped, if desired".

The Ekselsioro alphabet consists of all of the letters of the English alphabet except <q>, <w>, and <y> (though they do not all have the same phonetic values as in English; v. Table 2.2), and thus does not have "accented letters" (Greenwood 1906a:4), which Greenwood (ibid.) thinks are "crude subterfuges of double consonants: as, gh, hh, kh, ch, sh, etc., such compounds mostly indicating Asiatic gutturals and sounds totally foreign to the printed letters as regards Esperanto for instance". He continues (ibid.), On trying to pronounce such … one at once gets a cross between a gulp and a sigh, in fact, an utterly impossible pronunciation to Europeans". There are also no vowel letters with breves.

Modern Esperanto's alphabet consists of 20 letters: <a, b, d, e, v, g, h, i, j, k, l, m, n, o, p, r, s, t, u, w>. As can be seen, there are no letters with circumflexes,[21] nor is <ŭ> present – <w> is used instead of it. Those are changes that we have already seen in other modifications of Esperanto, but there is one change which to my knowledge is unique to Modern Esperanto: one will notice that <f> is missing from the alphabet, and that <v> has been moved to its place. It is not entirely clear to me how this letter is supposed to be pronounced: on the one hand Lahago (n.d.:23) states that "every letter … has one sound only, always the same"; on the other hand, he gives the English words *vault* and *fork* to illustrate the pronunciation of <f>. Could the fact that

---

[19] One might assume (although Antonius (ibid.) does not state it) that <g> always has the phonetic value [g], since <j> has the phonetic value [dʒ].

[20] It is not clear to me whether <zz> always has the phonetic value [ts] in Atlango. Antonius (2008c) says that its pronunciation in the word pizzo 'pizza' is "ts,dz". The Atlango word for 'jazz' is *jazo* or *jazzo*; I do not know whether the sequence <zz> in the latter should be pronounced [ts]. (Antonius (ibid.) does not give any information on the pronunciation of this word.)

[21] Further, unlike some other daughters of Esperanto in which this is also true, all of the sounds that they stand for in Esperanto, e.g. [ʃ], have been removed from Modern Esperanto.

in some accents of Dutch (which presumably was Lahago's first language) <v> is pronounced as a voiceless fricative be responsible for this?[22]

The alphabet of Perio is the same as that of English, except that <w> is not present. The letters <c> and <j> have the phonetic values [ʃ] and [ʒ] respectively. Couturat and Leau (1907/1979:4) state that <q> is "prononcé à peu près *gn*" and that <y> is equivalent to (French) <aï> and German <ei>, i.e. it has the pronunciation [aɪ]. The digraph <ch> has the phonetic value [tʃ]. Couturat and Leau (ibid.) indicate that "**zs** ou **sz**" has the pronunciation "dj", which one might take to mean [dʒ], while <ii> is equivalent to "yi". Capital letters are not used in the language.

Olingo also has almost the same inventory of letters as English; the only difference is that <k> is left out of its alphabet (<q> has the phonetic value [k]). The letter <c> is limited to occurring in the digraph <ch>. The other consonant letters have the same phonetic values as their English counterparts, "save that each letter has only one sound" (Jaque 1944:33),[23] while the vowel letters have the values that they do in Spanish. There are two other digraphs in the language, <sh> and <th>. Jaque (ibid.) states, "The digraphs are pronounced: ch-cheh, sh-sheh, th-theh". This seems to mean that the first two of these have the phonetic values of the English digraphs <ch> and <sh>, but it is not clear whether <th> stands for a voiced dental fricative or a voiceless one, or both. Olingo does not have diphthongs: Jaque (ibid.) says, "Where vowels appear together they are pronounced separately, never as diphthongs".

There are 25 letters in the Neo alphabet, namely the same letters as in the English alphabet except <q>. However, <q> can occur in Neo: Alfandari (1961:32) says, "La letter **q** ne se rencontre que des mots reproduits littéralement de leur langue d'origine (Albuquerque, Quevedo, Quinault)".[24] The letter <c> has the phonetic value [tʃ]; <sh> stands for [ʃ] and <x> for [ks]. Alfandari (ibid.) indicates that <j> has the same phonetic value that it does in *John*, by which I assume he means the name as said in English, although this work is in French; <g> stand for [g] and <w> has the same pronunciation as in English. Word-final <h> is silent (unless part of the diagraph <sh>); the motivation for its presence is to keep stress on the last syllable of some words which have a vowel as their last segment in their original form, e.g. *pashah* 'pasha', *cadih* 'cadi', *papah* 'daddy'. This <h> remains if the plural marker -*s* is

---

[22] The following paragraph in Lahago (n.d.:25), which might appear to be relevant, does not clear up the confusion (at least not for me):

> Note! In Old Esperanto the "word" – "vorto" came only to the closest comparison in the German and English language, each with their word "Wort" and "word". Any other language has a different word for it and is not to compare, except in a few smaller languages. Also in Old Esperanto was the word "forto" – "force", and still in use in more than seven living languages, but now abolished in Modern Esperanto, because there is no "f" letter in the Modern Esperanto alphabet. In Creative Esperanto now the word "vorto" is used for "force", strenght" [sic] etc.; and the new word "worto" for "word".

[23] Jaque does not clearly indicate what this "one sound" is for each consonant letter, his (ibid.) guide to their pronunciation being "b-beh, d-deh, f-feh, g-geh …". One might assume that <g> stands for [g], and probably <x> stands for [ks].

[24] Alfandari (ibid.) states, "On peut envisager de remplacer par cette même letter **q** le **k**, plus difficile pour l'écriture à la main".

attached, e.g. *pashahs*, but is deleted when derivational suffixes are added, e.g. *cadia* 'de cadi'.[25]

Romániço's alphabet is also made up of 25 letters, again the same letters as the English alphabet has, but with <k> left out. Most of these have the same pronunciation as in English; <g> always has the phonetic value [g]. The situation with respect to <c> is complex; Morales (n.d. i) rather confusingly states, "[it is pronounced] <u>k</u>ite before all letters except *e* and *i*, when it is [tʃ] as in *mi<u>ts</u>*. Written as **qu** to preserve the [k] sound before *e* and *i*, as **ç** or **cz** to preserve the [ts] sound elsewhere". That is, the sound [k] is represented by <qu> when immediately followed by [e] or [i], e.g. *quilogramo* 'kilogram' and, if I understand correctly, [ts] is represented by <ç> or <cz> (apparently one can choose either one) whenever it is not immediately followed by [e] or [i] (being represented by <k> when it is immediately followed by one of these vowels).[26] The pronunciation given for <j> in the table of the Romániço alphabet in Morales (ibid.) is [dʒ], but Morales (ibid.) says that it "[c]an also be pronounced [ʒ] is in French *Jacques*, whichever is easier for the speaker". There are three diagraphs, <ch>, <çh>, and <sh>, which stand for [x], [tʃ], and [ʃ] respectively; the first of these "is only used in a few words of non-Latin origin" (ibid.). Morales (ibid.) says the following about diphthongs:

> Ordinarily, when two vowels come together in a Romániço word, each is pronounced separately. (Eg., **coacter** is pronounced **co-ac-ter**.) Some vowels, however, combine with other vowels to form sounds pronounced as a single (or close to single) syllable, as in English *coin* and *couch*. These combination vowels sounds are called *diphthongs*.
>
> The letters **i** and **u**, when they are not the only vowel in a root and are immediately followed or preceded by another vowel in the same word, produce a diphthong. After the letters **c** or **g**, the letter **u** always produces a diphthong when followed by another vowel

The creation of diphthongs involving [i] is not compulsory under these conditions; Morales (ibid.) gives two possible pronunciations for some of the words provided to illustrate this process, e.g. *filiiso* 'daughter' can be pronounced [fi.ˈlji.so] or [fi.li.ˈi.so]; "[w]hichever is easier for the speaker" (ibid.) may be chosen. (Whether the same is true of diphthongs involving <u> when it does not follow <c> or <g> is not indicated by Morales (ibid.).) Vowels of different roots of compounds cannot join together to become diphthongs.

Novesperant displays some orthographical differences from Esperanto: Novesperant <j> and <y> correspond to Esperanto <ĝ> and <j> respectively, and the sequence <ku> corresponds to <kv> in Esperanto (meaning e.g. that the word for 'four' is *kuar* rather than Esperanto *kvar*). I do not completely understand the following statement from Cartier (n.d.): "'sc' (stz is pronounced as 'sh' in 'shape')".

---

[25] What Alfandari (1961:43) actually says is, "L'**h** muet disparaît dans les mots derives", but I assume that this would not happen if a derivational prefix were added.

[26] This represents a change in the orthography of the language; Morales (ibid.) says, "**c** represented [ts] in all positions, k [k] in all positions, which made spelling easier but more artificial-looking: il Greko parlen il Grekenso, il Franco parlen il Francenso instead of il Greco parlen il Grequenso, il Franço/Franczo parlen il Francenso".

However, I believe it means that the sequence <sc> has the phonetic value [ʃ], given that Cartier (ibid.) says, "the suffi[x] '-ej" becomes 'esc (esh)'". Cartier also states (ibid.), "There are no diacritical marks. therefore c=ch". He does not say what happens to the other Esperanto letters with circumflexes, i.e. <ĥ> and <ĵ> or the sounds that they represent. Novesperant <u> apparently corresponds to both <ŭ> and <u> of Esperanto, since the Novesperant word for 'car' is *automobil* (cf. Esperanto *aŭtomobilo*).

Henning (1995a) seems to indicate that the phoneme inventory of Sen:esepera is /a/, /e/, /i/, /o/, /u/, /p/, /t/, /k/, /b/, /d/, /g/, /f/, /s/, /h/, /m/, /n/, /l/, /r/, and /j/ (but v. note 27 below). I assume that the alphabet of the language consists of these symbols, except that there is no letter <j> (v. infra). Henning (1995a) comments as follows on this inventory: "Where Esperanto has 23 consonants, *Sen:esepera* has only the 14 most common consonants, based on Rick Morneau's analysis of a sample of 25 world languages ... Of the languages he surveyed, 76% contain every sound in Sen:esepera; their speakers will not need to master any new sounds, while speakers of the other 24% of the languages will have to master a few sounds." Henning (1995a) is one of the few presentations of an artificial language that explicitly brings up allophones; they are said to exist in Sen:esepera for "most consonants", though Henning does not describe most of them. The existence of these allophones is, according to Henning, due to the fact that the language "makes comparatively few distinctions between consonants". The allophones that he cites are [f] and [v] for /f/, [s] and [z] for /s/, [h] and [x] for /h/, while "the phoneme /r/ includes any retroflex or any alveolar flap or trill (ibid.). The phonetic value of <i> varies: when immediately after a vowel it stands for /j/, elsewhere it stands for /i/.[27] In Sen:esepera <c> stands for /k/, unlike in Esperanto. An unusual feature of Sen:esepera is that a colon is used to separate morphemes (except for the "class suffix" (Henning 1995a), for which v. section 4.0.1).; we see this in the name of the language itself: *sen-* 'without', *esepera* 'hope'. Other examples are *an:positifan* 'negative' (*an-* 'not', *positifan* 'positive') and *leren:loca* 'school' (*leren-* learn, *loca* 'place').

There are 28 letters in the Farlingo Alphabet: <a, b, c, ch, d, e, f, g, h, i, j, k, l, m, n, o, p, q, r, sh, t, u, v, w, x, y, z>. The letters <c>, <ch>, <j>, <sh>, and <y> have the phonetic values [ts], [tʃ], [ʒ], [ʃ], and [j] respectively. I do not know what sound <q> stands for: Farber and Faber (2005) who generally use Cyrillic letters to show pronunciation, indicates that it has the pronunciation "кh", which might make one think they mean [x], but the letter <x> has the same phonetic value as the Russian letter <x>, i.e. [x]. According to Farber and Farber (ibid.) the letter <w> is equivalent to the Cyrillic sequence <oy>.

The Hom-idyomo alphabet is: <a, b, k, c, c̃, d, e, f, g, h, i, y, j, l, m, n, ñ, o, p, ⱬ, r, s, s̃, t, u, w, v, z>. The capital letter counterparts of these are what one would expect, with the exception of <ⱬ>, the capital version of which is <Я>. This latter "is used only in inscriptions and titles, where all words are capitals, for as ⱬ cannot be the first letter of any syllable, no word begins with it" (Cárdenas 1923:I:3). Cárdenas (ibid.) makes the following, not precise, remarks about the phonetic value of <ⱬ>:

---

It appears that /i/ and /j/ are in complementary distribution, and thus allophones of the same phoneme; if this is the case, Henning's list of phonemes is not correct, having one too many members. (Henning does not explicitly say that /i/ and /j/ are phonemes, but since he uses slashes with them (and square brackets with allophones), one might think that he intends them to be understood as phonemes.)

"pronounced like Spanish and Italian *r*. It is somewhat stronger than English *r* but not so strong as German or French *r*. […] English speakers should be careful not to give it the faint, almost imperceptible sound which they often give to *r* at the end of a syllable, as in *hard, more*. The true sound is more like that of English *r* in *grass*."[28] The letters <č> and <š> have the same phonetic value as Esperanto <ĉ> and <ŝ>, while <ñ> stands for a palatal nasal. The letter <c> has a different pronunciation than it does in Esperanto, as it stands for [θ]. Cárdenas (1923:I:2) apparently allows for some variation in the pronunciation of <h>, saying that it "is always aspirated, as in English and German, or more strongly like German *ch* in *ach*, or like Spanish *j*". The phonetic value of <j> may be [dʒ], but I am not certain of this as Cárdenas' (ibid.) description of it is not entirely clear; he states that it "is pronounced as in English and a little less strongly then in French. This sound is similar to that of Spanish *y* in *yegua*, assuming that here y has a consonant sound different from that of *i*. In French and Italian, g followed by *e* or *i* has very nearly the correct sound of j here described".

The Hom-idyomo letters <w> and <y> are counted among the vowels; apparently they have the same phonetic values as <u> and <i> respectively, but are used in the representation of diphthongs.[29] Cárdenas (ibid.:I:1) states that <a> "is pronounced as in French, German, Spanish and Italian, and like English *a* in *father, man, nard*". According to Cárdenas (ibid.), <o> "is pronounced as in German, French, Spanish and Italian, or like English *o* in *go, word*. He later (ibid.:III:2) says that it "always sounds like English *o* in *follow, theory, not, odd, forest, comma, abhor, idiot or atom*, or as a in *hall, all*. It does not sound as *o* in *drown, flower, work*, visor, *do, lose* or *two*, nor becomes *oa* as in *fore, sore*". These instructions are confusing: on the one hand not all the example words have the same vowel in them (e.g. *comma* and *all*); on the other hand, w*ord* and w*ork* contain the same vowel but the latter is one of the example words for how not to pronounce <o>. There are also problems with some of Cárdenas' other statements about vowels.

Cárdenas was not fond of one kind of abbreviation: "In no case – not even in telegrams not transmitted in cipher -- should an institution or organization be referred to by the initials of its name, as that foolish custom is not consistent with clearness. Thus, do not write *C. P.* for 'Canadian Pacific' … *Ch. G. & Co.* for 'Chalmers, Goodry & Co.'" (1923:I:153). However, he did not ban all abbreviations from Hom-idyomo: "In commercial and private correspondence are used some common abbreviations, such as & for 'et cetera' … *nᵒ* for "number", *eks.* for 'example', v.g. [sic] for 'for instance'. It should be noted that & is not used for *kay* 'and'" (ibid.).

The Virgoranto alphabet consists of the vowels <a, e, i, o, u> and the consonants <b, c, d, f, g, h, k, kv, l, m, n, p, s, sh, t, v, x, z>. The letter <x> stands for [ç].

---

[28] Cárdenas (1923:III:4) explains the inclusion of <ɩ> in the Hom-idyomo alphabet:

> The distinction made in the pronunciation of those two letters [<r> and <ɩ>] , as having two different sounds, has raised much discussion between the author and his friends. Some of the friends affirm that the difference is merely imaginary, that *r* has exactly the same value in *four* and in *israelite*, in *free* and in *wrist*. Some others acknowledge there the existence of a real difference, but they consider the separation in [sic] r and ɩ to be a cause of greater confusion. The author argues that such difference is greater than that existing between *b* and *v*, for instance, and he requires the new language to be phonetic and free from any orthographic difficulty.

[29] Cárdenas (1923:I:1) says that <y> "is pronounced like i, and is used only to replace i in diphthongs".

According to Winkelhofer (2008a) <kv> "= Q", while in Winkelhofer (2000b) it is said to be "like Q in question"; I am thus not sure how this letter is to be pronounced, since the sequence <qu> has different pronunciations in German and English. Not suprisingly <sh> stands for [ʃ]. The other consonant letters have the same phonetic values that they have in Esperanto. Winkelhofer (2008a) does not give any directions on how the vowel letters are to be pronounced, but in Winkelhofer (2008b) is the following information:

(3)     A like in German "Alphabet"
        E like in energy
        O like in often
        I like in intention
        U like in good

If all of this information is accurate (and I suspect that some of it is not), then Virgoranto differs from Esperanto in the phonetic values of some of the vowels. For example, Esperanto <o> stands for [o], while the <o> of *often* is pronounced [ɔ]. Winkelhofer (ibid.) states, "There are no diphtongs [sic], when two vocals [sic] meet, they are pronounced seperately [sic]" and gives the example "E-u-ro-po".

The orthographic system of Linguna is complex and I shall not present every detail of it here.[30] The letter <c> is pronounced in two ways, as [ts] when it precedes <ae, e, i, j, y> and as [k] when it precedes <a, eu, o, u> or a consonant and at the end of a word. To represent [ts] before <a, eu, o, u> one uses <cs> or <ç> after a consonant, as in *prancsu* 'prance!' (cf. the spelling of the infinitive of this verb, *pranci*) and <zz> after a vowel, e.g. *grandezzo*, which I assume means 'largeness'. The sound [k] is represented by <q> when it precedes <ae, e, i, y>. (The letter <k> is not part of Linguna's alphabet.) According to Goeres (2004a) <ch> has the phonetic value [x] or [ħ];[31] <cz> and <ds> stand for [tʃ] and [ð] respectively. The digraphs <dj> and <gj>[32] both have the phonetic value [dʒ], the former "rarem" ('rarely', ibid.) occurring, the latter "prescau cziam" ('almost always', ibid.) being used. Goeres (ibid.) says that the <ds> is "prescau qviel" ('almost like') <gj>; he represents its pronunciation as "[dʃ/dƆ]", i.e. [dʃ]/[dʒ]; I do not know whether the slash means that one has a choice of pronunciations or that the phonetic value varies according to context. The digraph <jj> stands for "[Ɔ]", i.e. [ʒ].[33] The single letter <j> has an unrelated value, that of a "curta i" ('short i', ibid.). The letter <x> stands for [ks] and [gz]; it has the latter value when occurring in intervocalic position (I do not know whether it always has the other value otherwise). The letter <s> stands for [z], while [s] is represented by <ss> and <sz>; the latter is used at the beginnings of roots, the former cannot appear there. The digraph <sh> has the value [ʃ] and <z> stands for [θ].

The Linguna digraphs <ae> and <eu> have the phonetic values [æː] and [øː] respectively. The letter <y> stands for [y]. Sometimes a long vowel is indicated by a

---

[30] I shall describe the orthography as it is given in Goeres (2004a); Goeres (2008) presents a version which differs in a few respects.
[31] Goeres (ibid.) indicates that it replaces < ĥ> (which has the phonetic value [x]).
[32] As a capital letter it is <Gi>.
[33] As a capital letter it is <Ji>.

double letter, e.g. <oo> stands for [oː], but sometimes <h> is used, e.g. <uh> stands for [uː]. As we have seen, Goeres' indications of pronunciation do not always use symbols from the International Phonetic Alphabet (which may well have been due to difficulties in placing some of these symbols in his webpages); his (ibid.) indication about the phonetic value of the digraph <ao> is "[åː] (long vocal obtusa inter a: and ò:)" ('long dull vowel between a: and ò:').[34] A grave accent marks vowel letters standing for vowels which are "como aparte elparlendan" ('to be pronounced separately', ibid.), as in e.g. *villaò* 'villa (NOM)', which does not contain the digraph <ao>, but a sequence of vowels; Goeres (ibid.) gives the pronunciation of this word as "[viˈla-ò]".

In the table below the alphabet of Esperanto can be compared with those of some of its daughters; only the letters which have been changed in one of them are present. Note that this table is concerned with orthography only, i.e. when the letter used to represent a sound is different from that used in Esperanto – it is not concerned with changes in sounds (except when both a sound and the letter used to represent it have been removed in the creation of a daughter, as apparently happened in Ekeselsioro with the sound /dʒ/ and the Esperanto letter for it, <ĝ>, or when a sound has been removed and the letter which stood for it is used to indicate a different sound).

---

[34] Goeres (2008) states that its phonetic value is "aw, wie im .... Engl.: Bernard Shaw" and "gleich schwedischem a°/å".

| Esperanto | IPA | Ekselsioro | Ido | Mondezo | Mondolingvo | Neo | Sen:esepera |
|-----------|-----|-----------|-----|---------|-------------|-----|-------------|
| c | /ts/ | – [35] | c | c | z | – | – |
| ĉ | /tʃ/ | c | ch | ch | ĉ | c | – |
| ĝ | /dʒ/ | – [36] | | j | ĝ | j | – |
| ĥ | /x/ | – [37] | – | kh | ĥ | – | – |
| j | /j/ | i [38] | y | y | j | y | i |
| ĵ | | j | j | zh | ĵ | – | – |
| k | /k/ | k | k | k | k | k | c |
| s | /s/ | s | s | s | c | s | s |
| ŝ | | x | sh | sh | ŝ | sh | – |
| ŭ | | u [39] | w/u | w | ŭ | w | – |
| z | /z/ | z | z | z | s | z | – |

Table 2.2 *Changed Letters in Some Daughter Languages*

## 2.2    Omission of Sounds

Esperanto allows sounds to be omitted in certain circumstances. This is also true of some of its daughters, but the situations in which it happens (or is permitted to happen) are sometimes different.

Alfandari (1961:43) begins the section entitled "L'Elision" with the remark, "On a *la faculté* (non l'obligation) d'élider par euphonie et *tant que cela ne nuit pas à la clarté de la phrase,* le mots suivants". The first of these words is the definite article,

---

[35] I do not know whether /ts/ occurs in Ekselsioro, but if it does it would not be represented by a single letter of the Ekselsioro alphabet (and presumably would not be seen as an affricate, but a sequence of two sounds); as can be seen immediately below, the letter which stands for it in Esperanto, <c>, is used for another purpose.

[36] I assume that /dʒ/ is not part of the phoneme inventory of Ekselsioro, as Greenwood (1906a:9) states, "G in Gin, J in Judge … are not used". Couturat and Leau (1907/1979:90) say, "L'auteur [i.e. Greenwood] ne dit pas ce que devient [Esperanto] ĝ; le le remplace tantôt par g …, tantôt par j".

[37] Greenwood (1906a:9) says that "kh and hh gutturals are *not* used".

[38] In most contexts the <i> of Ekselsioro stands for the vowel /i/, but it "forms a glide or diphthong of one syllable by its position after [all vowels except /i/]" Greenwood (1906a:9). One might interpret this to mean that in the latter contexts it stands for what Esperanto <j> stands for. However, according to Greenwood (ibid.) the diphthong <oi> is pronounced "as *oey* in *joey*". This might mean that the sequence of letters <oi> in Ekselsioro is not pronounced identically to the Esperanto sequence of letters <oj>, since the latter has the sound of the diphthong in e.g. the English word *joy*; at least in my accent *joy* and *joey* are not identical in pronunciation. Greenwood (ibid.) indicates that the diphthong <ui> is pronounced "as *ouie* in *Louie*". As far as I know, in Ekselsioro /j/ does not occur at the beginnings of syllables (or words), or anywhere except after vowels, and it thus appears that whenever this sound occurs (i.e. after most vowels), the letter <i> is used to indicate it. Therefore we can say that Esperanto <j> is replaced by <i> in Ekselsioro, with <i> also standing for /i/ in the latter language. There can be two instances of <i> in succession (as in *metii,* cited but not glossed in Greenwood 1906a:9) and I do not know whether there would be a glide between them; Greenwood (ibid.) does not give any indication that there would be.

[39] Greenwood (1906a:9) says that <u> stands for "u in rule, (Fr. plus)." I assume the second part of this is an error, since French *plus* contains [y], and not [u]. Later on the same page he states, "Whenever *u* follows *a* or *e* it is short. […] And forms a glide or diphthong of one syllable by its position after: as in *ambau, neutra*". This may not be entirely clear, but it seems that the sequences <au> and <eu> in Ekselsioro are equivalent to the sequences <aŭ>and <eŭ> respectively in Esperanto: among the diphthongs listed (ibid.) are "**au**, as in ho*w*" and "**eu**, as in they *who*".

*lo*: when the sound either immediately before or immediately after the article is a vowel, its vowel can be omitted, and both the vowel and the -*s* of its plural form, *los*, can be deleted,[40] meaning that the shortened singular and plural articles have the same form, namely *l*. Unlike in Esperanto, deletion of sounds is not marked by an apostrophe. Thus *l omo and l omos* are 'the man' and 'the men' respectively (ibid.).

The vowel of the preposition *de* 'of' may be omitted when the following word has a vowel as its initial segment, e.g. *d un fem* 'of a woman' (ibid.). The -*o* which is the marker of nouns can also be deleted. This is also true of Esperanto, but in Neo nouns usually appear without their final -*o*.[41] For example, in the list of vocabulary relating to travel in Alfandari (1961:77) the words for 'train', 'plane', and 'hotel' are given as *tren, iv*, and *hotel*. This is not permitted with plural nouns.[42] The adjectival marker -*a*, along with the plural suffix -*s* if present, can be deleted from adjectives which are before their nouns (not necessarily immediately before them), e.g., *un gran(a) e bel(a) klezo* ' a big and beautiful church' (ibid.:43).[43] This also applies to demonstrative adjectives (though not, to my knowledge, with possessive adjectives), e.g. *et(a) dom* 'this house' (ibid.). The final -*a* of a substantivized adjective "employé … dans un sens absolute" (ibid.) is also omissible, e.g. *lo real* 'the real' (ibid.). Feminine forms of substantivized past participles can appear without the ending -*at* (which is the marker of such participles), e.g. *l akuzin* 'the accused (F)' (ibid.; cf. the masculine *l akuzat*). Finally, Alfandari (ibid.) says, "en poésie, n'importe quel mot, lorsque le sentiment le dicte ou lorsque la musicalité du vers le suggère". I do not know whether this overrules the limitations on omission that he previously gave, e.g. with respect to the adjectival -*a*, "*jamais il ne peut être élidé lorsqu'il* [the adjective] *suit le nom*" (ibid.). He concludes this section with the statement, "En ligne générale, l'élision est employée plus fréquemment dans le langage familier et en poésie qu'en langage scientifique ou technique, où la précision est de rigueur".

Vitek (n.d. b) mentions the possibility of dropping some suffixes in Arlipo (but the nominal suffix -*o* is not included among them): "En parolado au poezio esat ellasebla adjektiva au adverba finazho, anstate kvo on skribat apostrofo; akcento daurat sur la sama silabo" ('In speaking or poetry an adjectival or adverbial ending is elidable, instead of which one writes an apostrophe; [the] accent remains on the same syllable').

1919 Esperantida allows the deletion of a range of vowels in word-final position: de Saussure (1919:4) states, "En poetio, la fina vokalo de substantivo, pronomo, ajektivo or verbo povas esti apostrafa, kiam ji estas pleonasma, or ne necesa por la kompreno" ('In poetry, the final vowel of a noun, pronoun, adjective, or verb can be apostrophized, when it is pleonastic, or not necessary for understanding').

In Linguna one "prescau cziam" ('almost always', Goeres 2004a) deletes the masculine and feminine singular nominative nominal suffixes -*o* and -*a* "ubí la rádico finas en consonanto mola resp. non-abrupta" ('when the root ends in a soft or non-

---

[40] I assume that one must delete both, i.e. one cannot delete one and leave the other.

[41] Alfandari (ibid.:19) says, "nous renonçons à l'élision de l'**o** final d'un nom toutes les fois qu'un besoin d'emphase se fait sentir".

[42] There is a contrast between plural articles and plural nouns, the former, but not the latter, being able to drop their final -*os*. Perhaps Alfandari made this restriction so that plural noun phrases will have at least one instance of plural marking. Although he does not say it explicitly, it seems that when the last vowel of a plural form is omitted, the plural marker -*s* must also be dropped.

[43] This is not allowed in Esperanto; Wennergren (2005:95) states, "Oni ne povas apostrofi A-vortojn".

abrupt consonant', ibid.); these consonants include *l*, *m*, *n*, *f*, and *ss*. This deletion happens "foaje ancau post -ch, -s, -v" ('also sometimes after -ch, -s, -v', ibid.).

## 2.3    Stress

Some of the languages dealt with in this book, including Arlipo, Ekselsioro, and Mondlango, have the same stress rule as Esperanto (the penult is always stressed in words of more than one syllable). However, some other languages differ from Esperanto. Cartier (m.d.) says of Novesperant, "Accent is as in french no one syllable must be stressed [sic]". Cartier (p.c.) states, "Stress is unimportant". As in Esperanto, in Virgoranto all words are stressed on the same syllable, but it is the first syllable, not the penult.

The stress pattern of Ido is different from that of Esperanto, and more complicated. The stressed syllable in most words is the penult, as in Esperanto, but the last syllable of infinitives is the one that is stressed.[44] Many numerals represent exceptions to this pattern: Couturat (1925/2005:11) states, "En la nombri, inter 20 e 100, la acento restas sur la radiko *du, tri, quar* e. c. Ex. : **dûa-dek**, (o **dûadek**) ... Kompreneble en **dek-e-un, dek-e-du, dek-e-tri**, e. c. ne la konjunciono *e*, ma la nombro *dek* esas acentizata" ('In the numbers, between 20 and 100, the accent remains on the root *du, tri, quar* etc., e.g. : dûa-dek, (or **dûadek**) ... Of course in **dek-e-un, dek-e-du, dek-e-tri** etc. not the conjunction *e*, but the number *dek* is accented.').[45] With respect to words of one syllable, Couturat (ibid.:12) states that they "darfas esar acentizata o ne (tam en prozo kam en poezio) segun la kuntexto e l'intenco dil autoro" ('may be accented or not (both in prose and in poetry) according to the context and the intention of the author').

In Hom-idyomo the penult of polysyllabic words is usually the stressed syllable. However, the part of a verb comprising its inflectional marking (which will be the last part of the word) receives the stress, and so some (but not all) verb forms will have their stress on another syllable. When this part consists of one syllable, it (i.e. the ultima) is the stressed syllable, e.g. (using Cárdenas' way of marking stress) *do˞máy* 'sleep (PRES INDIC)'. (When this part is made up of two syllables, the first of these, i.e. the penult, receives stress, e.g. *do˞mívi* 'sleep (IMPER)'.) There is one other group of words which do not have penultimate stress; Cárdenas (1923:I:20), who classifies words containing derivational affixes as compounds, says, "There are a great many words which end with the same letters as a suffix, but are not compound. In order to avoid confusion, words compounded with a suffix are accentuated on the antepenultimate syllable, unless they are verbs, in which case they are, like all other

---

[44] Collinson (1924) criticizes this feature: "Ido ... has a stressed infinitive ending, which makes it somewhat jerky, and throws the emphasis on to the relatively unimportant part of the word."

[45] Some other words also appear to be exceptions to the Ido stress pattern, e.g. *filii* 'children', *misterio* 'mystery', which have their stress on the first and second syllable respectively. However, they are not seen as exceptions, since the vowels in the sequences *ii* and *ia* (among some others) in word-final position are often (considered to be) part of the same syllable, and thus these words have penultimate stress. The vowels of these sequences do not always belong to the same syllable, e.g. *dio* 'day' is a two-syllable word, with stress on *di*.

verbs, accentuated on the ending". Apparently these words with antepenultimate stress should have an acute accent over the vowel of the antepenult.[46]

Penultimate stress also applies in Romániço in most cases. The ultima of infinitives receives stress, as does the antepenult of some words; one can show that the latter situation holds by means of an acute accent, e.g. *ópero* 'opera'. This antepenultimate stress can be lost, with stress being placed on the penult, if what was the antepenult does not remain so after a suffix is attached. Morales' practice in his webpages on Romániço is to place a grave accent on the formerly stressed syllable, e.g. h*erèditanto* 'heir' (from *herédito* 'inheritance'). The use of the acute and grave accents is not compulsory; Morales (n.d. i) says, "These accent marks, while useful in print, need not be used in handwriting, and, if so desired, can be ignored altogether. (Words like **spectáculo** are generally more recognizable … with the accent mark left in, but the marks are not critical for understanding.)".

In Atlango as well, the stress generally falls on the penult. However, the ultima of words whose final component is the suffix *-all* or the suffix *-arr* receives the stress.[47] Aiola words have penultimate stress unless the last segment of the penult is [i] or [u], in which case the antepenult is the stressed syllable, as in e.g. *dikcionario* and *ambigua* (which presumably mean 'dictionary' and 'ambiguous'), the stress of which ARG (2005:6) represents as [dik-ci-o-NA-ri-o] and [am-BI-gu-a].[48]

Perio has a relatively complicated stress system. Words are usually stressed on the first syllable of their radical. Exceptions to this general rule are that passive verbs have their last syllable stressed and with proper nouns it is the penult that is stressed. The stress of the latter type of word is indicated by putting a grave accent mark not over the vowel of the stressed syllable, but over the vowel of the final syllable, e.g. *vaciqtonù* 'Washington'.[49]

Neo also has a more complex stress system than Esperanto: the general rule is that if a word ends in a consonant (including the silent <h>) its last syllable is stressed, while if it ends in a vowel the penult receives the stress. However, the plural marker *-s* does not count for this rule, i.e. a plural noun whose singular form ends in a vowel will be stressed on its penult both in the singular and in the plural. Compounds apparently are exceptional with respect to stress; Alfandari (1961:49) says, "*les mots composés sont censés avoir deux accents toniques:* **ristorAntvagOn**". Alfandari (ibid.:40) gives the following rule about stress in cardinal numerals, some of which do not follow the general stress pattern of the language: "*L'accent tonique des nombres se pose:* 1) *sur la dernière syllabe* lorsque le dernier chiffre est une unité ou un

---

[46] Cárdenas (1923) often also puts an acute accent above the vowel of verbs which have stress on the ultima, but he does this "only to guide the student" (ibid.:I:24) and says, "in practice that is not necessary" (ibid.).

[47] According to Antonius (2008b) these suffixes mean 'of, relating to'; words containing them can function as adjectives or adverbs.

[48] ARG (2005:6) contrasts words such as *dikcionario and ambigua* with some other words, including *kaloriyo* and *kontinuwa* (which presumably mean 'calorie' and 'continuous'), in which the penult is stressed since it does not have [i] or [u] as its final segment, but rather [ j] or [w]. However, the representation of the stress of these words (ibid.), e.g. [ka-lo-RI-yo], [kon-ti-NU-wa], makes it appear that the [ j] or [w] occurs in the ultima, in which case the last segment of the penult would be [i] or [u], in which case the antepenult should be stressed.

[49] Given this, I do not understand why some proper nouns appear without an accent mark, e.g. *penelopy, parizo* (from Couturat and Leau 1907/1979:11); perhaps Couturat and Leau (ibid.:4) have misstated or omitted something in their description of stress in Perio, or of the marking of it.

millier: isdU ['12'] ...dumIl ['2000'] ... 2) *sur l'avant-dernière syllabe* lorsque le dernier chiffre est une dizaine ou une centaine: dUis ['20'] ... Otek ['800'] ...”

Words in Esperloja apparently do not have to have a stressed syllable: Sulky (n.d.) states, “Emphasis is optional. If used, it is on the syllable that precedes the vowel-pair ending [i.e. the word class suffix]”.

In Linguna the penult of polysyllabic words usually is the stressed syllable; if another syllable is stressed, an acute accent is placed over its vowel. However, if the stress is on the ultima because of the deletion of the vowel of the last syllable (this will not cause the stress to shift), one need not have the acute accent, “condicze qve confús cun iu finagjo ne occasus” ('on condition that confusion with some ending not occur', Goeres 2004a).

## 2.4 Phonotactics

Sen:esepera is very restricted in terms of syllable structure; all syllables have the pattern (C)V(j)(N), that is, there is a maximum of one consonant in the onset, and there is a maximum of two consonants after the vowel, one of which must be /j/, and the other a nasal.[50] Ekselsioro does not allow some consonant clusters which exist in Esperanto: Greenwood (1906a.:10) states, “There are no ... *kn, ps, gv, ft, sf, shv,* and other forms of foreign difficulty”.

The phonotactic rules of Hom-idyomo are similar to those of English:

> As a general rule, a syllable consists of or begins with one consonant followed by a vowel, as in *kan-to,* “song”; *mul-ta,* “much”. The exceptions are the consonants b, k, d, f, g, p, t followed by l or *ɼ*, as in *ple-na,* “full”;
>
> *gloɼ -yo,* “glory”; *fɼu-e,* “early”; *dɼin-kiɼ,* “to drink”; *tɼo-no,* “throne”; ...
>
> Also as a general rule, at the end of a syllable there is but one consonant preceded by a vowel, as in *sem-peɼ,* “always”; *as-tɼo,* “star”.
>
> The exceptions are the combinations *bs, ks, ms, ns,* and *ts,* as in *abs-te-niɼ,*
>
> *eks-pɼe-s*a, *ins-piɼ-o, its-mo.* (Cárdenas 1923:I:4)

This apparently means that such Esperanto words as *knabo* 'boy' and *splito* 'splinter' could not occur in Hom-idyomo without being modified.

In Esperloja, a sequence of two vowels must form a word class suffix, which must be the last component of a word. Sulky (n.d.) gives some other phonotactic rules for his language, including one involving sounds in different words: “Vowel triplets never occur in a word; therefore, a spoken vowel triplet is necessarily a word-ending vowel pair [i.e. a word class suffix] followed by a vowel that begins a word. Identical vowels spanning a word boundary must be separated by a glottal stop, which is considered to be part of the pronunciation of the first word of the pair.” Further, a vowel cannot immediately follow another instance of the same vowel within the same word. While, as we have just seen, a glottal stop is sometimes required between vowels, a schwa can, but does not have to, break up a consonant cluster; Sulky (ibid.) states, “Between every two adjacent consonants, an optional unwritten schwa sound

---

[50] Henning (1995a) says, “Sen:esepera's morphology is designed to eliminate complex consonant clusters (i.e. /str/, /bl/, /pr/, /sp/), which are difficult for many speakers of Asian and African languages to pronounce”.

may be pronounced. Doubled consonants that are not separated by schwa buffering must be pronounced as a doubly-long single consonant".

## 2.5 Punctuation

Cárdenas (1923:154) gives the following instructions on punctuation: "… Homidyomo follows the general rules adopted in all other languages. Since, however, the use of the comma is not entirely uniform, it is well to state that all phrases and sentences not separated by a preposition, a conjunction or an adverb should be separated by a comma."

Vitek (n.d. b) says the following about "Uzazdo je komi" ('Use of commas') in Arlipo: "Arbitra, ma sekvanta signifio kaj voka divido di la frazo" ('Arbitrary, but following meaning and [?] division of the sentence'[51]). He presumably does not mean that comma placement is entirely arbitrary.

Sulky (n.d.) says of Esperloja, "Loglan's model is followed in pronouncing punctuation". *Fue* and *gue* are equivalent to the quotation marks which indicate the beginning and end of a direct quote, and the words *tue* and *sue* are the "left grammatical grouping parenthesis" (ibid.) and "right grammatical grouping parenthesis" (ibid.) respectively.

One of the devices used to make sentences in the DLT Intermediate Language "syntactically unambiguous" (Schubert 1992:89)[52] is the indication of boundaries between morphemes. To use the example from Schubert (ibid.), while in Esperanto *sendata* can mean 'undated' or 'being sent', in the DLT Intermediate Language *sen'dat'a* can only have the former meaning and *send'at'a* only the latter meaning.[53] In DLT there is also the possibility of having two spaces between words rather than one when a phrase boundary separates them. Schubert's (ibid.:88-9) example of this involves the sentence that in Esperanto would be written as *Ni acetas libron de Goethe*, which could mean 'We buy a book by Goethe' or 'We buy a book from Goethe'. The second interpretation would be expressed as follows in the DLT Intermediate Language:[54]

(4)     Ni acet'as libr'o'n #de Goethe

The second space shows that the PP *de Goethe* is not contained in the NP headed by *libr'o'n*. The first interpretation would be expressed by the sentence in (5), with only one space between *libr'o'n* and *de* (showing that there is no phrase boundary between them and thus that the direct object NP is *libr'o'n de Goethe*):[55]

(5)     Ni acet'as libr'o'n de Goethe

---

[51] I do not know how to translate *voka*; *vokon* is 'to call'.

[52] Recall that Schubert uses "syntax" for "all grammatical properties on the formal side of the linguistic sign" (ibid.), and it therefore includes morphology.

[53] Like Schubert (1986) I usually not use this marker in examples or words from the DLT Intermediate Language although presumably in principle it should always be present.

[54] I follow Schubert (ibid.) in using # to mark the second space.

[55] . This is a good example of the use of the double space for disambiguation, but it is not clear to me whether it would come up in the version of the DLT Intermediate Language presented in Schubert (1986), the version that I am focusing on, since Schubert (ibid.) states, "La aganton de la pasivo … signifas *far*, ne *de*"; (5) is not a passive construction, but *de* still has an agentive meaning.

# 3      Lexicon

In this chapter I shall treat differences in vocabulary from Esperanto, except for those involving derivational morphology or minor classes of words such as conjunctions; these will be dealt with in the next chapter. There is also some information on the vocabulary of several daughters of Esperanto in Chapter 1.

## 3.0      General Issues

In the "Vocabulary" section of his webpage on Esperloja Sulky (n.d.) states, "Wherever possible, Esperanto roots remain unchanged, as do Esperanto word-building prefixes and suffixes. As a rule, the second vowel of any vowel pair in Esperanto is dropped. An exception to this is vowel pairs in which the first vowel is a glide (Esperanto **j** is the only example); in this case the glide is dropped".

Alfandari (1961:12) criticizes Esperanto for its "emploi excessif d'affixes"; his language Neo has more roots than Esperanto, which allows improvement in this area. Some of the words of Neo are shorter than their equivalents in Esperanto. Among these words are the verbs of one syllable. Alfandari (ibid.:44) states, "Ces verbes sont la contraction d'une forme bisyllabique, employée de préférence dans le mots dérivés", as in *bevibla* 'drinkable'. Below are the verbs that Alfandari says are of this type, along with their full versions:

| contracted | full | meaning | contracted | full | meaning |
|---|---|---|---|---|---|
| i | avi | 'avoir' | pi | posi | 'pouvoir' |
| bi | bevi | 'boire' | pli | plazi | 'plaire' |
| ci | dici | 'dire' | pri | preni | 'prendre' |
| di | doni | 'donner' | ri | riri | 'retourner' |
| fi | fari | 'faire' | si | esi | 'être' |
| gi | igi | 'aller' | shi | shali | 'devoir' |
| ji | iji | 'devenir' | ski | aski | 'demander' |
| kli | klozi | 'fermer' | spi | sapi | 'savoir' |
| kri | kredi | 'croire' | sti | risti | 'se trouver, rester' |
| li | lati | 'laisser' | ti | meti | 'mettre' |
|  |  |  | vi | voli | 'vouloir' |

Table 3.1: *Neo "Verbes Monosyllabiques" Listed in Alfandari (1961:44)*

In fact, one could argue that the contracted root of the verb 'to have' does not consist of any segmental material, since the *-i* of all the above forms is the infinitive suffix, meaning that, for example, the contracted root of the verb 'to drink' is simply *b-*. Thus different tense forms of *(av)i* consist only of the tense endings, e.g. the present tense form is *ar* (the present tense suffix being *-ar*).

Perio also has short roots, at least most of them being a single syllable, and a large proportion of the vocabulary is *a priori*, with roots with similar meanings having the same consonants but differing in their vowel (one of the roots often being a posteriori). The semantic relationships holding among roots sharing consonants vary, as can be seen in the following table (in which word class suffixes are attached to the roots):

| | | |
|---|---|---|
| jalo 'throat' | julo 'neck' | jilo 'nape of neck' |
| dafo 'morning' | dufo 'noon' | difo 'evening' |
| date 'yesterday' | dute 'today' | dite 'tomorrow' |
| kladi 'to close | | klidi 'to open' |
| savi 'to know' | suvi 'to believe' | sivi 'to doubt' |
| maro 'floor' | muro 'wall' | miro 'ceiling' |
| cato 'hour' | vuto 'minute' | cito 'second' |

Table 3.2: *Some Items from the Vocabulary of Perio (after Couturat and Leau 1907/1979:8-9)*

Another language whose roots are short is E-speranto, as shown in the following passage from Holmes (n.d. a) (I believe that he means 'root' when he writes 'stem'); note also that E-speranto does not seem to have as many roots as Esperanto:

> E-speranto has a basic vocabulary of single syllable stems. Relatively few of these are needed because the agglutinative rules for forming compound words allow many if not most of the words needed in other languages to be built up from the stems in the basic vocabulary.
>
> Another factor that allows the basic vocabulary to be kept small is the provision in the orthography that allows words, particularly names, drawn from a particular culture to be marked - in the Latin alphabet by their initial letter being upper case, and by other measures. This marking reduces if not removes the tendency to follow the example of Esperanto in bringing words into the language with little justification.
>
> The basic vocabulary of E-speranto is drawn exclusively from that of Esperanto, but removing polysyllabic stems. However some useful stems in E-speranto are derived from Esperanto stems by abbreviation; for example the *sper* (hope) in E-speranto comes from Esperanto's *esper*.

A related fact is that in E-speranto vowels in some groups of morphemes are associated with particular meanings, as explained by Holmes (n.d. b):

> ... there are many syllables in which the effect or meaning is changed systematically by changing the vowel. This last feature is one of the measures used to allow the language to get by with far fewer basic stems to learn than it would otherwise need. [...]
>
> For the systematic shifts of meaning, the vowels should be thought of as arranged in a cross, as shown in the diagram.

$$O/o$$
$$U/u \qquad A/a \qquad E/e$$
$$I/i$$

The vowel *A/a* is neutral in this scheme of meaning, and the other vowels take a position in time or space relative to *A/a*, with *O/o* signifying ideas like *up* or *forward* or *north* or *beyond* or *future*, and *E/e* signifying ideas like *clockwise* or *right* or *east* or *certainty*. Of course, *I/i* is opposite to *O/o*, and *U/u* is opposite to *E/e*.

Some consonants are also involved in this sort of relationship (at least in 2008 E-speranto); Holmes (2008:96) states:

> This construction [it is not clear exactly what he is referring to here, the association of vowels with meanings or some subpart of it] can be simply extended to specify horizontal spatial placement by [vowel] (*m*) [*p*] and vertical by [vowel] (*n*)[*k*], where the *m* and *n* specify placement relations relative to the sentence's subject. […] Thus *la domompo* means the house ahead while *la domopo* means the front of the house. Such compounds can take some getting used to, but they are regular and powerful.

The elimination of letters with diacritics in Snifferanto led to changes in the forms of words and replacements of words. Hietala (2006a) states that the vocabulary was taken from Ido, Interlingua, Latin, or other languages, although many words are identical to their Esperanto counterparts. Hietala (ibid.) gives five methods (or "[t]ipoj de vokveksloj" 'types of word changes') for Esperanto words containing letters with diacritics, and one should attempt to apply them in the order given; Hietala. (ibid.) says: "Provu la unuan tipon. Se [olu] ne funkcias,[1] provu la duan, kaj tiel plu" ('Try the first type. If [it] does not work, try the second, and so on'). These methods are 1) simple removal of diacritics, e.g. Esperanto *ĝardeno* 'garden' becomes *gardeno*, 2) replacement of a letter with a diacritic by the equivalent digraph, e.g. Esperanto *ŝipo* 'ship' becomes *shipo*, 3) replacement of a letter with a diacritic with a letter having a similar sound, e.g. Esperanto *mesaĝo* 'message' becomes *mesazo*, 4) use of "[n]ovaj literkombinoj" ('new combinations of letters'), e.g. Esperanto *ĵaŭdo* 'Thursday' becomes *zovdo*, and 5) replacement of a word by a non-Esperanto word, e.g. Esperanto *neĝo* 'snow' is replaced with *nievo* (from Spanish).

Concerning Arlipo Vitek (n.d. a) says, "Multa changi esat farita en la vortstok Certe, elektado je vorti esat omnam influata da subjektiva gusto, ma me pensat, ke plejparte ti farita changi esat anke objektive motivebla" ('Many changes [from Esperanto, presumably] have been made in the vocabulary. Certainly, choice of words has always been influenced by subjective taste, but I think that most of those changes that have been made can also be objectively motivated').

The lexicon of Intero involves several changes (from that of Esperanto) which do not seem to be due to a desire to do away with difficult aspects of pronunciation (unlike some changes mentioned in section 2.1): *lino* 'flax' is changed to *leno* in Intero, *cimo* 'bug' is dropped and Intero has the word *vanco* instead of it; *celi* 'to aim at/for' is also dropped, with *peni* or *direti* (equivalent to Esperanto *direkti*?) being used instead of it. Thompson (2007a) says, "The Esperanto *lasta* may be used or may be replaced by the Esperanto *maluna*".

The "Vocabulary" section of Henning (1995a) contains the following statements: "***Sen:esepera*** is almost entirely derived from Esperanto and has approximately 1700 words, derived from around 1200 basic morphemes. The final version of the vocabulary will attempt to reduce the number of basic morphemes to 600."

---

[1] It is not clear to me what it means for a type not to work, except with regard to the second type.

The vocabulary of Reformed Esperanto is rather different than that of Esperanto. For one thing, roots of Germanic and Slavic origin were removed in favor of roots from Latin and Romance languages. According to Couturat and Leau (1907/1979:32) Zamenhof made these changes "[p]our donner plus d'homogénéité à son vocabulaire et aussi pour se passer des lettres proscrites". Thus for example Reformed Esperanto has *hiver-* 'winter' and a*prend-* 'learn' instead of Esperanto *vintr-* and *lern-*. Roots of Romance origin were not immune from removal: Couturat and Leau (ibid.) say that they "étaient souvent remplacées par des racines latines ou ramenées à leur forme étymologique". Further, "D'autres racines sont au contraire altérées dans le sens de l'évolution, et en générale raccourcies … Enfin il [= Zamenhof] substituait à quelques racines non romanes des dérivés ou composés … ou inversement il prenait des racines romanes pour remplacer des dérivés de racines non-romanes" (ibid.:32-3). The result of all this is that Reformed Esperanto has "l'aspect d'une langue néo-latine" (ibid.:33).

The same could be said of Romániço: Morales (n.d. b) gives the following procedure for vocabulary creation in this language:

> Romániço's lexicon is built using a method of "etymological Romance", which gives the language a consistently Romance look and sound, as well as an unvarying formula for introducing new words. This approach, used for existing as well as new words, can be summed up as follows:
> - Find the common root used by French, Spanish, Italian, and, where possible, English. For example, the words "ear", "nation", and "peace" are *oreille, nation,* and *paix* in French, *oreja, nación,* and *paz* in Spanish, *orecchio, nazione,* and *pace* in Italian — all of which come from Latin *auriculus, natio,* and *pax,* which appear in English *auricular, nation,* and *peace.*
> (Most planned languages simply adopt this or that national permutation of a word, eg. Esperanto and Ido *orelo* from French, Interlingua *aure* from Latin; Romániço adopts the *immediate source* form of modern Romance words, the ones in use before national spelling variations were applied to them.)
> - Recast the word into the ablative case (or past participle, in the case of verbs), and indicate irregular stress, if any: *aurículo, natione,* and *pace.*
> - Change hard *c* to **qu** before *e* and *i*, soft *c* to **ç** or **cz** at the end of a noun or adjective root; keep final *-que* as **-que** (not **-cue**); soft *g* to **j**; *-tius, -tia* (but not *-stius, -stia*) to **-cio**; *sce-, sci-* to **ce-, ci-**; *-cce-, -cci-* to **-ce-, -ci-**; *-nct-, -mpt-* to **-nt-**; *-atic-* to **-aj-**; double letters to single; the final vowel to **o**: **aurículo, naciono,** and **paço.**
> - Violate any of these rules to avoid homonyms: Latin *venire, vent-* ("to come") becomes **vener** in Romániço instead of *venter,* since **vento** (Latin *ventus*) already means "wind, breeze".

Ido differs somewhat from Esperanto with respect to the extent to which different sources have been drawn on in forming its vocabulary: Liu (2006:51) states, "Ido is distinctly more Romance (or Latinate) in its vocabulary than Esperanto". It is thus similar to Reformed Esperanto and Romániço in this respect. The thinking behind the construction of the lexicon has been briefly described as follows: "[The Ido lexicon] is based on the vocabularies of the main European languages since they are so widespread and have so many words in common (often those of Latin origin). The basic words in Ido were chosen with the primary aim of being intelligible to as many speakers of these languages as possible" (anon. n.d. h). Monnerot-Dumaine (1960:174) says that the vocabulary of Ido is "plus naturaliste [than that of Esperanto]".

Words taken from English form part of Mondlango's vocabulary; Mifsud (n.d. b) says:

> Mondlango ... for the purpose of making it easy, popular and useful, uses both English and Esperanto as sources of word roots. English, because this is the language everybody is trying to learn; and Esperanto because for more than a century of constant use it has proved to be the easiest language to learn quickly so far. Mondlango aims at simplifying and combining both to construct a new easy language for all.

> This, as can be expected, is no easy job. One of the main difficulties is the building of the vocabulary for beginners. The policy here is to take the English root, simplify it and phoneticise it. Thus, from photo (foto) we get foti, to photograph. Where the English root is not suitable enough, the Esperanto root is borrowed and once more, simplified if possible. Roots from other languages are also used when needed.

Other languages also provided items for the Mondlango vocabulary: according to anon. (n.d. c), "the words of Mondlango come mainly from English, German, French, Spanish and other Indo-European languages".

The Olingo lexicon comes from several sources. Jaque (1944:24-5) cites Olingo words drawn from various languages, including the following: from Arabic: *didebo* 'sentry', *surato* 'manuscript'; from Chinese: *chiho* 'paper', *wano* 'cask'; from English: *helpi* 'to help', *so* 'so'; from French: *adie* 'farewell', *pluvi* 'to rain'; from German: *gewaro* 'awareness', *nur* 'only'; from Greek: *chitono* 'undergarment', *qutalo* 'spoon'; from Hawaiian: *alohe!* 'salute of love!';[2] from Japanese: *quchiqo* 'destroyer (ship)', *sampo* 'trench'; from Latin: *arbo* 'tree', *ludi* 'to play'; from Malay: *getaho* 'rubber', *qarando* 'coffin'; from Portuguese: *pombo* 'pigeon', *surda* 'deaf'; from Russian: *palto* 'overcoat', *promi* 'to walk'; from Sanskrit: *labho* 'profit', *ratho* 'chariot'; from Spanish: *ajo* 'garlic', *maizo* 'corn'.

Linguna has also taken vocabulary items from a relatively large number of natural languages; Goeres (2004b) states:

> Der Vokabelteil (Linguna-Deutsch/Englisch) des Grundwortschatzes des LINGUNA besteht aus Elementen der Grundsprachen-Gruppen Latein, Griechisch, Romanisch, Slawisch, Germanisch und der indoeuropäischen Etymologie, sowie eiszeitlichen Wurzeln weltweiter Verwandtschaft. Die Wörter sind meist griechischen, lateinischen und russisch/bulgarischen Ursprungs. Manche stammen auch aus dem Sanskrit oder sind näher mit diesem verwandt.

---

[2] This is the only word from Hawaiian cited here.

With regard to loanwords in Sen:esepera Henning (1995a) says, "When a word is borrowed into Sen:esepera, it should conform to its phonology, morphology and class suffixes. […] Esperanto words are nativized according to standard rules, which are too involved to detail here". Among the examples that he gives are *linegefa* 'language' (cf. Esperanto *lingvo*) and *seterata* 'street' (cf. Esperanto *strato*).

Sabarís (2003) states, "Perhaps the main difference between Eo [= Esperanto] and UTL languages is the latter's possibility of using words imported from other languages. This means the user can introduce words from his or any other language, as long as it has been implemented in the translation software." The appropriate Esperanto word class (and inflectional?) suffixes will be attached to such words (connected by a hyphen), e.g.:

(1)     Via   explanation-o     klar-ig-is       niajn   dubojn.
        your  *explanation*-NN  clear-CAUS-PST   our     doubts
        'Your explanation cleared up our doubts.' (ibid., MT)

Sabarís (ibid.) says that this "'importing' function is a specially [sic] handy feature for beginners, but it should be used with care: homonymic words should be avoided".

## 3.1     Kinship Vocabulary

Henning (1995d) presents an elaborate system of kinship words in Sen:esepera, which can be, but does not have to be, very specific; it is based on his "detailed framework for defining kinship terms from different languages" (ibid.), KinDEEP (KINship Distinctive Elements, Exhaustive Profile), which is set forth in the same  paper. A guiding principle of both KinDEEP and the Sen:espera system seems to be to allow for the marking of any distinction that some natural language indicates in its lexicon. The system can indicate the person to whom the referent of the kinship term is related: the first possible part of a word in this system is *imun* 'my' or *tun* 'your', e.g.*imun:eman:u:sa* 'my brother', *tun:eman:dimin:pa* 'your grandson'. There is no parallel marker for third-person, since to Henning's knowledge no natural language has one.

The next possible part indicates sex, *eman* for males and *fem* for females, e.g. *eman:inten:pa* 'grandfather'. There is a third member of the system here, *sim*, for 'corresponding', i.e. for relations of the same sex of the reference person,[3] e.g. *sim:u:im:tempan:sa* 'younger sibling of my sex'. The third possible part gives information on the "side of family" (ibid.), and Henning (ibid.) gives five members of the set marking this (though he may allow for other possibilities to be marked): *pam* 'paternal', *fam* 'maternal', *duen* 'half', *tepim* 'step', and *belim* 'honorary',[4] e.g. *fem:pam:in:ta* 'paternal aunt', *fem:fam:in:ta* 'maternal aunt', *eman:tepim:u:sa* 'step-brother'.

The next part which can appear (and one which I believe will be present in the vast majority of cases) indicates the relation in terms of generations of the relative to the reference person. The morphemes of this set are *intensin* 'three generations

---

[3]  KinDEEP includes this notion because Hawaiian can express it lexically.

[4]  On the last of these Henning (1995d) says, "Families often have unofficial members, as English recognizes by encouraging the use of *Aunt* and *Uncle* for close family friends of the same generation as a child's parents. […] to support this almost metaphoric use of Aunt and Uncle, KinDEEP keeps the value {Honorary} as part of the semantic component of Side of Family".

before', *inten* 'two generations before', *in* 'one generation before', *u* 'same generation', *dim* 'one generation after', *dimin* 'two generations after', and *diminten* 'three generations after', as in *intensinpa* 'great-grandparent', *fem:inten:ta* 'great aunt', *fem:in:pa* 'mother', fem:u:sa 'sister', and *eman:dim:pa* 'son'. To indicate a generation beyond three in the past or future one uses *afo*, which precedes *intensin* and *dimenten*, e.g. *afo:intensin:pa* 'great-great-grandparent'. When *afo* precedes *in* or *dim* it has a different, general, meaning, e.g. *afo:in* 'all ancestors', *afo:in:coganta* 'ancestor', *afo:dim:coganta* 'descendant' (*coganta* being the general term for 'relative by blood or marriage'). *Inten* and *dimin* can occur together: *inten:dimin:coganta* means 'anyone two generations removed'.[5]

The fifth possible part of a Sen:esepera kinship word is an indicator of "[r]elative birth order" (ibid.), *tempan* and *im:tempan* meaning 'older' and 'younger' respectively, as in *fem:u:tempan:sa* 'older sister' and *fem:u:im:tempan:sa* 'younger sister'. As Henning (ibid.) points out, natural languages overwhelmingly apply this marking only to brothers and sisters, while in KinDEEP (and presumably Sen:esepera) one can indicate this notion for other relatives; the example he gives is 'younger uncle'. The final possible part indicates the type of "lineage" (ibid.); Henning (ibid.) gives four members of the set of morphemes indicating this (and again he may allow for other possible members of the set): *pa* 'direct', *ta* 'ablineal', *sa* 'colineal', and *coganta* 'unspecified'. His notions of ablineal and colineal, which he does not explicitly define, seem to be different from those used by others: Wallace and Atkins (1960:61) cite Ward H. Goodenough's conception of these terms: "lineals are persons who are ancestors or descendants of ego; co-lineals are non-lineals all of whose ancestors include, or are included in, all the ancestors of ego; ablineals are consanguineal relatives who are neither lineals nor co-lineals". This means that aunts and uncles (in the narrowest sense) would be colineal relatives, as would brothers and sisters, while cousins would be ablineal relatives since a person's cousins has ancestors that he does not have. However, Henning (1995c) states, "lineage would be either direct, colineal (as in siblings) or ablineal (as in uncles and aunts)". To get a sense of the use of these morphemes compare *in:pa* 'parent' and *in:ta* 'parent's sibling', or *u:sa* 'sibling', *u:ta* 'child of aunt or uncle', and *u:coganta* 'sibling or cousin'. More than one of these morphemes can appear in a word, giving a disjunctive meaning, e.g. *eman:in:ta:pa* 'father or uncle', *fem:fam:in:ta:pa* 'mother or mother's sister' (although I assume that *coganta* could not appear with one of the other lineage morphemes).

In the table below are kinship words from some other daughters of Esperanto:[6]

---

[5] This term was presumably inspired by a word from the Australian language Njamal that Henning (1995d) mentions, *maili* 'any relative two generations distant'.
[6] In this and the following tables in this chapter an empty cell usually means that my source or sources for the language do not provide a word with the meaning in question.

|  | Esperanto | Farlingo | Hom-id. | Neo | Olingo | Romániço | Virgor. |
|---|---|---|---|---|---|---|---|
| father | patro | patro | patżo | patro | patro | jènitintiçho, patro | fato |
| mother | patrino | matra | mateżno | matro | patrino | jènitintiso, matro | mato |
| husband | edzo |  | mażito | sposo | andro | sposiçho |  |
| wife | edzino | femina[7] | mażitino | spozin | andrino | sposiso |  |
| son | filo | filo | filyo | filyo | filo | filiiçho | sono |
| daughter | filino | fila | filino | filyin | filino | filiiso | doxto |
| brother | frato | brato | fżatżo | frat | frato | jermaniçho, fratro |  |
| sister | fratino | sista | fżátżino | sor | fratino | jermaniso; sororo | sisko |
| uncle | onklo | onklo | onklo | onklo | uqo | avùnculiçho | onklo |
| aunt | onklino | tanta | ónklino | tant(o) | uqino | avùnculiso | tanto |
| nephew | nevo | nevo | nevo | nep |  | nepiçho | nefo |
| niece | nevino | neva | névino | nepin |  | nepiso | nixto |
| cousin | kuzo[8] |  | kusino | kuz(o)[9] |  | consobrino |  |

Table 3.3: *Some Kinship Words in Esperanto and Some Daughter Languages*

## 3.2    Body Part Terms

One might find it interesting that Neo has single-word names for the different fingers: *index*, *medel*, *anelel*, and *letel* ('index finger', 'middle finger', 'ring finger', and 'pinky' respectively), none of which contains the word meaning 'finger'.

In the following table it can be seen that across languages words for some body parts are the same or quite similar, while those for other parts contain different roots:

---

[7] The word for 'woman' in Farlingo is *fema*.
[8] This is the word for 'male cousin'; 'female cousin' is *kuzino*.
[9] This is the word for 'male cousin'; the word for 'female cousin' is *kuzin*.

|  | Esperanto | Far-lingo | Hom-id. | Ido | Mond-lango | Neo | Olingo | Romániço |
|---|---|---|---|---|---|---|---|---|
| head | kapo | kapo | kapo | kapo | hedo | cef, kap | qapo | cápito |
| face | vizaĝo | faso | faco | vizajo | faso | vizo | vizajo | facio |
| fore-head | frunto | frento | fronto | fronto | frunto | front |  | fronto |
| eye | okulo | okulo | okulo | okulo | okulo | ok | oqulo | óculo |
| nose | nazo | nazo | naso | nazo | nazo | nazo | nazo | naso |
| mouth | buŝo | boko | boko | boko | buxo | mund, bok | boqo | buco |
| lip | lipo | lipo | labyo | labio | lipo | labyo, | lipo | labro |
| ear | orelo | audo[10] | orelo | orelo | orelo | orel | orelo | aurículo |
| chin | mentono | mentono | mentono | mentono | mentono | menton | mentono | mentono |
| neck | kolo | neko | kolo |  | kolo | kol | quelo | colo |
| arm | brako | armo | braco | brakio | brako | bras | braqo | braquio |
| wrist | pojno, manradiko | polso | risto | karpo | risto | polso | qarpeo | carpalo |
| hand | mano | hando | mano | manuo | mano | man | mano | mano |
| finger | fingro | fingro | digito | fingro | fingro | fingo | fingro | díjito |
| leg | kruro |  | gambo | gambo | kruro | gambo | qruro | gambo |
| thigh | femuro |  | kwiso | kruro | femuro | kosh | femuro | coxo |
| foot | piedo | futo | pyedo | pedo | pedo | ped | piedo | pedo |
| toe | piedfingro | tao | pyeda-digito | ped-fingro | pedfingro | ortelyo | dedo | pedodíjito |
| bone | osto | osto | osto | osto | osto | osto | ostro | oso |
| brain | cerbo | sterbo | cerebro | cerebro | cerbo | cerebro, cervel[11] | serbo | cerebro |
| heart | koro | kuoro | koro | kordio | koro | kor | qoro | cordio |
| lung | pulmo |  | pulmono | pulmono | pulmo | pulmo | pulmo | pulmono |
| liver | hepato | hepato | hepato | hepato | hepato | ep |  | fígato, hépato |
| kidney | reno |  | reno | reno |  | ron, nefro |  | reno |

*Table 3.4: Body Part Terms in Esperanto and Some Daughters*

It is worth pointing out that the word for 'thigh' in Ido is the word for 'leg' in Esperanto. (The word for 'thigh' in Esperanto is the word for 'femur' in Ido.)

### 3.3    Color Terms

Cárdenas (1961:I:97) expresses a desire for more precise terms for colors: "It would be very useful to adopt a numerical scale to denote the different shades of colours, as the terms now used in trade do not differentiate them clearly enough. There are at least twenty shades of pink, and as many of other colours. We suggest that some

---

[10] Although *audo* is the word for 'ear' in Farlingo, its term for 'ear-ache' is *orele doloro*.
[11] On p. 84 Alfandari (1961) gives *cerebro* as the equivalent of French *cerveau*, and *cervel* as the equivalent of French *cervelle*, but on p. 914 he gives both *cerebro* and *cervel* as equivalents to French *cerveau*, and also gives both of them as equivalents of French *cervelle*.

chemist who makes a specialty of colours take the first step towards filling this want." Some color terms of Esperanto and some daughters are given in the table below:

| | Esperanto | Arlipo | Farlingo | Hom-id. | Mond-lango | Neo | Olingo | Romániço |
|---|---|---|---|---|---|---|---|---|
| white | blanka | blanka | blanke | blanka | wayta | alba | blanqa | blanca |
| yellow | flava | flava | yelove | flava | flava | jala | flava | flava |
| red | ruĝa | ruzha | rede | rusa | reda | ruba | ruja | rúbea |
| purple | purpura | viola[12] | violete | puɹpuɹa | purpla | purpa | purpura | púrpura |
| blue | blua | blua | lazure[13] | blua | blua | blu(a) | blua | blava |
| green | verda | verda | grine | veɹda | verda | verda | verda | vírida |
| brown | bruna | bruna | brune | bɹuna[14] | bruna | bruna | bruna | bruna |
| grey | griza | griza | grize | gɹisa | griza | griza | gra | grisa |
| black | nigra | nigra | nigre | nigɹa | blaka | nera | nigra | nigra |

Table 3.5: *Words for Colors in Esperanto and Some Daughters*

## 3.4 Vocabulary Relating to Time

Couturat and Leau (1907/1979:88) says that the Esperanto words for the seasons were 'barbares' in the opinion of the designer of Mondlingvo, who suggested new words for them, and for the days of the week, in his language. The ones for the season are *flortempo, varmtempo, fruktempo,* and *neĝtempo* or *froatempo* and those for the days of the week include *ripozdio* 'Sunday', *duadio* 'Monday', *kvaradio* or *mezodelsemajno* 'Wednesday', and *sepadio* or *finodelsemajno* 'Saturday'.

Neo has single words for phrases such as *next week*. The nominal forms are *pasvek, pasmes,* and *pasanyo* for 'last week', 'last month', and 'last year' respectively and *narvek, narmes,* and *naranyo* for 'next week', 'next month', and 'next year' respectively. To create adverbs from them one attaches the usual adverbial ending -*e*.[15] In the two examples below we see examples of a nominal and an adverbial form in use:

(2a)   Narmes      sar   lo    gran   mes     de   turismo.
       next.month   is    the   big    month   of   tourism
       'Le mois prochaine est le grand mois de tourisme.'

---

[12] Arlipo *viola* is equivalent to English *violet* and *purple*.

[13] Farber and Farber (2006) give *lazure* as the equivalent of both *blue* and *light blue*, and *blue* as the equivalent of *dark blue*.

[14] Cárdenas (1961:I:97) indicates that *fulva* is the word for 'brown', but he later (ibid.:II:144) gives *fulvous* as the English equivalent of *fulva* (with *braun, fauve, pardo,* and *fulve* being the German, French, Spanish, and Italian equivalents), and (ibid.:III:42) gives *bɹuna* as the Hom-idyomo equivalent of English *brown*. Further, he (ibid.:II:44) gives *brown* as the equivalent of *bɹuna* (with *braun, brun, bruno* and *moreno,* and *bruno* being the German, French, Spanish, and Italian equivalents).

[15] The adverbial form of *pasanyo* is *pasanye*; thus when the -*e* is attached the final -*o* is deleted. I assume that the same thing happens with *naranyo*.

(2b)  Narmes-e        el    fest-or        sa    issita    nasid.
next.month-ADV   she   celebrate-FUT  her   sixteenth birthday
'Le mois prochaine, elle fêtera sa seizième anniversaire.' (Alfandari
1961:72)

Neo has a prefix *yo-* meaning 'ago', e.g. *yovek* 'a week ago'.[16] The Neo abbreviations equivalent to 'a.m.' and 'p.m.' are *a.m.* and *d.m.* respectively (for *antemid* and *domid*; cf. Esperanto *atm.* and *ptm.*).

In the table below are terms for periods of time:

| | Esper-anto | Atlango | Hom-idy. | Ido | Mond-lango | Neo | Olingo | Romániço |
|---|---|---|---|---|---|---|---|---|
| second | sekundo | sekundo | sekondo | sekundo | sekondo | sekund | sequndo | secundo |
| minute | minuto | minuto | minuto | minuto | minuto | minut | minuto | minuto |
| hour | horo | horo | hoꞯo | horo | horo | or | horo | horo |
| day | tago | | dio | dio | tago | id | tago | dio |
| week | semajno | semango, viko | semayno | semano | weko | vek | semeno | septimano |
| month | monato | menso | menso | monato | mono | mes | buluno | menso |
| year | jaro | anyo | anwalo | yaro | yero | anyo | yaro | anuo |

Table 3.6: *Words for Time Periods in Esperanto and Some Daughters*

The next table shows names of days of the week. Some of the Atlango words in it are quite different from their Esperanto equivalents, though two are identical to them; the Virgoranto words are also quite different:

| | Esperanto | At-lango[17] | Hom-id. | Neo | Olingo | Romániço | Virgor. |
|---|---|---|---|---|---|---|---|
| Sunday | dimanĉo | soldo | dominiko | dominiko | dimancho | Domínico | sondago |
| Monday | lundo | lundo | lundo | lundo | lundo | Lundio | mondago |
| Tuesday | mardo | mardo | maꞯdo | tud | mardo | Martedio | tusdago |
| Wednesday | merkredo | sredo | meꞯkꞯedo | mirko | | Mercuridio | midveko |
| Thursday | ĵaŭdo | jodo | jovedo | jov | jeudo | Jovedio | tordago |
| Friday | vendredo | frado | vendꞯedo | venso | vendredo | Venerdio | fredago |
| Saturday | sabato | lerdo | sabato | sab | samedo | Sábato | saturdago |

Table 3.7: *Names of the Days of the Week in Esperanto and Some Daughters*

In the following table are the names of the months in Esperanto and some daughter languages; one will notice that the Olingo names all have the ending *-bo*:

---

[16] This word appears to be a noun.
[17] Antonius is inconsistent with respect to capitalization of names of days. I give the forms as they appear in the list of days of the week in Antonius (2008b). In Antonius (2008c) they are: Soldo, lundo, Mardo, Sredo, Jodo, frido, and Lerdo.

| | Esperanto | Atlango | Hom-id. | Ido | Mondlango | Neo | Olingo |
|---|---|---|---|---|---|---|---|
| Jan. | januaro | Jenayo[18] | janwaɾo | januaro | januaro | januar | Janubo |
| Feb. | februaro | febrayo | febɾwaɾo | februaro | februaro | februar | Februbo |
| March | marto | marco | maɾzo | marto | marto | marso | Marbo |
| April | aprilo | aprilo | apɾilo | aprilo | aprilo | april | Apribo |
| May | majo | mayo | majo | mayo | mayo | meyo | Mayebo |
| June | junio | juno | junyo | junio | juno | junyo | Junbo |
| July | julio | yulo | julyo | julio | julio | yul | Julbo |
| Aug. | aŭgusto | agosto | agosto | agosto | awgusto | agost | Agubo |
| Sept. | septembro | septembro | septembɾo | septembro | septembro | septembro | Septebo |
| Oct. | oktobro | oktobro | oktobɾo | oktobro | oktobro | oktobro | Oqtobo |
| Nov. | novembro | | novembɾo | novembro | novembro | novembro | Novebo |
| Dec. | decembro | decembro | dicembɾo | decembro | decembro | decembro | Desebo |

Table 3.8: *Names of the Months in Esperanto and Some Daughters*

Next we see words for the season of the year:

| | Esperanto | Hom-id. | Ido | Mondlango | Neo | Olingo | Romániço |
|---|---|---|---|---|---|---|---|
| spring | printempo | pɾimaveɾo | printempo | printempo | primaver | printempo | primavero |
| summer | somero | estivo | sumero | somero | zom | somero | estato |
| autumn | aŭtuno | autumno | autuno | awtuno | erso | atuno | autumno |
| winter | vintro | hibeɾno | vintro | wintro | yem | brumo | hiberno |

Table 3.9: *Names of the Seasons in Esperanto and Some Daughters*

## 3.5  Vocabulary in Some Other Semantic Fields

In this section I present some words in Esperanto and some daughter languages from some other semantic fields:

---

[18] As can be seen, none of the Atlango names of months is capitalized except that of the word for 'January'. (I have given the words as they appear in Antonius (2008c), which does not contain the word for 'November'.) One might assume that the capital <J> in January is an error.

|  | Esperanto | Atlango | Hom-id. | Mondlango | Neo | Olingo |
|---|---|---|---|---|---|---|
| artichoke | artiŝoko | | artičuko | | articok | |
| asparagus | asparago | | asparago | asparago | aspargo | |
| Brussels sprouts | rozbrasiketoj | | | | kabolos | |
| cabbage | brasiko | kawlo | brasiko | brasiko | kab | qavalo |
| carrot | karoto | karoto | karoto | | karot | qaroto |
| cauliflower | florbrasiko | | kolifloro | | florkab | qarnabo |
| celery | celerio | | celeryo | selerio | apyo | apo |
| cucumber | kukumo | | kukumo | kukumbo | gurko | ququmbo |
| lettuce | laktuko | | laktuko | letuso | latugo | letuqo |
| onion | cepo | sibolo, onyo | onyono | cepo | cipol | sipolo |
| potato | terpomo | potato | patato | | terpom | tato |
| radish | rafano | | radiŝo | napo | rapanel | |
| spinach | spinaco | | espinačo | | spinaso | |
| tomato | tomato | tomato | tomato | tomato | tomat | tomato |

Table 3.10: *Words for Vegetables in Esperanto and Some Daughters*

|  | Esperanto | Arlipo | Hom-id. | Linguna | Mondlango | Neo | Olingo |
|---|---|---|---|---|---|---|---|
| apple | pomo | pomo | aplo | pomm | pomo | pom | pomo |
| banana | banano | | banano | | banano | banan | |
| cherry | ĉerizo | cherizo | ceriso | czeriso | cerio | kirso, kirsel | cherizo |
| grape | vinbero | vinbero | viño | [19] | grapo | uv | vinbero |
| grapefruit | grapfrukto | grepo | pamplemuso | | pampelmuso | grep | |
| lemon | citrono | citrono | citrono | | lemono | limon | sitrono |
| peach | persiko | persiko | persiko | pérsico | persiko | pic | picho |
| pear | piro | piro | pero | apiso | piro | pirso | piro |
| pomegranate | granato | granato | granado | | granato | grendo | dalimo |
| raspberry | frambo | frambo | frambweso | | | frambol | |

Table 3.11: *Words for Fruit in Esperanto and Some Daughters*

---

[19] In Goeres (2004b) there is an entry for the Linguna word *bótryo*, which means "Weintraube / bunch of grapes   [Hell.: bótrys,bótryos]".

| | Esperanto | Farlingo | Hom-id. | Linguna | Mondlango | Neo | Olingo |
|---|---|---|---|---|---|---|---|
| shirt | ĉemizo | kamiso | kamiso | czemiso | | kamizo | qamiso |
| pants | pantalono | pantalono | pantalono | | | pant(alon) | pantalo |
| skirt | jupo | skarto | jupo | | jupo | jup | jupo |
| sock | ŝtrumpeto | sokos[20] | kalcetos[21] | | | kalsel | strumpeto |
| shoe | ŝuo | [22] | ŝuo | zapato | suo | sut | paduqo |
| slipper | pantoflo | pantuflo | pantuflo | | pantoflo | pantoflo | paduqeto |
| hat | ĉapelo | kepelo | kapelo | | | cap(el) | qapelo |
| glove | ganto | | ganto | | ganto | gant | |

Table 3.12: *Words for Clothing in Esperanto and Some Daughters*

| | Esperanto | Atlango | Hom-id. | Ido | Mondlango | Neo | Olingo |
|---|---|---|---|---|---|---|---|
| dog | hundo | hundo | dogo | hundo | dogo | kanyo | hundo |
| cat | kato | gato | kato | kato | kato | kat | qato |
| horse | ĉevalo | kavalo | kabalo | kavalo | horso | ip, kaval | chevalo |
| jackal | ŝakalo | | ŝakalo | shakalo | jakalo | shakal | rigalo |
| bird | birdo | foglo, ornito | biʐdo, avo | ucelo | birdo | ezo | birdo |
| fish | fiŝo | fixo | fiŝo | fisho | fixo | pesh | fisho |
| bee | abelo | abelo | abeylo | abelo | abelo | ap | abelo |
| fly | muŝo | mosko | mosko | musho | muxo | mosko | mosqo |
| mosquito | moskito | | moskito | moskito | moskito | moskito | zanzaro |

Table 3.13: *Words for Animals in Esperanto and Some Daughters*

## 3.6 Proper Nouns

Ido treats personal and place names in a different manner than Esperanto does: while in Esperanto one may, but does not have to, change proper nouns to conform to the orthographic (and case marking) system of the language, in Ido one tries to keep them as they are in their original language,[23] even to the point of retaining accent marks and

---

[20] The English-Farlingo Dictionary (Farber and Farber 2006) only gives this plural form, the equivalent of English *socks*.

[21] Only this plural form is given in the dictionary parts of Cárdenas (1923). This word also means 'stockings'.

[22] Farber and Farber (2006) give *buto* as the equivalent of shoe, and *botinok* (i.e. ботинок) as its Russian equivalent, but *shuos* as the equivalent of *shoes*, and *tufli* (i.e. туфли) as its Russian equivalent.

[23] In the case of countries and major areas of the world, if they have a "Latina formo historiala" ('historical Latin form'; de Beaufront 1925/2005:19), it is generally used, e.g. *Afrika* 'Africa', *Amerika* 'America', Oceania 'Oceania', Suedia 'Sweden'. Further, de Beaufront (ibid.:20) says, "Por simpligar e generaligar, Ido uzas ta formo (-*ia*) anke en **Chinia, Japonia, Brazilia, Mexikia**" ('to simplify and generalize, Ido also uses that form (-*ia*) in **Chinia, Japonia, Brazilia, Mexikia** '). Note that in the case of *Afrika* and *Amerika* a change has been made in the orthography: the <c> of the original Latin has become <k>. This change is made in other cases also, e.g. *Kanada* 'Canada', which goes against the principle of not altering the original language spelling. De Beaufront (ibid.:21) justifies this as follows: "La c transskribesas per k en **Nikaragua, Kanada, Maroko**, pro ke en Ido ni havus (kun *c*) *Nitsaragua, Tsanada, Marotso*, quo certe ne konkordus kun l'internaciona sono di ta vorti. Ma qua homo, vidante li kun *k*, vice *c*, havas mem ombro di hezito por rikonocar li?" ('The *c* is transcribed with *k* in **Nikaragua, Kanada, Maroko**, because in Ido we would have (with *c*) [the pronunciations]

umlauts (which do not generally occur in Ido), e.g. *München* 'Munich', *Genève* 'Geneva'. De Beaufront (1925/2005:18) states:

> La *propra nomi* omnaspeca devas principe konsideresar kom « vorti stranjera » a la linguo. La nomi personal precipue ... devas restar netushebla. [...] On riproduktas, se on povas, la diakritika signi ed on indikas, *segun quante on povas*, la pronunco inter parentezi. Se li apartenas a linguo ne uzanta l'alfabeto Romana, on transskribas li fonetike (*maxim bone posible*).
>
> ('*Proper nouns* of every type must in principle be considered as "foreign words" to the language. Foreign names especially ... must remain untouchable. [...] One reproduces, if one can, the diacritic signs and one indicates, *to the extent that one can*, the pronunciation between parentheses. If they belong to a language not using the Roman alphabet, one transcribes them phonetically (*as well as possible*).') [Italics are as in the original]

Arlipo also usually does not change proper nouns; Vitek (n.d. a) states that they "daurat plunombre en sia origina formo, nur ikva, zhenerale uzata, povat havon Arlipa ortografio kaj substantiva finazho -o' ('remain for the most part in their original form, only some, generally used, can have Arlipo orthography and [the] nominal ending - o').

A rule of Mondezo is that names of countries must serve as the stem for creating the names of their people (by means of *-an*) (only sometimes is this the case in Esperanto), e.g. *Anglano* 'Englishman' from *Anglo* 'England' (cf. Esperanto *anglo* 'Englishman', *Anglujo* 'England'. Language names are formed with *-ez-*, e.g. *Svedezo* 'Swedish'.

Greenwood (1906a:11) says the following about how names of people are to be treated in Ekeselsioro:

> *Proper names*, *Persons*, should retain their original form, according to [the] Ekselsioro alphabet, that it [sic] may be recognisable, enclosed in quotation marks: as, Beaufront, "Beaufront"; Chefech, "Cefec"; O'Conner, "O'Konnor"; merely changing the *ch*, *sh*, *w*, and *q* sounds for c, x, v, and ku: as Wilhelm, "Vilhelm"; Edward, "Edvard"

In Perio proper nouns are spelled with "une orthographe phonétique approximative" (Couturat and Leau 1907/1979:11) and they have Perio affixes, e.g. *cicerù, penelopy, londono* (recall that capital letters do not occur in the language).

ARG (2005:29) says, "In Aiola proper names from other languages are approximated by the string of Aiola sounds which is closest to the native pronunciation, and are spelled using the twenty-eight symbols of the Aiola alphabet along with the acute accent ( ´ ) over the vowel of the stressed syllable to indicate irregular stress. Sometimes the Aiola approximation is identical or nearly identical in sound to the native version". Among the examples then given are *Deiv* 'Dave' and

---

*Nitsaragua, Tsanada, Marotso*, which certainly would not agree with the international sound of those words. But who, seeing them with *k* instead of *c*, has even a shadow of hesitation in recognizing them?').

*Kustó* 'Cousteau'. However, sometimes a name will be changed because Aiola lacks a sound occurring in it, e.g. *Smit* 'Smith', *Bak* 'Bach'.

ARG (ibid.:29-31) discusses three other kinds of names in Aiola (i.e. three types of names which it apparently considers not to fall under the heading of proper names); these names include titles of e.g. books. "Simple derived names" (ibid.:29) are names or titles created from nouns (including nominal forms of cardinal and ordinal numerals) by capitalization and attachment of the suffix -*n*, e.g. *Belon* 'Beauty' (from *belo* 'beauty'), *Profesoron* 'Profesor' (from *profesor* 'professor').[24] "Simple derived name combinations" (ibid.) contain a simple derived name and at least one other name, a proper name or an additional simple derived name, e.g. *Sinyorono Katon* 'Mister Cat' (simple derived name + simple derived name), *Ruton Trion* 'Route Three' (simple derived name + simple derived name), *Profesoron Djailiz* 'Professor Giles' (simple derived name + proper name), *Redjon Tcarlz Martelon* 'King Charles the Hammer' (simple derived name + proper name + simple derived name). "Complex derived names" (ibid.:30) are phrases and sentences which have been made into names: if these phrases or sentences contain derived names, i.e. names ending with -*n*, this final -*n* becomes -*m*; as far as I can determine proper nouns contained in such phrases do not undergo any change; all other words in the phrase or sentence (e.g. adjectives, conjunctions) receive the suffix -*n*. All words in the phrase or sentence must begin with a capital letter. Examples of complex derived names are given below:

(3a)     Honesta-n    Eib
            honest-NF   Abe
            'Honest Abe'

(3b)     Vizitajo-n   Jyalu-n  La-m     Blantca-m     Hauso-m
            visit-NF     to-NF    the-NFD  white-NFD   house-NFD
            '*A Visit to the White House*' [title of a book] (ibid.)

As ARG (ibid.) points out, if the suffix -*m* on the last three words of (3b) were -*n*, i.e. *Lan Blantcan Houson*, we would have the book title '*A Visit to the White House* (a definite white house but not the one in Washington)'; this is because the complex derived name would then not have been constructed from a phrase containing a simple derived name combination (*Lan Blantcan Houson*) but from a phrase containing an ordinary noun phrase (*la blantca houso*).

In Hom-idyomo, as in Esperanto, the suffix -*o* is the marker of nouns. However, names of people are exceptions, as Cárdenas (1923:8) states in the following apparently contradictory remarks, which give an idea of how they are dealt with in this language:

> This rule [that nouns are marked with the word class suffix -*o*] does not include personal proper nouns, in which it is better to preserve the spelling of the respective national languages, as in *Byron, Pasteur, Cervantes, Michel Angelo*. However, it seems advisable to adapt their spelling to

---

[24] ARG's (2005:29) definition of *simple derived noun* is: "A simple derived noun designates something which is a member of the class designated by its underlying noun. Thus **Profesoron** names a professor, **Monton** names a mountain, **Redjon** names a king, etc." This may be a misleading definition because instances of common nouns very often refer to specific individuals.

Hom-idyomo pronunciation, for the sake of uniformity, writing, for instance, *Mikel Angelo* for "Michel Angelo"; *Čaıles* for "Charles"; *Kaılos* for "Carlos"; *Pol* for "Paul"; *Fıedʑik* for "Fredric".

On the other hand, place names do have *o* as their final segment: it is attached to those whose original form does not already have it, e.g. *Londono, Sinaio*. Those original forms whose final sound is "a non-emphatic vowel (ibid.)", with the exception of *o*, have this sound deleted when *-o* is attached, e.g. *Filadelfyo*.

With respect to toponyms in Neo, Alfandari (1961:56) says, "Les noms géographiques ont été établis, il faut le dire tout de suite, de façon forcément arbitraire; ils sont sujets à modifications, suivant les preferences et les gouts locaux, ou pour d'autres raisons imprévisibles".

The general procedure for forming names of countries in Virgoranto seems to involve the attachment of *-lando*: *Austrolando* 'Austria', *Kinlando* 'China', *Germanlando* 'Germany', *Japanlando* 'Japan', *Spanlando* 'Spain', *Svedlando* 'Sweden'.

In the table below one can see how names of some countries differ, or do not differ, in Esperanto and some of her daughters:

| | Esperanto[25] | Ido | Mondlango | Neo | Olingo | Romániço |
|---|---|---|---|---|---|---|
| Austria | Aŭstrio | Austria | Awstrio | Austrio | Astrio | Austria |
| Denmark | Danlando, Danujo | Dania | Denmarko | Danmark | Denio | Dania |
| Germany | Germanujo | Germania | Germanio | Germanio | Germio | Alemania |
| Greece | Grekujo | Grekia | Greko | Grek, Grekio | Greqio | Grequia |
| Hungary | Hungarujo | Hungaria | Hungario | Majario, Ungrio | Hungio | Hungaria |
| Ireland | Irlando | Irlando | Irlando | Irland | Irlio | Irlandia |
| Norway | Norveguujo | Norvegia | | Norgo | Norwio | Norvejia |
| Poland | Pollando | Polonia | Polando | Polno | | Polonia |
| Scotland | Skotlando | Skotia | Skotlando | Skotyo, Skotland | Sqotio | Scotia |
| Spain | Hispanujo | Hispania | Espanio | Espanyo | Spanio | Hispania |
| Switzer-land | Svislando | Suisia | | Swiso | Swisio | Helvetia, Suicia |
| Burma | Birmo | Burma | Burmo | Birmanio | | Birma |
| Mexico | Meksikio | Mexikia | Meksiko | Mexik | Mexio | México |
| United States | Usono | Usa | Unita Statos | Usio, U.S.A. (Unat Statos d Amerik) | Usamio | Unionita Statos, Usonia |
| New Zealand | Nov-Zelando | Nov-Zelando | | Nuvzeland | Nuzelio | Nov-Zelandia |

Table 3.14: *Names of Countries in Esperanto and Some Daughters*

---

[25] Esperanto allows a fair amount of freedom with respect to names of countries. For example, Wennergren (2005:504) says, "Neniam estas eraro uzi UJ aŭ I anstataŭ sufikseca LAND". I do not give all the possibilities in this table.

# 4        Morphology

## 4.0        General Issues

### 4.0.1        Markers of Parts of Speech

Perhaps one of the most salient features of Esperanto is that several of the parts of speech are indicated by particular suffixes. Many of its descendants have the same feature, but the particular endings are not always the same. The table below shows some such differences:[1]

| | Noun | Personal Pronoun | Cardinal Numeral | Adjective | (Derived) Adverb | Preposition |
|---|---|---|---|---|---|---|
| Esperanto | -o | -i | – | -a | -e | – |
| Aiola | -o | – | – | -a [2] | -e | -u |
| Farlingo | -o, -a | – | – | -e | -en | – |
| Neo | -o | – | – | -a | -e | – |
| Sen:esepera | -a | -u | -in | -an, -en, -in, -m | -e | -o |

Table 4.1: *Part of Speech Markers in Esperanto and Some Daughters*

There are two kinds of differences here: 1) a marker for a part of speech may differ, and 2) a language may have a marker of a part of speech in a daughter of Esperanto, while Esperanto does not have one for that particular word class, or vice-versa. Note for example that Sen:espera has a suffix marking prepositions, while Esperanto does not. In Reformed Esperanto the adjectival and adverbial suffixes are the same, *-e*.

Most Farlingo nouns have *-o* as an ending, the only exceptions to my knowledge being nouns denoting female entities; their suffix is *-a*, e.g. in *sista* 'sister', *chika* 'girl'. Although Farber and Farber (2005) indicate that *-en* is the suffix of adverbs in Farlingo, there are adverbs which do not end with it, e.g. *tre* 'very (much)'. In Farber and Farber (2006) the Farlingo word *true* is given as an equivalent of English *very*, as well as being the equivalent of English *true*; with the former meaning it would be another adverb without the adverbial word class suffix.

The situation with respect to the Sen:esepera "class suffixes", as Henning (1995a) calls them, is rather complex. Henning gives the class suffixes for adjectives as in the table above, but states (ibid.) that "Adjectives typically end in /-an/". He is not explicit about when they do not have that ending, but numerals have *-in* as their class suffix,

---

[1] Both in Esperanto and some of the other languages that have them, such suffixes are often not the last morphemes of the word; for example, when an Esperanto word has a plural suffix, that suffix will follow the word class marker. For that matter, it is possible for a word of a particular class to lack the suffix of that class. As we have seen in section 2.2, and as will be discussed later in this section, some daughters of Esperanto allow the omission of word class suffixes in some circumstances (as does Esperanto itself). Further, if we take *-o* to be the marker of nouns in Arlipo, Ido, and Reformed Esperanto, then plural nouns will appear without this marker, since with them the plural suffix *-i* occurs instead of it. It also sometimes happens that words which do not belong to a word class characterized by a part of speech marker end in the same way as words of that class. For example, Esperanto infinitives, as well as pronouns, end in *-i*, and in Sen:esepera prepositions are not the only words which end with *-o*.

[2] "Relational adjectives" (v. section 4. 4) have *-i* added to this suffix, i.e. they end in *-ai*.

as shown in Table 4.1.[3] However, the marker of fractional numerals is *-en*, according to Henning (1995a).[4] There is a non-numeral adjective in Henning (1995b) which also ends in the sequence *in*, *interin* 'inner' and a word which is not a fraction that ends with the sequence *en*, *pelen* 'full'. The vast majority of adjectives in Henning (1995b) end in *-an*, but the words for 'same' and 'different' do not, being *sam* and *emalsam* respectively. The same is true of *fem* 'female' (which is labelled an adjective), though not of *eman* 'male', and of *perocsim* 'near' (which is an adjective; there is also a preposition meaning 'near', *perocsime:alo*). As indicated in Table 4.1, the class suffix for pronouns is *-u*, but not all pronouns have this ending; personal pronouns do, but the class marker for correlatives is *-o(n)*, and pronouns that belong to this set will have that ending and not *-u*.

Although *-o* is the marker of nouns in Neo, many nouns in the language have a consonant as their final segment: Alfandari (1961:33) states, "Le noms se terminant par une consonne ont simplement subi l'élision de l'o final, qu'on peut rétablir toutes les fois qu'un besoin de clarté, d'euphonie ou d'emphase le suggère". Somewhat similarly, Novesperant nouns usually do not have the *-o* suffix: Cartier (n.d.) states, "There is no final -O on nouns unless it [omission of *-o*] makes pronunciation difficult or impossible, ar[t]istic reasons are allowed."

Esperloja has a larger set of part of speech markers than other languages discussed here. They all consist of two vowels; Sulky (n.d.) says, "To ease learning and machine parsing, every word ends in a vowel pair, which cannot occur elsewhere in a word. The different pairs mark a word as noun, verb, etc." His (ibid.) table of these endings is below:

| | |
|---|---|
| -oi | noun |
| -au | proper noun (name) |
| -iu | verb |
| -ai | adjective / adverb |
| -ia | quantifier |
| -ui | modifier of modifier |
| -ua | preposition / particle |
| -ue | conjunction / punctuation |
| -io | interjection |
| -ei | lowercase or numeric glyph |
| -eu | non-lowercase or non-numeric glyph |

Table 4.2: *Word Class Markers of Esperloja*

There are no words with the ending *-ui* appearing in Sulky (n.d.), so I do not know what is meant by "modifier of modifier". One might think that they are adverbs which modify adjectives and other adverbs (such as English *very*), since Sulky (ibid.) defines "modifiers" as "adjective and adverbs", but such words in e.g. English are generally classified as adverbs, and adverbs in Esperloja end in *-ai*. If I understand correctly, "glyph" here means the name of a letter, number, or other symbol, e.g. *pei* is the name

---

[3] Henning seems to consider numerals both a separate word class and a type of adjective. He says (1995a), "the first 10 ordinal numerals are, when used as adjectives, *unin, duin ... decin*". However, *unin* means 'one' according to Henning (1995b), not 'first', and *decin* means 'ten' and not 'tenth', although they and other cardinal numerals which appear in Henning (1995b) are labelled as adjectives.

[4] In Henning (1995b) *une:din* is given as the word for 'half', which is not consistent with this.

of the letter <p> (e.g. if one were reciting the alphabet), and *tirei* means the name of the number 3 (perhaps used e.g. when saying a telephone number or a credit card number?), but if one were using 'three' to state a quantity, one would say *tiria*, which has the suffix of quantifiers.[5]

## 4.0.2    Derivational Morphology

Several of the derivational suffixes of Reformed Esperanto are different from their Esperanto equivalents, as can be seen in the table below:

| Esperanto | Reformed Esperanto |
|-----------|--------------------|
| -aĵ-      | -e-                |
| -ec-      | -it-               |
| -iĝ-      | -isk-              |
| -uj-      | -i-                |

Table 4.3: *Some Derivational Suffixes of Reformed Esperanto*

As one would expect, Ido has many of the same derivational affixes as Esperanto. However, it also has some which Esperanto does not have (with the same meaning). The following table shows some of these:

| | |
|---|---|
| des- "indikas la kontreajo dil koncepto expresata sen olu." ('indicates the opposite of the concept expressed without it'; de Beaufront 1925/2005:103) | desavantajo 'disadvantage' |
| mi- 'half' | miklozita 'half-closed' |
| para- 'protection against' | parafairo 'fire-guard, fire-screen' |
| -atr- 'like' | metalatra 'metallic' |
| -ed- 'la quanto qua plenigas X (la radiko) o korespondas ad X') ['the quantity which fills X (the root) or corresponds to X'] (ibid.:121) | glasedo de vino 'glass of wine' (ibid.) |
| -eri- 'establishment' | bakerio 'bakery' |
| -if- "indicates production or generation of something" (anon. n.d. i) | sudorifar 'to sweat' |
| -ik- 'sick with/in/because of' | kordiika 'heart-diseased', koleriko 'a person with cholera' |
| -yun- 'offspring of [an animal]' | hundyuno 'puppy' |

Table 4.4: *Some Derivational Affixes of Ido*

We shall see that some later daughters of Esperanto also have some of these affixes, and one might suspect that they were borrowed from Ido.

Lahago (n.d.:46-7) lists *ek-* and *eks-* among the prefixes of Modern Esperanto, but has a negative view of them, as he states (ibid.:46), "Note! Words starting with ek- or eks- do a lot of harm to the language movement of Esperanto ... Suggestions about this matter are really appreciated!" Lahago changed the form of the prefix *re-*, which led to changes in the form of some words: "The prefix re- is replaced for [i.e. by] ri ...

---

[5] Sulky (n.d.) defines *tirei* as "three (glyph)" and *tiria* as "three (of something)".

To stop confusion, Esperanto words starting with re-; like ripeti, rigardi etc. will be changed to re-; repeti, regardi".

The Novesperant suffix -esc is equivalent to Esperanto -ej, e.g. *automobilesc* 'garage'.

Ekselsioro has the prefix *ma-* instead of Esperanto *mal-*, e.g. *mavarma* 'cold'.

In Esperloja there is a prefix *net-*, which "marks something as having an average amount of the measured quantity" (Sulky n.d.).

Many of the derivational suffixes of Snifferanto are the same as in Esperanto. Two are different as a result of orthographic/phonetic changes from Esperanto: *-ats-* and *-itz-* correspond to Esperanto *-aĵ-* and *-iĝ-* respectively.

Among the derivational affixes of Mondlingvo which were not inherited from Esperanto are the verbal prefixes *ab-* and *be-*; the former corresponds to *ver-* and *ent-* of German, and the latter to German *be-*, *ge-*, and *er-*. The meaning of *-av-* is 'science', e.g. *naturavo* 'natural history'. The suffixes *-ilm-* and *-ov-* have the same meanings as Esperanto *-ar-* and *-em-* respectively, e.g. *homilmo* 'humanity'.

In the following table are some of the derivational affixes of Romániço (definitions and examples from Morales n.d. 1):

| des- 'opposite of'[6] | desbona 'bad' |
|---|---|
| par- 'completely and utterly' | parlecter 'to read from cover to cover' |
| -ac- 'suffering from' | cànceraco 'a cancer victim' |
| -astr- 'relationship by re-marriage' | fratrastro 'a step-brother' |
| -ed- 'direct object' | manjedo 'food', dicedo 'a saying' |
| -esc- 'relating to, concerning, depending on, appropriate to' | Pushquinesca poetajo 'a poem concerning Pushkin', nacionesca criso 'a national emergency' |
| -isc- 'in the style of, resembling' | blavisca 'bluish', Tarantino-isca película 'Tarantino-esque film' |
| -ol- 'young of' | catolo 'kitten' |
| -uz- 'moral inferiority' | combatuzer 'to fight dirty' |

Table 4.5: *Some Romániço Derivational Affixes*

Like Modern Esperanto, Romániço has *ri-* 'again' rather than Esperanto *re-*. Also, to mean 'worthy of' Romániço has *-and-* in place of Esperanto *-ind-*, e.g. *laundanda* 'praiseworthy'. The suffix *-ez-* is equivalent to Esperanto *-iĝ-*.

In Mondlango the prefixes *dis-* and *mal-* have different meanings than they do in Esperanto; oppositeness and 'bad' respectively, e.g. *disbiga* 'small' (from *biga* 'big'), *malinsekto* 'bad insect' (from *insekto* 'insect'). Other derivational affixes of Mondlango include *-or-* 'human', e.g. *yunoro* 'youth' (from *yuna* 'young'), *edukoro* 'teacher' (from *eduki* 'to teach'),[7] *-od-* 'like', e.g. *kidoda* 'childlike' (from *kido* 'child), and *-ub-* 'position', e.g. *sidubo* 'seat' (from *sidi* 'to sit'), *prezidentubo* 'presidency' (from *prezidento* 'president').

In Intero *ge-* does not have the same meaning as in Esperanto: Thompson (2007a) states that it "indicates half way [sic] between a word and its opposite. It could also indicate a monistic combination of a word and its opposite". Intero has taken the

---

[6] Morales (n.d. 1) states, "This prefix is especially handy for creating *ad hoc* words for which one does not know the standard form".

[7] This suffix can be deleted before the suffixes -ul- and -in- (v. section 4.1.2) without changing the meaning the the word. For example, *edukulo*, like *edukuloro*, means 'male teacher'.

following derivational affixes from Ido: *para-*, *-atr-*, *-ed-*, *-eri-*, *-if-*, *-ik-*, and *-iv-*.[8] The Intero suffix *-by-* is equivalent to the Esperanto suffix *-ĉj-*.[9]

Arlipo has many of the same derivational affixes as Esperanto, but some which are different, including *des-* which conveys the meaning of oppositeness, and *ej-*, which Vitek (n.d. b) indicates means "komenco au kurtatempezo" ('beginning or short time'), *-aj-*, 'place' (cf. Esperanto *-ej-*), and *-er-* 'apparatus, machine'.

The derivational affixes of Olingo which do not exist in Esperanto (taking orthographical differences into consideration include *un-*, which seems to be equivalent to Esperanto *mal-*,[10] e.g. *unamiqo* 'enemy' (from *amiqo* 'friend'), *unlevi* 'to sink' (from *levi* 'lift, raise'), *unsana* 'ill' (from *sana* 'healthy'), and *-eri-* 'the trading place', e.g. *florerio* 'flower shop' (from *floro* 'flower'). The suffixes *-ev-* and *-it-* correspond to Esperanto *-eg-* and *-id-* respectively, e.g. *vagonevo* 'truck, van' (from *vagono* 'wagon'), *qatito* 'kitten' (from *qato* 'cat'). The suffix *-um-* means 'language of', e.g. *Angliumo* 'English language' (from *Anglio* 'England') and thus is not the equivalent of *-um-* in Esperanto.

Hom-idyomo has some affixes not present in Esperanto. The table below presents some of these:

| bene- "denotes goodness or kindness" (Cárdenas 1923:13) | bene-fakanto 'benefactor' |
|---|---|
| bovo- "denotes castration" (ibid.) | bovo-bovino 'steer' |
| magni- "means an augmentative of the substantive" (ibid.:14) | magni-kato 'big cat' |
| paᵤa- "denotes protection" (ibid.) | paᵤa-pluvyo 'umbrella' |
| undeᵤ- "denotes incompleteness or insufficiency" (ibid.:15) | undeᵤ-alimentiᵤ 'underfeed' |
| -aj- "indicates the use made of the substantive, or its restriction to denote a special thing" (ibid.:19) | pontajo 'bridge toll', long-ajo 'joist' |
| -az- 'blow struck with' | maᵤtazo 'hammer blow' |
| -el- "an endearing diminutive" (ibid.) | fᵤatᵤelo 'little brother' |
| -eᵤ- 'container' | tabakeᵤo 'cigar case' |
| -iš- "denotes similarity" (ibid.:20) | blankiša 'whitish' |

Table 4.6: *Some Derivational Afixes of Hom-Idyomo*

Hyphens are to be inserted between a prefix and the root to which it is attached, in order to distinguish prefixes from homophonous word-initial sequences which are not prefixes.[11] Cárdenas (ibid.:20) says the following about affixes in Hom-iydomo: "It is to be remarked that words composed with prefixes and suffixes may not be used in preference to international words having equivalent meanings. Thus we say either *pᵤesidanto* or *nacyón-čefo*, either *kapitano* or *naví-čefo*, but *pᵤesidanto* and *kapitano* are preferable."[12]

---

[8] The last of these, *-iv-* 'able to, capable of', is also an unofficial Esperanto suffix.

[9] Thompson (2007a) says, "An Esperanto *-cj* becomes an Intero **-by**", but I assume by "-cj" he means '-ĉj-'.

[10] Jaque (1944:34) glosses it as "the complement".

[11] The same does not apply to suffixes (because of the stress rule applying to words with derivational suffixes; v. section 2.3), and so I have removed the hyphens which Cárdenas had placed ("merely as a means to explain the formation of words", ibid.:20) in his example words for suffixes.

[12] Cárdenas considers *-čef-* to be a suffix.

There are some derivational affixes in Neo which either do not have an affixal equivalent in Esperanto or are different from their Esperanto equivalent. Some of these are in the following table, with glosses and examples from Alfandari (1961:41-2):

| ju- 'qui vient de' | junasat 'nouveau-né', juparsat 'qui vient de paraître' |
|---|---|
| -ior 'navire, avion, voiture' | peskior 'bateau de pêche', delior 'destroyer', bombior 'bombardier', konvegior 'convoyeur (bateau, avion)' |
| -ol 'jeune d'animal', diminutif | bovol 'veau', ipol 'poulain', lepol 'lapereau', dorfol 'hameau' |
| -on augmentatif | domon 'grande maison', shopon 'grand magasin' |
| -ori- 'fabrique' | brosorio 'brosserie (fabrique)', kordio 'corderie' |
| -oy- 'meuble' | klozoyo 'armoire', noxoyo 'table de nuit' |
| -ul diminutive | omul 'homunucule', infanul 'mioche', manul 'toute petit main' |
| -un 'individu' | un kuryozun 'un type curieux', un sagun 'un homme sage' |
| -yes 'fréquence, occasion' | mulyes 'beaucoup de fois', idyes 'un jour', shakidyes 'chaque jour', belidyes 'un beau jour'[13] |

Table 4.7: *Some Derivational Affixes of Neo*

It will be noticed that there are two diminutive suffixes; Neo also has the diminutive suffix of Esperanto, -*et*, e.g. *boyet* 'garçonnet', *fresketa* 'frisquet'. To my knowledge Alfandari does not indicate the differences of meaning or function among them (if there are any), except that -*ol* can also mean 'young (of an animal)'. In Neo *mal*- is a pejorative prefix, and thus different in meaning than Esperanto *mal*-. The prefix *ne*- "marque une négation pure et simple" (Alfandari 1961:54), e.g. *noposibla* 'impossible', while *di*- "a un sens privatif correspondant à celui du préfix français *de*-" (ibid.), e.g. *dikalci* 'decalcify', and *sen*- "indique un manque" (ibid.), e.g. *senviva* 'inanimate, without life'.

The table below shows some affixes of Atlango which do not exist in Esperanto, or do not have (exactly) the same form as in Esperanto (with glosses, descriptions, and examples from Antonius 2008b; the affixes with plus signs before them are or may be "Neofisyala kay prondata afiksoy" ('unofficial and proposed affixes' (ibid.)):[14]

---

[13] As we shall see, -*yes* also occurs in a few of the words that are equivalent to some of the correlatives of Esperanto.

[14] I say "are or may be" because it is not entirely clear where in Antonius (2008b) the list of such suffixes ends.

| be- "about, concerning. As prefix with nouns and verbs - besimini - sow (a field) [in verbs] used to mean that someone or something is treated in particular way. to coronate - **be**-krun-I (like in Dutch: bekroning)" | |
|---|---|
| gran- "intensive or emphatic (for verbs)" | granpregi 'beseech' granpyori 'bewail' |
| + porte- 'partial container' | porteovo 'egg cup', portevoco 'spokesman' |
| -ab- augmentative | domabo 'a big building', bonaba 'excellent' |
| + -efr- 'be afraid of' | |
| + -iklang- 'sound of, resound, howl' | gatiklango 'mewing', vyentiklango 'wailing of the wind' |
| -ikol- 'small particle of a whole' | aqikolo 'drop of water', brotikolo 'a crumb of bread' |
| + -ob- 'make a movement with' (from mobi 'to move') | manobi 'make a movement by hand' |
| -ud- 'descendant of' | hundudo 'puppy' |
| -ur- 'result or product of action' | pikturo 'drawing', pinturo 'painting' |
| -yun- 'young animal' | gatyuno 'kitten' |

Table 4.8: *Some Derivational Affixes of Atlango*

Some of the derivational affixes of Perio have been created following an *a priori* type pattern (which, as we have seen, is also true of much of the vocabulary of the language), with semantically related items being phonetically similar. This is shown in the table below (definitions from Couturat and Leau 1907/1979:10):

| af- 'commencement' | | uf- 'milieu' | if- 'fin' |
|---|---|---|---|
| -ab- 'ce qui porte' | | -ub- 'ce qui tient' | -ib- 'ce qui contient' |
| -ad- augmentative | | -ud- perjorative | -id- diminutive |
| -ac- 'plein de' | | -uc- 'riche en' | -ic- 'vide de' |
| -ag- 'faire' | -og- 'préparer' | -ug- 'fabriquer' | -ig- 'faire'[15] |

Table 4.9: *Some Derivational Suffixes of Perio*

The *ab-* and *ad-* series derive nouns, the affixes of the *-ac-* series create adjectives and those of the *-ag-* series create verbs (although *-ug-* and presumably the other affixes of the series can also be contained in nouns: Couturat and Leau (1907/1979:10) mention words ending in *-ugo* which have the meaning 'la machine à fabriquer').

Linguna has a large number of derivational prefixes and suffixes, most of which are not in Esperanto. Some of them are in the tables below (glosses and explanations from Goeres 2007):

---

[15] I believe that the difference between *-ag-* and *-ig-* is that the former means 'make' in the sense of 'create' while the latter is a causative suffix, like *-ig-* in Esperanto. Couturat and Leau (1907/1979:10) do not give any examples of words containing *-ag-*, but for *-ig-* they give the example *savigi* 'faire savoir', from *savi* 'to know'.

| anqí- | 'very close to, as near as that you can touch it, tangibly near', e.g. *anqísala* 'near the sea' |
|---|---|
| argyro- | 'silver-, silverlike, silvery' |
| atro- | 'dark shade of' |
| ari- | 'very, strongly, utmost' |
| chrys(o)- | "prefix denoting the golden aspect", e.g. *chrysofasán* 'golden pheasant' |
| gam- | '-in-law', e.g. *gampatr* 'father-in-law' |
| omb- | 're- (changing), trans-, ex-', e.g. *ombscribi* 'to rewrite' |
| plagi- | "transverse, cross(-), denoting transversal position, broad, athwart, at right angles to (G[erman]: quer-)" |
| puan- | 'whole of, Pan-' |
| rody- | 'both sexes together', e.g. *rodyalumnoi* 'pupils: boys and girls' |

Table 4.10: *Some Derivational Prefixes of Linguna*

| -ab- | 'utensil or device of common use' |
|---|---|
| -ador- | 'apparatus, machine-like contrivance'[16] |
| -ead- | 'squash/drink of fruit, juice (without alcohol)' |
| -ell- | 'very good, noble, fine, pleasant, agreeable' |
| -enc/q- | 'tremendously deep, profound, abrupt, abyss, definitive obstacle' |
| -ent- | "denotes the superior or abstract or else metaphorical meaning, subject to definition or context. E.g.: 'pezenti' (feel happy being in one's element, like fish in water, {la pez = fish}" |
| -icz- | "rare suffix distinctly denoting the male" |
| -íli- | 'boat, vessel, ship', e.g. *papyrilio* 'papyrus boat' |
| -ops- | 'looking like' |
| -uc/q- | "suffix indicating castrated animal/person" |
| -uld- | 'carrying much or great, having done great/important; victorious, rich harvest of' |
| -úlli- | "denoting a very little person or an extremely small matter, or a thoroughly tiny object … (almost a double diminutive)" (ibid.), e.g. *ovúllio* 'a tiny egg, little egg' |
| -und- | "stressing the origin, the coming from and provenance" |
| -uos- | "points to a disease, sickness (because) of" |

Table 4.11: *Some Derivational Suffixes of Linguna*

As can be seen with *-ent-*, some of Linguna's derivational affixes have meanings or functions which are complex and/or difficult to understand, or which at least are not clearly explained. To take another example, Goeres (2007) says of *ga-*: "prefix originating [from] the Gothic: finding s.o./s.th., meeting s.o., getting, to comment/judge/find, and find oneself together with". Among the examples then given is *gavulni*, defined in Linguna as "obteni vulnon" ('get a wound'?) and later in the same work given the German and English gloss "Verletzung davontragen, verwundet werden / get injured".

---

[16] Nouns formed by this suffix are feminine. Goeres (2004b) explains this as follows: "all machines are considered as feminine because of their aspect of sophisticated profoundness as well as extended contrivance and shrewd configuration".

### 4.0.3 Compounds

There is a large number of compounds in Esperanto, very many of which are nouns. However, Greenwood (1906a:11) says with respect to Ekselosioro, "Compound Nouns should be avoided if possible, and single words used instead".

Jaque (1944:34) gives the following rule of Olingo: "When a thing [= noun] is used for a quality it is joined to the thing it modifies by a hyphen. Example: oro-lado–gold plate." Another example is *animo-qiso* 'soul kiss'.

Romániço has a suffix *-ig-* which is restricted to compounds and whose function is to clearly mark compounds as such. For example, the compound *unóculo* 'a one-eyed person' is phonetically identical to the sequence *un óculo* 'one eye', but if *-ig-* is affixed to the former, the result, *unòculigo* 'a one-eyed person', can only be interpreted as a compound.

Unlike in Esperanto, in Esperloja non-final members of a compound never have a word class ending; Sulky (n.d.) states, "Compound words are formed by adjoining the roots of the constituent words, adding the grammatical suffix only at the very end of the word. Doubled consonants may be formed by this process".

Cárdenas (1923) has an unusual notion of compounds: he apparently considers words containing a root and a derivational affix (as well as words containing two roots) to be compounds. This is shown by the following passage:[17] "Compound words are divided [into syllables] as if they were simple, but it is better to hyphenate them, for clearness. [...] Compound words in which the first element is a prefix should be hyphenated: *retʐo-vendo*, 'reversion-sale'... Those in which the ending is a suffix need not be hyphenated, as the accent on the ante-penultimate syllable is a sufficient distinguishing mark" (Cárdenas 1923:I:5).

ARG (2005) distinguishes three types of Aiola compounds, XX→ X, XY → Y, and XY → Z. With compounds of the first type the two component words and the resulting compound all belong to the same word class. Examples of this type of compound are *sofleto* 'sofa-bed' (NN → N), *bluverda* 'blue-green' (AA → A), and *rulvibrare* 'to roll-vibrate (to roll back and forth)' and *andvenare*' to go-come (to make a round trip)' (VV → V). The first of these examples seems similar to a type of compound which does not exist in the language: ARG (ibid.:33) states, "The largest group of compound words which is *not* permitted in Aiola comprises most noun-noun combinations, in which one noun modifies a second noun. Two examples are 'bookstore' in which the second noun 'store' is a simple noun and 'bookseller' in which the second noun 'seller' is a derived noun". (One uses phrases containing "attributive" or "relational" adjectives to express such meanings; v. section 4.4). On the following page, in the discussion of the XX → X type of compound are the following remarks:

---

[17] Another non-standard aspect of Cárdenas' concept of compounds comes out in the following passage (1923:I:15): "In order that a word may be considered as compound, it is necessary that each of its parts should have the meaning it has in Hom-idyomo, and that the resulting word should combine the two meanings, as in *semi-plena*, 'half-full'. Thus the word *kanindento*, 'eye-tooth', 'fang', is not compound, because the so called tooth belongs not only to dogs." This means that Cárdenas would not consider the English word *blackboard* (often cited in discussions of compounds) to be a compound, since it is not necessarily black.

Compounds of this type may denote either mixtures of the two individual meanings (housbarko, bluverda, rulvibrare) or sequential combinations of them (andvenare …).

Note the important difference between the mixture compounds [i.e. compounds of this type] and the two-word combinations discussed previously [e.g. the equivalent of English *bookstore*]. A houseboat is *partly* a house and *partly* a boat; northwest is *partly* north and *partly* west, etc. In contrast, a bookstore is a type of store and a bookseller is a type of seller but neither one is a type of book.

Words of the XY → Y type of compound involve words belonging to two different word classes; the compound belongs to the same class as the second of these, e.g. *undertaso* 'saucer' (PN → N), transandare 'to cross' (PV → V). The word class of compounds of the XY → Z compounds is not that of either of its component words (each of which belongs to a different word class), e.g. *enkosta* 'offshore' (PN → A). In all of these types of compouns the first word loses its word class suffix, although in some situations a vowel is inserted after the first component "in order to make the combination pronounceable" (ARG ibid.:35); this vowel is *a* with XX → X compounds and *i* with the other two types of compound.

## 4.1 Nouns

### 4.1.1 Number

Esperanto marks plurals with *-j*. EsF does not have this suffix, i.e. there is no morphological means of distinguishing between singular and plural nouns. There is no number marking on nouns (or pronouns) in Sen:esepera. The same is true of Esperloja nouns, but the meaning of plurality can be conveyed by a quantifier; Sulky (n.d.) says, "A commonly-used quantifier … means 'more than one'". Mondezo does have a plural suffix, but a different one than Esperanto has, *-s*. The plural marker of Farlingo, Hom-idyomo, Mondlingvo, Neo, Perio, Romániço, and Virgoranto is also *-s*; in Perio this suffix occurs after the case suffix, if there is one, e.g. *homuls* 'of the men' (Couturat and Leau 1907/1979:4). Mondlango has the same plural marker, but according to the *Basic Grammar of Mondlango* (anon. n.d. b), "The plural form is optional, for example: tri domo = tri domos".

Atlango's nominal plural suffix is *-y* (i.e. it is phonetically identically to that of Esperanto). The plural marker of 2008 E-speranto is also *-y* but its use is not required; Holmes (2008:96) states, "the optional *y* signals plurality".

Cartier (n.d.) says of Novesperant, "Plurals end with 'OS' or 'S' (Generally the former on nouns ending in consonants and the latter [on nouns] ending in vowels, not a strict rule)". In both the 1919 and 1923 versions of Esperantida the plural suffix is *-n*, as it is in Nov-Esperanto and Olingo.

The plural suffix of Reformed Esperanto, Ido, and Arlipo is *-i*, and it replaces the nominal ending *-o*, rather than following it, e.g. Arlipo *silabo* 'syllable', *silabi* 'syllables'. One could thus perhaps say that *-o* is a singular marker in these languages. Aiola's plural suffix is also *-i*, but it does not replace the nominal word class suffix, e.g. *katoi* is the plural of *kato* 'cat'.

In the small amount of textual material in Perilo in Horváth (n.d.) no nouns with the plural suffix occur. There are only two contexts where the plural suffix would have appeared in Esperanto, both in NPs introduced by definite articles, and it seems to be the case that in plural NPs with definite articles plurality is marked on the article and not on the head noun (v. (3a-b) below).

The plural suffix of Ekselisoro is spelled <-i>, which appears to be a consequence of an orthographic difference between Esperanto and Ekselsioro; the sequence <oi> of Ekselsioro is at least similar in sound to the sequence <oj> of Esperanto (v. note 38 of Chapter 2).

Linguna has different forms in all cases for singular and plural nouns, with the plural form usually, but not always, having *i* where the singular form lacks it (v. section 4.1.4).[18]

### 4.1.2 Sex and Gender

Esperanto has been accused of being sexist because stems for female entities are made by adding a suffix (*-in-*) to a stem which means a male entity, e.g. *patrin-* 'mother', from *patr-* 'father'. Mondezo eliminates this supposed sexism by making the roots free of indication of sex and having affixes for the formation of stems for both male and female entities, *-ich* and *-in* respectively. For example, in Mondezo *patro* means 'parent', not 'father'; *amiko* means 'friend', unspecified for sex, while *amikicho* means 'male friend' and *amikino* 'female friend'. Intero has the same type of solution, with *-ab* being the male suffix.

Nouns in Perio have the suffix *-o*, with some exceptions: those denoting male and female entities are marked by *-u* and *-y* respectively. Couturat and Leau (1907/1979:4) give the following example illustrating this: *homo* 'man' (as a generic term), *homu* 'man (male human being)', *homy* 'woman'. These suffixes can be attached to verbs, e.g. from *vidi* 'voir' can be formed *vidu* 'le voyant'. Also, "substantifs de qualité" (ibid.) have the suffix *-i*, which is also the infinitival suffix, thus for example *nami* means both 'être grand' and 'grandeur' (ibid.).

According to Winkelhofer (2007b), in Virgoranto nouns denoting people carrying out professions are "neutral" regarding sex; the affixes *-ma-* and *-fe-* can be used to express 'male' and female' respectively. Thus for example, *sekretaro* means 'secretary (neutral as to sex)', while *sekretamaro* and *sekretafero* are 'male secretary' and 'female secretary' respectively.[19] Winkelhofer (2007a) says something different about the meaning of the forms wihtout the sex-specific affixes: "Berufsbezeichnungen [sind] neutral oder weiblich, bei Männern Einschub –ma und bei Frauen -fe (sekretaro = SekretärIn, sekratamaro = männlicher Sekretär, sekretafero = weiblich)".

In Romániço it appears that nominal roots denoting animate beings do not contain any inherent meaning with respect to sex (and there are no default rules about sex); the suffixes *-içh-*[20] and *-is-*, 'male' and 'female' respectively, can be attached to them.

---

[18] There is a "sehr seltenen" (Goeres 2007) dual suffix in Linguna, *-oá*. The example of its use in Goeres (ibid.) is *la páchyai polecoá* 'die beiden dicken Daumen einer Person'.

[19] Note that in this example (the only one given) *-ma-* and *-fe-* are placed not immediately before the part of speech suffix *-o*, but before the *r* which precedes it and which occurs in at least some other words for people performing particular jobs, e.g. *enginero* 'engineer', as well as in some other words denoting people, e.g. *statbirgero* 'citizen of a state', *mordero* 'murderer'. I do not know whether the latter words can also take these affixes, although I suspect that they can.

[20] Cf. the unofficial Esperanto suffix *-iĉ-*, whose use is advocated by Riismo (and which was adopted by the DLT Intermediate Language).

For example, *jermano* means sibling, while *jermaniçho* and *jermaniso* mean 'brother' and 'sister'.[21]

Roots of Esperloja also have no inherent meaning regarding sex, and again there are suffixes for indicating sex, *-un-* and *-in-* for male and female respectively.

Mondlango also has suffixes for indicating the sex of a noun denoting a person or animal, *-ul-* and *-in-* for male and female respectively; as anon. (n.d. b) says, "most word roots are neutral [concerning sex]". Thus for example *frato* means 'sibling', with *fratulo* and *fratino* meaning 'brother' and 'sister' respectively. However, this is not the case for the words for parents: *patro* is 'father' and *matro* is 'mother'. The suffix *-ul-* may have come from Ido, which uses it for the same purpose (and which also has sex-neutral roots).

Linguna has grammatical gender, which affects the set of case forms that a noun has (v. section 4.1.4) and the personal pronoun used to stand for it (v. section 4.2). Goeres (2007) gives the following list of feminine nouns (v. also note 16):

> All names of countries, states, territories, regions, provinces, beaches, woods, islands, moons, planets, plains, towns, and counties, - and the nouns of country, county, homeland, beach, banks, island, hilly country, mountainous country, countryside, moon, town, city, wood, duchy, native country, plateau, tableland, high mountain region, mead, grounds, fields, depression/hollow, valley, landscape, region, prairie, plain, territory, terrain, foreign country/ ~ countries, etc. themselves as nouns are regarded as feminine (except for the words planet, desert, continent, because of being too mighty) and therefore follow the feminine declination ... like the females. ... -((But: regno, Estato, império, deserto, monto, continento, planedo, mondo, capitólio {all strong entities of administration, rule and power, or of summary, comprehension are masculine}))- ... also those in figurative sense of extension and livelihood/liveliness: vita, ánima, esperanza, synfónia, ...

### 4.1.3 Definiteness and Articles [22]

There are no articles in Mondezo, Reformed Esperanto, Sen:esepera, or Virgoranto. Modern Esperanto has an indefinite article (in addition to the definite article), *un*, unlike Esperanto. Lahago (n.d.:25) says, "The Russian language and some others have no indefinite articles and do they get by real well [sic] without it. But an article denotes the definiteness or indefiniteness of a noun! So why not use it? [...] It will specify the noun better and beautifies the sentence more". However, he allows beginners to omit the articles, stating (ibid.), "People who find a difficulty in the use of the articles need not at first use it [sic] at all".

Atlango's definite article is *le*, and it is also optional to some extent; Antonius (2008b) states, "People for whom use of the article offers difficulties (e.g. speakers of Chinese, Russian, Polish) may at first elect not to use it at all". In addition he says (ibid.) "Article LE are [sic] usually dropped in headlines".

---

[21] Morales (n.d. k) says, "Note that **-içh-** and **-is-** should only be used to avoid potential confusion. When speaking about **Senioros Smith** ("Mr. and Mrs. Smith"), for example, one might need to distinguish between **Senioriçho Smith** ("Mr. Smith") and **Senioriso Smith** ("Mrs. Smith"), but not when addressing either one of them directly (both are **Senioro Smith**)".

[22] For contractions of articles and prepositions occurring together v. section 4.7.

Perilo has an indefinite article:

(1)     Ni   logx-as      en una nova   domo.
        we live-PRES    in  a   new    house
        'We live in a new house.' (Horváth n.d, MT.)

However, it does not appear in the following sentence; one might have expected it to
be present before *besto*:

(2)     La   hundo estas  besto.
        the  dog   is      animal
        'The dog is an animal.' (ibid., MT)

Perilo apparently has a plural form of the definite article, *lo*; note that the nouns in the
following examples remain in their singular form:

(3a)    Paulo  ka   Anna estas  lo    infano.
        Paul   and  Anna are    the   child
        'Paul and Anna are the children.'

(3b)    Fero   ka   oro   estas  lo    metalo.
        iron   and  gold  are    the   metal
        'Iron and gold are the metals.'  (ibid., MT)

The Neo definite article agrees in number with its nominal head; its singular and
plural forms are *lo* and *los*. However, there will be no (overt) agreement when the
article appears in its shortened form, *l*, or is contracted with a preposition. Alfandari
(1961:33) states, "L'emploi de l'article n'est pas aussi fréquent qu'en français.
Comme en anglais, il est omis devant les mots pris dans leur sens général: **Franso** la
France; **omeyo** 'l'humanité; **riligo** la religion; **astronomio** l'astronomie". There is an
indefinite article in Neo, *un*, but it does not have a plural form.

Ido has the same definite article as Esperanto, *la*, and, as in Esperanto, its vowel
can be deleted, yielding *l'*.[23] It can also be contracted with the prepositions *a* 'to', *da*
'by', *de* 'from', and *di* 'of', creating the forms *al*, *dal*, *del*, *dil*. The definite article has
a plural form, *le*, but this is only used where the plurality of a NP is not marked or
expressed anywhere else, e.g. *le Cato* 'the Catos' (de Beaufront 1925/2005:13).

There are definite and indefinite articles in Olingo, *la* and *una* respectively. Arlipo
has only a definite article, *la*, but there is a plural form of it, *le*. Novesperant has an
indefinite article, *e*; it is "optional" (Cartier n.d.). Intero has both definite and
indefinite articles, *u* and *o* respectively, but Thompson (2007a) says of the latter, "The
use of this word is optional because it is not a necessary deviation from Esperanto".

The definite article of 1919 Esperantida is the same as that of Esperanto, *la*. In
addition 1919 Esperantida has what de Saussure (1919:3) calls a "difinita artiklo
substantivigita" ('a substantivized definite article', *lo*; it "expresas la jenerala
substantiva ideo (abstrakta) en definita senco" ('expresses the general (abstract)

---

[23] De Beaufront (1925/2005:13) says, "on atencez ne elizionar la artiklo, se ol destruktas la aspiro di la
litero *h*. Do ne uzez **l'homo**, **l'hosti**, ma **la homo**, **la hosti**" ('let one take care not to elide the [vowel of
the] article if it destroys the aspiration of the letter *h*. Therefore do not use *l'homo*, *l'hosti*, but *la homo*
['the human being'], *la hosti* ['the hosts']'.

substantive [i.e. nominal] idea in a definite sense') (ibid.:3). It is thus similar to Ido *lo*, and occurs with adjectives, e.g. *lo agrabla* (which I assume means 'agreeability' or something similar), from *agrabla* 'agreeable', as well as with participles and infinitives, e.g.:[24]

(4)  lo      paf-i[25]          dawr-is      tre      long-e.
     the     shoot-INFIN        last-PST     very     long-ADV
     'The shooting lasted for a very long time.' (ibid.:20, MT)

Ekselsioro also has the same definite article as Esperanto. In comparative correlatives a similar word, *le*, occurs, e.g.: *le pli vi legadas le pli saga vi ijos* 'the more you read the wiser you become' (Greenwood 1906b:18). Thus the first and second instances of *le* in this construction correspond to Esperanto *ju* and *des* respectively. Presumably *le* would also be used in comparative correlative constructions containing *mapli* 'less'.

*La* is also the main definite article of Romániço, appearing with both singular and plural nouns, but a plural form of it, *los* (which is the same in form as the general 3rd person plural pronoun), can occur, "to emphasize that an adjective is describing something in the plural" (Morales n.d. h) when that adjective is in a noun phrase with no overt nominal head. An example is given below:

(5)  Éviten los       vírida.
     avoid  the.PL    green
     'Avoid the green ones.' (Morales n.d. h)

There is also a generic article, *il*:

(6a)  Li es il        servisto cua     prensen pecunio.
      it is GART      servant  who     takes   money
      'It's the servant (as a class) who takes money.'

(6b)  Mi odien il infanto.
      I hate GART child
      'I hate kids' (Morales n.d. j)

---

[24] The following sentence occurs in de Saussure (ibid.:14):

(i)   Lo   hav-ata                       estas   pli   bona,   ol    lo
      The  have-PRESPASSPARTIC           is      more  good    than  the

      hav-ota
      have-FUTPASSPARTIC

I would have expected active rather than passive participles here, under the assumption that the sentence means 'To have is better than to be going to have'; if the participles are indeed meant to be passive, then the sentence means 'To be had is better than to be going to be had', which is, in my view, a less likely meaning.

[25] De Saussure (ibid.:20) gives *la tiro* as an alternative to *lo pafi* in this sentence.

Notice that the noun is in its singular form in (6b). This article also occurs before abstract nouns in Morales' webpages on Romániço, e.g. *ye nómino di il paço* 'in the name of peace' (Morales n.d. c).

There also a generic article in Aiola, *lo* (in addition to the definite article *la*).[26]

According to Couturat and Leau (1907/1979:87) in Mondlingvo, "La déclinaison porte sur l'article". Below are the examples that they give (ibid.) of it:

|         | SG           | PL            |
|---------|--------------|---------------|
| NOM     | la patro     | las patros    |
| GEN     | del patro    | dels patros   |
| DAT     | al patro     | als patros    |
| ACC     | lan patro(n) | lans patro(n)s |

Table 4.12: *Examples of Declined Articles and Nouns in Mondlingvo*

The genitive and dative forms of the definite article look like preposition-article contractions, as occur e.g. in Italian. Couturat and Leau (ibid.) state, "On ne dit pas comment se décline un substantif qui n'a pas d'article défini". However, from their examples, the accusative seems to be optionally marked on the noun. The article agrees with its noun in number, taking the same plural suffix as nouns, *-s*.

There are definite and indefinite articles in Perio, *il* and *un* respectively.

Hom-idyomo also has both definite and indefinite articles; in fact, according to Cárdenas (1923:I:27) it has two of the latter, since he considers *otza* 'another' to be an indefinite article, along with *una* 'a'. As with nouns, the suffix *-s* marks plurality, i.e. articles agree with their nouns in number; thus we have *las* as in *las vocistos* 'the spokesmen' (ibid.I:61) and *unas* as in e.g. *unas infantos* 'some children' (ibid.:I:27). Cárdenas' view on the word class of the indefinite articles is that "They are true adjectives having special offices" (ibid.).

Linguna has a relatively large number of forms of the definite article, since this language has several cases and articles agree with their nouns in case and to some extent in natural gender, though they have the same form for singular and plural:

|                                            | M   | General | N               |
|--------------------------------------------|-----|---------|-----------------|
| NOM, ACC                                   | le  | la      | lo (NOM), lon (ACC) |
| GEN                                        | les | las     | –               |
| DAT                                        | il  | il      | –               |
| instrumental ablative, locative ablative   | yl  | yl      | –               |

Table 4.13: *Definite Articles of Linguna*

The masculine forms are limited to occurring with nouns denoting male entities. The neuter article does not have forms for cases other than the nominative and accusative; prepositions are used to express the other cases, e.g. *al lo* for the dative. Further, Goeres (2004a) indicates that the accusative form of it is restricted to occurring before

---

[26] ARG (2005:37) says, "In Aiola there are three types of articles: definite, indefinite, and generic". This is misleading since Aiola does not have an (overt) indefinite article; on the same page of ARG it is stated that "Aiola marks an indefinite noun form with the absence of an article".

infinitives.[27] According to Goeres (2004b) *lo* "very seldom" occurs; I believe that it is the article which is to be used with infinitives. Two examples of its appearance in another type of context in Goeres (ibid.), with glosses as given there, are *lo reala* 'das Wirkliche / the real things', *lo vera* 'das Wahre / the true thing'. Linguna also has an indefinite article *un*, which "can be omitted" (ibid.); it is inflected for case, gender, and number.

The DLT Intermediate Language has the word *le*, about which Schubert (1986) says the following:

> La speciala artikolo le estis enkondukita ne kiel vera artikolo, sed kiel signo de komenco por tiaj substantivaj sintagmoj kun atributo, kiuj bezonas tian signon, sed ne havas ĝin en la formo de iu el tiuj determiniloj, kiu povas aperi nur komence de sintagmo (ekz. la, tiu, mia). Ekzemplo:

> [43]    La flughaveno posedas ok elektrajn le pasaĝerojn portantajn veturilojn.

> kie ne temas pri 'elektrajn pasaĝerojn'.

That is, *le* (which is not translated) indicates that *pasaĝerojn* is not modified by *elektrajn* (which rather modifies *veturilojn*), but makes up a separate NP (which is the object of *portantajn*). Although with respect to this example real world knowledge tells us that this is the more likely interpretation, one could imagine other examples for which our real world knowledge would fail to do this, and therefore for which *le* would be helpful in choosing the intended interpretation.

### 4.1.4    Case

Esperanto has an accusative suffix, *-n*. An accusative suffix does not exist in Aiola, Arlipo, EsF, Mondezo, Reformed Esperanto, Romániço, or Virgoranto. Esperloja, Hom-idyomo, and Novesperant nouns also are not inflected for case.[28] E-speranto has the same accusative suffix as Esperanto, but apparently its use is not obligatory; Holmes (2008:96) states, "the optional *n* signals accusativity". Harrison (2004) says of EsF, "Word sequence (subject-verb-object) will normally indicate which noun is the object of the verb. The preposition *na* will indicate the accusative when it is necessary to mark it".

Medrano (2002) indicates that Mondezo has as its "standard word order" SVO, and this is used to indicate which NPs are direct objects. In Baza the Esperanto accusative affix is "not required" (Hoover n.d.), the direct object will be again identifiable through SVO order. Hoover (ibid.) states, "However, well established words may retain the *n* in common usage, such as, 'Bonan tagon'".

There is no accusative suffix in Intero (on nouns or pronouns), but there is a suffix for the genitive case, *-es*. It follows the plural marker, which is spelled <y>, and thus genitive plural noun end with *-yes*.

---

[27] When they are preceded by *lo*, as apparently in general when they have a nominal function, active infinitives have the ending *-ejn* rather than *-i*, Goeres (2004b) says that *-ejn* is "[the suffix of the] infinitive of participle, which may be used like a noun, but without change of ending".

[28] V. section 4.7 for prepositions indicating objects in Hom-idyomo and Romániço and subjects and objects in Esperloja.

Ido has the same accusative suffix as Esperanto (for both nouns and pronouns), but it should only be used with some non-basic word orders and in other contexts where it would not otherwise be clear whether a NP was a subject or a direct object;[29] this suffix is referred to as the "*n* inversigala" ('inversional *n*') by de Beaufront (1925/2005). He (1925/2005:88) says: "Kompreneble la **n** inversigala esas necesa nur kande la komplemento direta preiras la subjekto. Ma, mem se ol preiras la verbo, nula **n** devas uzesar, kande la subjekto konservas l'*unesma plaso*. Ex. : **tua fratulo me odias** = *tua fratulo odias me*. Ico precipue aplikesas al pronomi : **el vu amas, il me vidis** = *el amas vu, il vidis me*." ('Of course the inversional *n* is necessary only when the direct object precedes the subject. But, even if it goes before the verb, no *n* has to be used when the subject keeps the *first place*. E.g.: … This is mainly applied to the pronouns: …')[30]

Atlango also has the same accusative suffix as Esperanto, and like Ido it does not appear on direct objects when a clause has a basic order, but it does with an "inverted sentence structure" (Antonius 2008b), e.g. *mi vida le purto* 'I see the port', *mi le purton vida* (ibid.). Antonius (ibid.) states, "In alga okazo se poda uzili akuzativa partikolo – **an**" ('On any occasion one can use an accusative particle – **an**').

1919 Esperantida does not have an accusative suffix; it marks direct objects with the preposition *e*, but it is not always present; de Saussure (1919:9) states, "Kiam la vorton seqas su en la natura ordo (subjeko, verbo, komplemento), la prepozicio akuzativa estas forlasata, konforme al principo de sufito (ex.: *li amas shi*). En omnin alian kazon la uzo de la prepozicio *e* estas deviga (*li e shi amas*; *e shi li amas*; *e shi amas li*; *amas li e shi*; *amas e shi li*)" ('When the words follow each other in the natural order (subject, verb, complement) the accusative preposition is omitted, conforming to the principle of sufficiency … In all other cases the use of the preposition *e* is obligatory …'). Note that there is a difference from Ido here: with the order SOV Ido does not require accusative marking on the object, but 1919 Esperantida requires *e*.

1923 Esperantida has an accusative suffix, *-u*,[31] and as in Esperanto, it appears on all nouns which are direct objects, regardless of the word order of the clause, e.g.:

(7)     Mi  leg-as        libr-u
        I    read-PRES   book-ACC
        'I read a book'  (de Saussure 1923:14, MT)

---

[29] It is also attached to "inverted" (de Beaufront 1925/2005:88) NP subject complements when it would not otherwise be clear that they were not subjects.

[30] Collinson (1924) makes the following remarks on Esperanto and Ido accusative case marking:

> It is quite true that the use of the accusative requires some study on the part of the English, Scandinavians, Romance nations, and the Chinese, and that the ending is sometimes inadvertently dropped in conversation. But the issue between Esperanto and Ido is not as to the absolute desirability of having the case, but simply as to whether it is better to lay down a rule of universal application (Esperanto standpoint) and tacitly condone minor breaches in colloquial speech, or provide for the use of the inflection only in a specified contingency (Ido). It is not fair of De Beaufront to claim that the accusative makes Esperanto harder than Ido, while he still retains the case at all -- at any rate it is just as hard for an Englishman to grasp the use of the accusative before the noun as after. On the whole -- for the written form at any rate -- the balance of advantage would seem to be with the regular employment of the accusative.

[31] This becomes *-w* when following the *-a* suffix of adjectives or the *-e* suffix of adverbs (when marking motion towards), e.g. *mi iras domew* 'I am going home' (de Saussure 1923:8, MT).

Note a morphological difference from Esperanto presumably due to the different form of the accusative suffixes in the two languages: the Esperanto suffix is added to the end of the noun stem (which ends in *-o* in the singular), while the 1923 Esperantida suffix replaces the *-o* with which the stem ends. Thus for example the stem (and nominative form) of 'book' is *libro* in both languages; the final *-o* is retained in the Esperanto accusative form *libron*, but lost in the 1923 Esperantida accusative form *libru*. The order of the plural and accusative suffixes is also different: in Esperanto the former precedes the latter, e.g. *librojn*, while in 1923 Esperantida the reverse order holds, e.g. *patrun* 'fathers (ACC)' (recall that *-n* is the plural marker in this language). In Nov-Esperanto the accusative suffix is also *-u*,[32] and again it precedes the plural suffix.

There is no morphological case marking of nouns in Sen:esepera; Henning (1995a) says, "What Esperanto would express with the accusative case, *Sen:esepera* expresses with the preposition *ano*". However, one might claim this is not accurate, since it does not seem to be required on direct objects (unlike *-n* in Esperanto); in fact it never occurs in the sample text in Henning (ibid.). Apparently it is optional, or perhaps it is only required when the word order is not SVO.

Olingo does not have an accusative case suffix, but it does have a possessive marker, the same one as in English, *'s*, e.g. *lingo's* 'language's', *rexino's* 'queen's'. However, Jaque (1944:34) states, "*Possession* is better indicated by use of the prepositional form: *la qiso de mia patrino* ['the kiss of my mother']". Perio has genitive and accusative case suffixes for nouns, *-l* and *-n* respectively; these follow the nominal suffixes such as *-o*.

We have seen in the preceding section that in Mondlingvo the definite article bears (what Trischen and/or Couturat and Leau consider) marking for the genitive, dative, and accusative cases (although the forms for the first two of these resemble contracted forms of prepositions with the article in some Romance languages) and the noun appears to have an optional accusative suffix *-n*.

Although Neo lacks a nominal accusative suffix,[33] it has an ending, *-ye*, which at least resembles a case affix: Alfandari (1961:55) states that it "remplace les prépositions *à, en, dans, vers, chez* lorsqu'on emploie un mot *dans un sens général*, qu'il y ait repos ou mouvement". Some of his (ibid.) examples are below:

(8a)  mi  s-ar,      mi  g-ar      dom-ye
      I   be-PRES  I   go-PRES  house-*ye*
      'je suis, je vais à la maison'

(8b)  il  no   v-ar        g-i        skol-ye
      he  not  want-PRES  go-INFIN  school-*ye*
      'il ne veut pas aller à l'école'

When a noun phrase refers to a particular house, school, etc., a preposition is used rather than *-ye*:

---

[32] As in 1923 Esperantida this becomes [w], written *-ù* in the relevant examples in de Saussure (1926), after the adjectival suffix *-a* and the adverbial suffix *-e*, e.g. *mi iras domeù* 'I am going home' (ibid.:8, MT).

[33] The original (1937) version of Neo did have one.

(9)     mi   g-ar     al     skol    del    dorf
         I     go-PRES  to.the  school  of.the  village
         'je vais à l'école du village' (ibid.)

Ekselosioro has a possessive case for nouns (which Esperanto does not have), marked by *-es*, e.g. *la hundes vosto* 'the dog's tail', *la reges arboi* 'the king's trees' (Greenwood 1906b:17). Note that this ending replaces the *-o* which is the marker of nouns, rather than being attached to it. However, in the plural, it is joined to the plural affix, which follows the *-o*, and the latter is retained, e.g. *la hundoies okuloi* 'the dogs' eyes' (ibid.). Greenwood (1906b) mentions both a possessive and a genitive case (the latter marked by the preposition *de*), and it is not clear to me whether they have different meanings and/or functions or are alternative ways of indicating the same set of relations. He states (ibid.:17) that the former "signifies – belonging to, possession or ownership" while the latter means 'of or arising from' (ibid.). He gives (ibid.) the examples for the latter *la frukto de la arbo* 'the fruit of the tree' and *la vaporo de la akvo* 'the vapor of the water' (ibid.). In the glossary appearing later in the same work the entry for *de* (p. 24) says, "*of* or *from*. Forms the Genitive, *by, since, among*". The function of structures with the possessive case such as *la homes mano* 'the man's hand' is "to obviate" (ibid.:17) phrases such as *la mano de la homo*; does this mean that the latter are incorrect? In any case, among the occurrences of *de* in Greenwood (1906:b) are *"Edvard" VIII, rego de Anglando* 'Edward VII, kind of England' (p. 17) and *estro de la xipo* 'ship captain' (p. 19). There is also apparently a locative case marker in Ekselsioro but my primary sources on the language have very little information on it: Greenwood (1906b:17) states "All [cases] end in *-o* excepting Possessive and Locative" and later on the same page says, "Locative–vide 'N' function, to follow" and "all inflections are superseded by respective prepositions, except the Possessive, *es*, and *-n*, to follow". However, in the rest of this work, at least what I have of it,[34] there is nothing about a locative case or on the suffix *-n*, but it seems that the latter is the marker of the former. Ekselsioro does not have an accusative marker; Greenwood (ibid.) states that the accusative is "same as nom[inative]".

Linguna has a relatively large number of case forms, as shown by the following paradigm:

---

[34] My photocopy of it ends unexpectedly on p. 24, and it is not clear to me whether this is in fact the end of the work.

| | SG | PL |
|---|---|---|
| NOM | la colombo blanca | pl.: la colomboi blancai |
| GEN | de la colombo blanca / (las) colombes blanqes | de la colomboi blancai / (las) colombois blancais |
| DAT | al la colombo blanca / (il) colombim blanqim | al la colomboi blancai / (il) colombins blanqins |
| ACC | la colombon blancan | la colomboin blancain |
| Instrumental Ablative | (yl) colombom blancom | (yl) colómboiom bláncaiom / (yl) colómboimy bláncaiom |
| Locative Ablative | blanca-colombe[35] (yl) colombe blánqaé | blancai-colómboie (yl) colómboi-bláncaie |
| DIR | blanca-colomben | blancai-colómboien |

Table 4.14: *Paradigm for the Phrase* la colombo blanca *'the white dove' (from Goeres 2004a, with changes)*

It can be seen that to express some case meanings has a choice of using a preposition or case inflection. There is also a separative ablative suffix, *-oth*. Feminine nouns are declined in a somewhat different way, as the table below illustrates:

| NOM | adelfida |
|---|---|
| GEN | adelfidaes |
| DAT | adelfidaem |
| ACC | adelfidan |
| Instrumental Ablative | adelfidaom |
| Locative Ablative | adelfidae |
| DIR | adelfidaen |

Table 4.15: *Singular Forms* of adelfida *'niece' (from Goeres 2004a, with changes)*

## 4.2 Pronouns and Related Words

### 4.2.1 Personal Pronouns and Possessive Pronouns and Adjectives

The table below shows the (nominative) personal pronouns in three of de Saussure's languages:

---

[35] I do not know why the article is missing with the items in this line, or with the directional forms. I also do not know why the article is in parentheses with forms in some cases. Note that here the adjective has been attached to the noun, and since it is now not a separate word but the first component of a compound, it does not need a case ending; the same thing happens in the directional case (which Goeres (2004a) calls the *diréccio locativa* ('locative direction')), and perhaps this is the only option in this case for an attributive adjective.

|  | 1SG | 2SG | 3MSG | 3FSG | 3NSG | 1PL | 2PL | 3CNPL | 3MPL | 3FPL | 3NPL |
|---|---|---|---|---|---|---|---|---|---|---|---|
| 1919 E-tida | mi | vi | li | shi | ji | nu | vu | lu | lin | shin | jin |
| 1923 E-tida | mi | vi (ci) | li | shi | ji | ni | vi | illi | – | – | – |
| Nov-Esp. | mi | vi (ci) | li | shi | ji | ni | vi | hili | – | – | – |

Table 4.16: *Personal Pronouns in de Saussure's Languages*

In 1919 Esperantida pronouns, like nouns, are not inflected for case, so the forms in the above table are the only forms of the personal pronouns. In 1923 Esperantida and Nov-Esperanto the accusative pronouns end in -u instead of the -i of the forms above, e.g. *hilu* is the 3rd person plural pronoun of Nov-Esperanto. In Nov-Esperanto possessive pronouns consist of possessive adjectives (which are constructed from nominative personal pronouns and the adjectival ending -*a*) and the suffixes -*y* or -*ù* (for nominative and accusative forms respectively), e.g. *viay* 'yours (NOM)', *viaù* 'yours (ACC)'. The possessive pronouns of 1923 Esperantida seem to be constructed in the same sort of way, e.g. *liaw* 'his (ACC)'.

The DLT Intermediate Language has eliminated the pronoun *ci*. *Li* has become a sex-neutral pronoun, while a specifically male 3rd person singular pronoun has been added, as have male and female 3rd person plural pronouns (but not a specifically 3rd person neuter one). This yields the following array of personal pronouns:

| 1SG | 2SG | 3CSG | 3MSG | 3FSG | 3NSG | 1PL | 2PL | 3CNPL | 3MPL | 3FPL |
|---|---|---|---|---|---|---|---|---|---|---|
| mi | vi | li | hi | ŝi | ĝi | ni | vi | ili | ihi | iŝi |

Table 4.17: *Personal Pronouns of the DLT Intermediate Language*

There is also *lo* (with the accusative form *lon*), which Schubert (1986) calls a "nepersona pronomo", although originally it was considered an article; Schubert (ibid.) says, "ĝi kondutas ekzakte kiel pronomo el la korelativa vico *tio*". As for its function, "Ĝi enkondukas atributon, kiu en Esperanto dependas de nenio, kaj por kiu ankaŭ ne estas trovebla reganto ie en apuda propozicio" (ibid.). One of the examples of its use given by Schubert (ibid.) is:[36]

(10) Lo unua, kion ni povas fari, estas esploro.
　　 *lo* first what we can do is investigation
　　 'The first thing that we can do is to investigate.' (MT)

---

[36] Schubert (ibid.) states that it does not occur in cases such as the following:

(i) Ĉi-tiu kalkulilo estas la plej malgranda, kiun mi iam vidis.
　　 this calculator is the most small, which I ever saw
　　 'This calculator is the smallest that I have ever seen.' (MT)

Here the head of the second NP has been deleted under identity with *kalkulilo*; such a process did not occur in (10).

In addition it is a dummy subject pronoun.

Webpage E-speranto has a pronoun not present in Esperanto, *xli* 'he/she'.[37] In 2008 E-speranto the prefixes *i-* and *o-* serve "to widen the scope [of pronouns]" (Holmes 2008:94) and "to abstract it" (ibid.) respectively. The examples that Holmes (ibid.) provides of this are *ili* (i.e. *i-* and *li* 'he') 'he and his associates, they' and *omi* (i.e. *o-* and *mi* 'I') 'someone like me, one'. (It is possible to attach these prefixes to correlatives as well.).

Mondezo has added a member to Esperanto's set of pronouns, *gi* 'he/she', "when the sex is not known or is unimportant" (Medrano 2002). Unlike in Esperanto, in Mondezo *vi* only has a plural meaning; the 2nd person singular pronoun is *ci*. Like nouns, pronouns are not marked for accusative case.

The singular personal pronouns of Virgoranto are *me* 'I', *ju* 'you', *hi* 'he', *shi* 'she', and *gi* 'it'. All of these have plural counterparts, ending in *-s*, e.g. *mes* 'we', *jus* 'you (PL)', *his* 'they (M)'. They have the same form in all grammatical functions.

The singular "nominal" personal pronouns of Intero are given in the following table:

| 1SG | 2SG common | 2SG rare | 3MSG | 3FSG | 3SG common | 3NSG | 3SG impersonal |
|-----|-----------|----------|------|------|------------|------|----------------|
| mo | to | co | labo | lino | lo | xo | no |

Table 4.18: *Intero Nominal Pronouns (after Thompson 2007a)*

I am not certain why these are called "nominal", but they seem to be equivalent to personal pronouns, e.g. *xo* means 'it'. I am also not sure what the meaning of "rare" is in relation to the 2nd person pronouns, but since the 2nd person common form begins with *t-*, it might mean 'polite/formal', with "common" here meaning 'familiar/informal' (i.e. not meaning 'common gender', although I think that "common" does have this meaning when applied to the 3rd person pronons). All of these pronouns, including the impersonal pronoun, have a plural form, constructed with the same suffix as plural nouns have, namely *-y*, e.g. *moy* 'we'. The singular possessive forms are the same as the nominal pronouns except that they end in *-es* rather than *-o*, while the plural possessive forms have the *-es* added to the end, e.g. *loyes* 'their'. (These forms seem to correspond to possessive adjectives; I do not know whether they also correspond to possessive pronouns such as *theirs*.) There are also "descriptive" pronouns, the singular ones all ending in *-a* rather than *-o*, e.g. *ma*, *laba*, the plural ones having the *-a* after the plural marker *-y*, e.g. *moya*. Their meaning/function is not explained by Thompson (2007a).

Sen:esepera pronouns (like nouns) do not show a distinction between singular and plural, nor do they bear accusative marking. Thus *imu* means both 'I' and 'we', as well as 'me' and 'us'. *Tu* is 'you' and the third person pronoun, for all numbers, genders, and cases, is *hu*. As we have seen, the characteristic ending for pronouns in this language is *-u*. Henning (1995a) states that "All possessive pronouns (e.g. *mine*, *yours*, *his*) are formed by appending /n/". The words created in this way also apparently can have the function of possessive adjectives, as shown by the phrases *hun lingifa* 'their language' (ibid.) and *Hun enoma* 'its name' (ibid.). Henning (ibid.)

---

[37] This pronoun is not in Holmes's (2008) list of singular pronouns of 2008 E-speranto.

says that "possessive pronouns are treated as adjectives", which might account for this fact, although I do not know whether this is what he means.

Concerning Novesperant Cartier (n.d.) states, "There are no Cases, except for object pronouns if necessary". The fact that *mi* means both 'I' and 'my' in the following example may follow from this:

(11)    mi  ne  pov  trovi  mi   automobil.
        I   not can  find  my   car
        'I cannot find my car.' (Cartier n.d., MT)

The personal pronouns of Ekselsioro are the same as or similar to their Esperanto counterparts; I assume that what differences exist are a consequence of differences in the sound and spelling systems of the two languages:[38]

| 1SG | 2SG | 3MSG | 3FSG | 3NSG | 1PL | 2PL | 3PL |
|-----|-----|------|------|------|-----|-----|-----|
| mi  | zi  | li   | xi   | gi   | ni  | vi  | ili |

Table 4.19: *Personal Pronouns of Ekselsioro (after Greenwood 1906b:19)*

Possessive adjectives and pronouns are identical, both formed by attaching *-es* to the above words, e.g. *mies libro* 'my book' *la libro estas mies* 'the book is mine' (ibid.). The table of personal pronouns in Greenwood (1906b:19) contains "Objective" forms, e.g. *mia, zia*, along with the possessive forms such as *zies*. However, it is not clear that these are in fact objective or accusative forms. For one thing, the section heading immediately before this table begins, "**VIII.**–*Possessive Pronouns,–Sia, Lia, &c.*", making it seem as though e.g. *lia* is a possessive form (although the nominative forms such as *mi* are also in the table, and labelled as such). Second, the form *sia* (from the 3rd person reflexive pronoun *si*) acts as a possessive adjective in the following passage from Greenwood (1906a:8):[39]

(12)    ...  oni  pov-as      esprim-i         si-a        propra  penso-i
             one  can-PRES    express-INFIN    self(3)-*a*  own     thought-PL
        '... one can express his own thoughts' (MT)

Further, in the sentence *mi aldonis gi* 'I added it' (Greenwood 1906b:23), which occurs in the entry for *al* 'to, toward' in the Ekselsioro - English glossary, the direct object pronoun has no suffix.[40] On the other hand, the entry for *gi* in this glossary (ibid.:24) is: "**gi**, *it*; **gia**, *it (obj.)*; **gies**, *its*."

---

[38] From the table we see that Ekselsioro has *zi* instead of Esperanto *ci*. Ekselsioro does have the letter <c> but it stands for [tʃ], not [ts] as in Esperanto, thus the sequence <ci> in Ekselsioro would not sound the same as <ci> in Esperanto. Greenwood chose to give this pronoun the form *zi* (instead of *tsi*, which would sound the same as Esperanto *ci*).

[39] Greenwood (1906b:19) says of the personal pronouns (among which he includes *si*), "except *si*, all take possessive *-es*. (see partial license as we proceed)".

[40] Couturat and Leau (1907/1979:91) state, "L'accusatif devient facultatif, soit pour la direction, soit même pour la régime direct ... Mais on conserve l'accusatif dit «de clarté»: **mi amas xi pli ol vi** (sous-ent.: **amas xi**); **mi amas xi pli ol vin** (sous-ent.: **mi amas**)". However, in my primary source material on Ekselsioro, which seems to include the work that Couturat and Leau (ibid.:90) cite, Greenwood says nothing like this. In fact he says something which is incompatible with this, if Couturat and Leau are speaking of nouns as well as pronouns, v. sec. 4.1.4. As mentioned in that section, Ekselsioro has a

The personal pronouns of Atlango are shown below:

| 1SG | 2SG | 3CNSG | 3MSG | 3FSG | 3NSG | 1PL | 2PL | 3PL |
|-----|-------|-------|------|------|------|-----|-----|-----|
| mi | ti, tu | li | hi | xi | to | mu | Tu[41] | lu |

Table 4.20: *Atlango Personal Pronouns (after Antonius 2008b)*

There are alternative forms of these pronouns: Antonius (ibid.) says, "For euphonious purposes or to avoid misunderstandings between pronouns we can add **- e -**. For example: **mi = emi - I, mu = emu -we**, and so on". Just before this he states that one may use *teno* 'this woman' instead of *xi*, also "[f]or euphonious purposes". A 3rd person neuter plural pronoun, *tadoy*, is given in Antonius' (ibid.) table of personal pronouns; it apparently is the plural form of *tado* 'that thing' (which does not appear in this table). There is also a "nepersona pronomo" ('impersonal pronoun', ibid.) *lo*, about which Antonius (ibid.) says,

> 1. **Lo** refers to an indeterminate object **- to a fact, action** or **situation** rather than to a thing:
> Prin(es) ta pomo, mi dezira **lo**, Take this apple, I desire it (= I desire you to do so ).)
> 2. **Lo** as an **impersonal "it" with adjectives:** it's cold - **Lo**-s kolde (frige)
> 3. **Lo** as an **impersonal "it"**(dummy subject) **with verbs:**
> **Lo** pluva **-it rains - it is raining.**
> **Lo**-s le qina -It's five o'clock
> **Lo** esto sredo morge - It will be Wednesday tomorrow.

*To* can also be a "dummy subject" (ibid.):

(13)    To-s    facil-e        kritik-i
        it-is    easy-ADV    criticize-INFIN
        'It is easy to criticize'  (Antonius 2008b)

The plural personal pronouns of Perio also end in -*u*:

|      | 1  | 2  | 3M | 3F | 3N |
|------|----|----|----|----|----|
| SG | mi | vi | li | la | lu |
| PL | mu | vu | | lu | |

Table 4.21: *Personal Pronouns of Perio (after Couturat and Leau 1907/1979:4)*

As in French and various other natural languages, the 2nd person plural pronoun is used as a polite form of the 2nd person singular pronoun. The definite article (*il*) also serves as an impersonal pronoun and *ii* is equivalent to the French pronoun *on*.

---

case ending -*n*, but it is not the accusative case marker. This is not the only apparent discrepancy between Couturat and Leau and Greenwood (1906a, b), v. sec. 2.1.

[41] I have capitalized the 2nd person plural pronoun, but not the singular ones, because this is what Antonius (ibid.) does in his table of personal pronouns. However, he is inconsistent in this respect, for example he (2008c) gives *Tu* as both the singular and the plural form, so I would not assume that *tu* is capitalized only when it is a plural pronoun.

Personal pronouns have the same accusative suffix as nouns, *-n*, e.g. *min*, *vun*. Possessive adjectives consist of the nominative pronouns and *-l* (i.e. the suffix which marks the genitive case of nouns), e.g. *mil*, *lil*, and possessive pronouns are made of these latter forms and one of the nominal endings *-o*, *-a*, and *-u*, depending on gender. Couturat and Leau (ibid.:5) give the examples *il milo* 'le mien' (N), *il vulu* 'le vôtre' (M), and *il muly* 'la notre' (F).

The singular personal pronouns of Mondlingvo are the same as in Esperanto, but the plural ones differ since they are formed by suffixing *-s* to the singular forms (and thus there are masculine, feminine, and neuter forms in the plural), e.g. *mis* 'we', *vis* 'you (PL)', *ŝis* 'they (F)'. In Modern Esperanto there are the following changes to the personal pronouns of Esperanto: *ŝi* 'she' becomes *ŝji*, *ĝi* 'it' becomes *gi*, and *ni* 'we' is replaced by *wi*.

Some of the personal pronouns of Hom-idyomo are identical to their Esperanto equivalents, but some are not, and there are more personal pronouns than in Esperanto, since there are masculine, feminine, and neuter 3rd person plural pronouns:[42]

| | 1SG | 2SG | 3MSG | 3FSG | 3NSG | 1PL | 2PL | 3MPL | 3FPL | 3NPL |
|---|---|---|---|---|---|---|---|---|---|---|
| NOM | mi | tu, bi[43] | li | ŝi | ji | nos | vos | ili | eli | esi |
| ACC | me | te, be | le | ŝe | je | nes | ves | ile | ele | ese |

Table 4.22: *Personal Pronouns of Hom-Idyomo (after Cárdenas 1923:I:29)*

The procedure by which a nominative form is turned into an accusative one is that "it changes its vowel (or its second vowel, if there are two) to *e*" (ibid.).

The 3rd person plural pronouns of Mondlango also indicate gender, again yielding a relatively large array of personal pronouns:

| 1SG | 2SG | 3CSG | 3MSG | 3FSG | 3NSG | 1PL | 2PL | 3CPL | 3MPL | 3FPL | 3NPL |
|---|---|---|---|---|---|---|---|---|---|---|---|
| mi | yi | li | hi | xi | ji | mu | yu | lu | hu | xu | ju |

Table 4.23: *Personal Pronouns of Mondlango (after anon. n.d. b)*

Mondlango nouns do not take an accusative suffix, but anon. (ibid.) states, "If necessary, personal pronounces [sic] have accusative case"; the accusative forms end in *-m*, e.g. *mim* 'me'. Mondlango has distinct possessive adjectives and possessive pronouns; the former consist of personal pronouns and *-a*, e.g. *mia* 'my', while the latter are made up of possessive adjectives and *-s*, e.g. *mias* 'mine'.

The "baza" ('basic', Vitek n.d. b) personal pronouns of Arlipo are shown below:

---

[42] Hom-idyomo also has a word *an* 'of him/her/it/that, here, there', which Cárdenas (1923:I:39) considers to be a relative pronoun, but which seems rather to be a personal pronoun and perhaps also an adverb; it appears to be at least partly equivalent to French *en*, as in e.g. *tu an paroley* 'thou spokest of him' (ibid.).

[43] *Tu* is glossed as 'thou' and *bi* as 'you (sing.)' in Cárdenas (1923:I:29).

|   | SG | PL |
|---|----|----|
| 1 | me | ni |
| 2 | vu |    |
| 3 | il | ili |

Table 4.24: *Arlipo Basic Personal Pronouns*

If one wants to be more specific about number for the 2nd person and sex for the 3rd person one can use the pronouns *tu* and *vi* (2nd person singular and plural respectively), *ul* and *in* (3rd person singular masculine and feminine respectively), and *uli* and *ini* (3rd person plural masculine and feminine respectively).

Romániço has a quite large set of personal pronouns, even though pronouns do not take case affixes. The 1st person singular and plural pronouns are *mi* and *nos*, and those for the 2nd person singular and plural are *vi* and *vos*. There is an additional 2nd person pronoun: Morales (n.d. g) says, "Those wishing to express a higher degree of familiarity or antiquarian flavor when addressing a single person (e[.]g., to family and very close friends) can use the secondary pronoun **ti** ('thou/thee')". The general 3rd person singular and plural pronouns are *li* and *los*. There are more specific 3rd person singular pronouns: *ili* (male), *eli* (female), *hi* (human), *uli* (sentient), and *oli* (insentient). *Los* can serve as the plural version of any of these, but there are also specific 3rd person plural pronouns, e.g. *ilos* 'they (M)'. In addition Romániço has the pronoun *lo*, which Morales (ibid.) says "means 'the business, thing, fact' and refers to the entire content of a previous clause"; he gives the following example:

(14)  Vi   desíderen ecuila focilo,  Zed, no? Advancien et   leven   li.
      you  desire    that   gun      Zed  no  advance   and pick.up
      3SG

      Mi   desíderen lo.
      I    desire    lo
      'You want that gun, don't you, Zed? Go ahead and pick it up. I want you to.'

This pronoun is equivalent to the English impersonal *it* in e.g. *lo pluven* 'it's raining' (ibid.), *lo semblen ad mi que…* 'it seems to me that…' (ibid.).

Ido has more 3rd person personal pronouns than Esperanto. The basic 3rd person pronouns, *lu* and *li* (for singular and plural respectively) are unspecified for sex. One can be specific about the sex of the referent(s) with the masculine, feminine, and neuter singular pronouns *il(u)*, *el(u)*, and *ol(u)* respectively, and with their plural counterparts *ili*, *eli*, and *oli*. The 1st person singular and plural pronouns are *me* and *ni*. There are three 2nd person pronouns, *vu* (singular), *tu* ("familiar" (de Beaufront 1925/2005:25) singular), and *vi* (plural). All of these pronouns can have the accusative suffix *-n* under the same conditions in which nouns would have them (v. section 4.1.4). In addition, Ido has a word *lo*, considered an article by Collison (1924) but labelled a pronoun by de Beaufront (1925/2005:32). It can stand for a clause as in *Il esas mortinta de tri monati, e vu ne savas lo!* [*ke il esas mortinta*] 'He has been dead for three months, and you do not know it! [that he has been dead]' (ibid., MT). It can precede adjectives (and thus seem to behave like an article) in NPs without nominal heads, as in *La etiko docas lo bona, la cienco serchas lo vera, l'arto kultivas* *lo bela* 'ethics teaches the good, science seeks the true, art cultivates the beautiful' (ibid.:169, MT).

Snifferanto's set of personal pronouns is slightly different from that of Esperanto:

| 1SG | 2SG | 3MSG | 3FSG | 3NSG | 1PL | 2PL | 3PL |
|-----|-------|------|------|------|-----|-----|-----|
| mi  | tu, vi | li  | shi  | olu  | ni  | vi  | ili |

Table 4.25: *Snifferanto Personal Pronouns*

I assume that the difference between *tu* and *vi* as 2nd person singular pronouns is that the former is informal and the latter is formal. The pronoun *olu* comes from Ido.

Sulky (n.d.) gives a fairly long list of Esperloja personal pronouns. The singular pronouns are *moi* 'I, me', *toi* 'thou, thee', *lunoi* 'he', *linoi* 'she', *loi* 'it'. The plural pronouns are shown in the table below (from Sulky n.d. with minor changes):

| motoi | 'I and thou' (inclusive) |
|-------|--------------------------|
| moloi | 'I and it' (exclusive) |
| mototoi | 'I and you' |
| motoloi | 'I and thou and it' |
| mololoi | 'I and they' |
| totoi | 'you (thou and thou)' |
| toloi | 'you (thou and it)' |
| loloi | 'they (it and it)' |

Table 4.26: *Plural Pronouns of Esperloja*

Some of the personal pronouns of Olingo have been borrowed from English, as can be seen in the following table:

|       | 1SG | 2SG | 3MSG | 3FSG | 3NSG | 1PL | 2PL | 3PL |
|-------|-----|-----|------|------|------|-----|-----|-----|
| NOM   | I   | vi  | hi   | shi  | ji   | wi  | vin | lin |
| ACC   | mi  | vi  | hu   | shu  | [44] | wiu | [45] | linu |

Table 4.27: *Olingo Personal Pronouns*

Possessive adjectives end with *-a*, e.g. *hia* 'his', *lina* 'their'. It is not clear to me how possessive pronouns are formed: they do not occur in texts in Jaque (1944) and in the Olingo-English and English-Olingo vocabularies in that work only two unambiguous possessive pronouns occur: *miona* 'mine' occurs in the latter vocabulary (cf. *mia*

---

[44] I would think that the accusative form of the 3rd person neuter pronoun is also *ji*, but I am not sure because to my knowledge it never appears in any Olingo texts in Jaque (1944) and he does not say anything about it.

[45] I would assume that *vin* is both the nominative and accusative form of the 2nd person plural pronoun, but I cannot be certain because Jaque (1944) says nothing explicit about this (only giving *vin* as the word for 'you (plural)' on p. 58 the "English-Olingo Vocabulary" section, and 'you (plural)' as the meaning of *vin* on p. 46 of the Olingo-English Vocabulary section) and because to my knowledge *vin* does not occur in any of the Olingo sentences of texts in this work. (I was able to determine that the 2nd person singular pronoun is the same in the nominative and accusative because it occurs as an object in three sentences on p. 35, e.g. *La OLINGA QODO helpota vi* 'The Olingo Code will help you' (MT).)

'my'; ona as a separate word means 'own') and *shia* 'hers' is found in both. The word for 'her' is also *shia*, so unless Jaque has made an error, it appears that possessive pronouns are not formed in a uniform manner: some may be identical to possessive adjectives, but at least one is not.

The personal pronouns of Aiola are shown in the table below:

|     | SG  | PL  |
| --- | --- | --- |
| 1   | mi  | moi (inclusive) mai (exclusive) |
| 2   | vu  | voi |
| 3M  | deo | deoi |
| 3F  | dea | deai |
| 3   | da  | dai |

Table 4.28: *Aiola Personal Pronouns (based on ARG 2005:44)*

Like other words of the language, they are not inflected for case. As can be seen, there are inclusive and exclusive 1st person plural pronouns, which to my knowledge is a rare feature among artificial languages. *Da* is both the 3rd person singular neuter pronoun and the pronoun used "to denote something of which the [sex] is unknown" (ibid.). The following example shows the latter use:

(15)  Da        dev-as         aport-are      daza      libro   alu   la    klaseo.
      he/she  must-PRES  bring-INFIN  his/her   book   to    the   class
      'He/she must bring his/her book to class.' (ibid.)

As for the 3rd person plural pronouns, *deoi* and *deai* occur when the referents are all male and all female respectively, while *dai* is the neuter plural pronoun and also occurs when the referents are a mixture of males and females. Ailola has what ARG (2005:47) calls ["t]he [t]ypical [p]ronoun", which is equivalent to 'one' in English:

(16)  Tyo  dev-as         omnibwande  dirare         "gratsia".
      one   must-PRES  always          say-INFIN  thank.you
      'One must always say "thank you".' (ibid.:47)

Aiola has a dummy subject pronoun *tsi* 'it' (called the "delayed-subject pronoun" in ARG (2005:86)) which "is used in sentences in which the subject of the sentence is clause or an infinitive whose occurrence is delayed until after the verb for stylistics" (ibid.), e.g.:

(17a)  Tsi  est-as        importenta  ke   vu   kompren-as          tibwo.
       it     be-PRES   important   that  you  understand-PRES  this
       'It is important that you understand this.'

(17b)  Tsi  estas          bona  ambul-are      djornuale.
       it     be-PRES   good   walk-INFIN   daily
       'It is good to walk daily.' (ibid.:86)

It is not necessary to use this construction, i.e. the clause can occur in subject position, e.g.:

(18)  Ke vu komprenas tibwo estas importenta.
      'That you understand this is important.' (ibid.)

There are 4th person pronouns, possessive adjectives, and possessive pronouns in Aiola (referred to as "#2 pronouns", "#2 possessive adjectives", and "#2 possessive pronouns" in ARG (2005)). They are derived from 3rd person personal pronouns and posessive adjectives (which are "#1 words" (ibid.:82)) by placing -w- immediately after the *d-* of the latter forms. For examples the #2 pronouns 'he' and 'they' (F) are *dweo* and *dweai*. ARG (ibid.:83) gives the following instructions concerning them: "first identify the two persons or things that will be represented with pronouns within a single sentence or paragraph. Apply the #1 pronoun to the first-mentioned person or thing and apply the #2 pronoun to the second-mentioned person or thing."[46] If we follow this procedure with respect to the English example passage that they give (ibid.:82), *Jenn telephoned and told me about Linda. She said that she was very excited about her work*, we can get the following four different sentences (with the referents added in parentheses):

(19)  Djen telefoniris ce diris alu mi pertu Linda. Dea diris ke dea (Djen) estis
          mutce ekcitata pertu deaza (Djen) laborajo.
      Djen telefoniris ce diris alu mi pertu Linda. Dea diris ke dea (Djen) estis
          mutce ekcitata pertu dweaza (Linda) laborajo.
      Djen telefoniris ce diris alu mi pertu Linda. Dea diris ke dwea (Linda) estis
          mutce ekcitata pertu dweaza (Linda) laborajo.
      Djen telefoniris ce diris alu mi pertu Linda. Dea diris ke dwea (Linda) estis
          mutce ekcitata pertu deaza (Djen) laborajo. (ibid.:83)

In Neo most of the personal pronouns are different from their Esperanto counterparts and there are different accusative and dative forms for some pronouns:

---

[46] These instructions are not completely accurate, if we consider some more complicated cases, such as those given in ARG (ibid.:83) itself:

(ia)  Sali cwe Fred ce Keit cwe Djordj faros bwoi tinokte. Dai andos alu la butikario ice dwai
      andos alu la teatro.
      'Sally and Fred and Kate and George are going to do things tonight. They will go to the mall
      and they will go to the theater.'

(ib)  Ei vu vidas la dusa animaloi? Da estas kato ice dwa estas hundo.
      'Do you see the two animals? It is a cat and it is a dog.'

The "first-mentioned person" in (ia) is *Sali*, and the "second-mentioned person" is Fred, but it is not the case that the #1 pronoun, *Dai*, refers to *Sali* and that the #2 pronoun, *dwai*, refers to Fred. This is obvious, and it might appear that I am bringing up a trivial point, but one might desire a more precise rule. (ib) represents a different problem: the noun phrase *la dusa animaloi*, to which *da* and *dwa* each refer to a member of, cannot be said to have a "first-mentioned" and a "second-mentioned" member, since both animals are originally referred to simultaneously (this noun phrase not containing conjoined noun phrases).

|      | 1SG | 2SG | 3MSG | 3FSG | 3NSG | 1PL | 2PL | 3MPL | 3FPL |
|------|-----|-----|------|------|------|-----|-----|------|------|
| NOM  | mi  | tu  | il   | el   | it   | nos | vu  | zi   | zel  |
| DAT  | me  | te  | lu   | luy  | lu   | ne  | ve  | zu   | zuy  |
| ACC  | me  | te  | le   | ley  | it   | ne  | ve  | ze   | zey  |

Table 4.29: *Neo Personal Pronouns (after Alfandari 1961:33)*

There are two possessive forms each corresponding to each of these, except the 3rd person singular neuter:

| 1SG | 2SG | 3MSG | 3FSG | 1PL | 2PL | 3MPL | 3FPL |
|-----|-----|------|------|-----|-----|------|------|
| ma/mia | ta/tua | la/lea | la/leya | na/nosa | va/vua | za/zea | za/zeya |

Table 4.30: *Neo Possessive Pronouns and Adjectives (after Alfandari 1961:34)*

The shorter forms occur only in prenominal position (and function as adjectives), while the latter function as adjectives after the noun (and there will be a definite article before the noun) and, with the definite article but without a noun, as pronouns, e.g. *ma libro* 'mon livre' (ibid.), *lo libro mia* 'mon livre à moi' (ibid.), *konar tu lo mia?* 'connais-tu la mienne?' (ibid.). Both forms take the plural marker *-s*, e.g. *em mas floros* 'voici mes fleurs' (ibid.).

Farber and Farber (2005) give four forms for Farlingo personal pronouns, e.g. for the 1st person singular pronoun there are the forms *yo, me, mey,* and *mue*, glossed respectively "я", "меня", "мне", and "мой". Thus *yo, me,* and *mey* are the nominative, accusative, and dative forms, i.e. equivalent to 'I', 'me', and 'to me', and it appears that *mue* serves as both a possessive pronoun and a possessive adjective (it is given as the equivalent of both 'my' and 'mine' in Farber and Farber (2006)).

Linguna has several different case forms for personal pronouns (as it does for nouns):

|              | 1SG  | 2SG  | 3MSG | 3FSG  | 3CSG | 3NSG | 1PL     | 2PL     | 3PL           |
|--------------|------|------|------|-------|------|------|---------|---------|---------------|
| NOM          | mi   | dzi  | li   | shi   | to   | id   | ni      | vi      | illi          |
| GEN          | mies | tues | lies | shies | toes | ées  | nostres | vestres | lores         |
| DAT          | me   | tu   | luj  | sher  | toj  | ei   | nu      | vu      | illur, leur   |
| ACC          | min  | dzin | lin  | shin  | ton  | djin | nin     | vin     | illin         |
| Instrumental Ablative | meom | tuom | lujom | sherom | tojom | eom | nostrom | vestrom | illurom |

Table 4.31: *Lingunua Personal Pronouns (after Goeres 2004a)*

Apparently *vi* can also be used as a 2nd person singular pronoun; I do not know whether a *tu/vous* type system is involved here. The 3rd singular feminine pronouns are used not only for female entities but also for anything which is denoted by a grammatically feminine noun, e.g. *urba* 'city'. There is also a specifically feminine 3rd person nominative plural pronoun, *illai*.

### 4.2.2    Reflexive and Reciprocal Pronouns

In Mondlingvo there is a plural form of the reflexive pronoun *si*, formed with the same suffix as for plural nouns and personal pronouns, *-s*, hence *sis*. The reflexive pronoun of Arlipo is *si*, but unlike Esperanto *si* it is not restricted to referring back to 3rd person pronouns; Vitek (n.d. b) says it is "uzebla ma ne uzenda por omna tri personi di tak singularo, tak pluralo" ('usable but not obligatorily used for all three persons of both singular and plural').

Modern Esperanto replaces the Esperanto reflexive pronoun *si* with *di*. The singular and plural "nominal" (Thompson 2007a) reflexive pronouns of Intero are *zo* and *zoy* respectively, while the singular and plural possessive reflexive pronouns are *zes* and *zoyes*, and the singular and plural "descriptive" (ibid.) reflexive pronouns are *za* and *zoya*; thus the reflexive pronouns are formed on the same pattern as the personal pronouns.

Perio has both a 3rd person reflexive pronoun and a reciprocal pronoun, *si* and *hi* respectively.[47] They do not take case endings, "car ils sont essentiellement au cas indirect" (Couturat and Leau 1907/1979:6).[48]

Olingo, like English, appears to use the same words as reflexive and emphatic pronouns, given the following examples:

(20a)    La eldega    virino,    ahonta    al ur-qortita    di una viro
    the elder    woman, ashamed    to be-courted    by a    man

    junega    zan shiaego …
    younger than herself
    'The older woman, ashamed to be courted by a man younger than herself …'
    (Jaque 1944:28)

(20b)    I    miaego    ur-i    bonfortuna
    I    myself    be-PRES    good.fortune
    'I myself am good fortune' (ibid.:29, "Excerpt from 'Song of the Open Road' by Walt Whitman")

As can be seen, these pronouns consist of a possessive adjective and *ego* 'self'; the complete set of such pronouns is not given in the glossaries in Jaque (ibid.), but one which is given, *linaegon* 'themselves', indicates that reflexive/emphatic plural pronouns end in *-n*, the plural marker.

Mondlango reflexive pronouns are made up of a personal pronoun and *-self*, e.g. *yiself* 'yourself', *yuself* 'yourselves', *hiself* 'himself'.

The reflexive pronoun of Hom-idyomo is *se*. There is also a word *sua*, which is something like a reflexive possessive adjective. Cárdenas' (1923:I:33-4) instructions concerning these words make them seem unusual in terms of their behavior:

> The use of some of the third-person possessives may give rise to ambiguity. In order to avoid it, use is made of the substitute possessive *sua*,

---

[47] As we shall see, Perio also has synthetic reflexive verb forms.

[48] Perio also has reflexive verb forms, e.g. *sapiq* 'to wash oneself', *min sapiqt* 'I wash myself' (Couturat and Leau 1907/1979:7). I do not know whether Perio has any rules allowing or requiring co-occurrence of reflexive pronouns and reflexive verb forms.

which governs the complement[49] of a sentence or clause having two subjects, provided (1) the two subjects are of the third person; (2) they have the same number and gender; (3) the complement refers only to the first of the two subjects.

Let us take an example: *Maɽy kay Kate iɽey a sua domo* "Mary and Kate went to her house". Whose house? – The possessive *sua* indicates that it belongs to Mary, first subject.

Second example: *La fɽatɽo kay lia amiko kaɽesay a lias infantos,* "The brother and his friend caress his children." Whose children? The possessive *lias* indicates that they are the friend's, the second subject. In case the the children belong to the brother, first subject, it must be told [sic] *suas infantos.* Why not *sua amiko?* In the first place, because the regular possessive lia does not cause any ambiguity, and in the second place, because *amiko* is not a complement.

It may happen that there are more than two subjects and that neither the first nor the second denotes the possessor. In that case it is necessary to change the construction so as plainly to indicate the possessor. *Peteɽ, John kay James lesonay a las infantos de la ultima* ['Peter, John, and James teach the children of the last']; *Peteɽ, John, James kay Andɽew lesonay a las infantos de James* ['Peter, John, James, and Andrew teach the children of James'].

The same rules apply to the reflexive *se*.

If the above directions mean that *sua* and *se* only appear under these circumstances, we would expect them to occur less often than its counterparts in other languages, e.g. Esperanto *sia* and *sin*. This might appear to be the case, given examples such as the following, in which Esperanto would have *sia*:

(21)  La señoɽo    doney a  las  dogos en pikolas fɽagmentos lia
       the gentleman gave o the  dogs  in small   pieces      his

      poɽcyono
      portion
      'The gentleman gave his portion to the dogs in small pieces'  (ibid.:I:59, tr.
      I:60; *La señoɽo* and *sua* are coreferential)

However, *se* appears in the following sentence, in which there is only one subject:

(22)  La   maɽito   adɽesey se   a  una  tɽanspoɽt-agentio ...
       the  husband  betook  RP  to a    transportation-agency
       'The husband betook himself to a transportation agency ...'  (ibid.:I: 116, tr.
       117)

---

[49] Neither *govern* nor *complement* appears to be used in the usual grammatical sense here; I interpret "govern the complement" to mean something like 'occurs in the determiner position of the object'.

There are other such examples, e.g. *Julian moᴢtey se ipse* 'Julian killed himself' (ibid.:114), *James anojay se* 'James is annoyed' (ibid.:I:113).

Consider finally the following example, in which *sua* appears where Esperanto *sia* would not, because it corefers with something outside of its own clause, namely with the subject of the matrix clause:

(23)  Li alegay   ke    las  bestos  havay  lia  maᴢko, ke   la
      he alleges  that  the  animals have   his  mark   that the

      vendando[50] robey  se    fᴢom  sua  granjo ...
      seller             robbed them  from  his   grange
      'He alleges that the animals have his mark, that the seller stole them from his
      grange ...' (ibid.:I:38, MT; *Li* and *sua* are coreferential )

There are three subjects in this part of the sentence, *Li*, *las bestos*, and *la vendando*, but only the first and the third are the same in number and gender and the presence of *sua* indicates that the former of these two is the owner of the grange. (If *sia* were present in the Esperanto equivalent of this sentence, it would indicate that the seller stole the animals from his own grange.)

### 4.2.3    Correlatives

Esperanto has a group of words called correlatives, which include most pronouns and related adverbs, e.g. demonstratives and interrogatives/relatives. Some reformed versions of it have the same sort of system, although sometimes considerable changes have been made to it. Discussion about particular kinds of correlatives will be made in the appropriate sections below, but here I shall discuss systems of correlatives (or of equivalent words) that have significant differences from that of Esperanto.

The table of correlatives of 1919 Esperantida in de Saussure (1919:5) has only three columns, for demonstratives, interrogatives, and indefinites. Most of the words in the first two columns are the same as or very similar to their Esperanto counterparts (the main difference involving words in the manner series, which end in *-e*, e.g. *kie* 'how' (cf. Esperanto *kiel*); words in the place series end in *-ey*, e.g. *tiey*, there (cf. Esperanto *tie*). The same is true of words in the column of indefinites, except that they all begin with *n-*, e.g. *nio* 'something' (cf. Esperanto *io*). The indefinites act as the stems for the negative prefix *ne-* (yielding words which are usually the same as their Esperanto equivalents, e.g. *nenio* 'nothing') and for the universal prefix *om-*, e.g. *omniam* 'always' (cf. Esperanto *ĉiam*). There are also two words, *irg* and *sirt* which modify or change the meaning of the indefinites when placed before or after them; the former "pliigas la nedefiniteco til PLENA NEDEFINITECO" ('increases the indefiniteness to FULL INDEFINITENESS', ibid.), the latter "minigas la nedefiniteco til DEFINITECO" ('reduces the indefiniteness to DEFINITENESS', ibid.). One of the examples de Saussure (ibid.) gives involves libro 'book': *sirt ni libro* ("difinita" ('definite')), *ni libro* ("nedefinita" ('indefinite')), *irg ni libro* ("tute nedefinita" ('completely indefinite')).[51] The words of the demonstrative series can be modified by the words *ci* and *ca*, the former adding the meaning of nearness, the latter of distance, e.g. *ci tiey/tiey ci* 'here',

---

[50] I believe that this is an error for *vendanto*.

[51] It is not clear to me what the difference between "indefinite" and "completely indefinite" is.

*ca tiey/tiey ca* 'there (distant)'. (One might therefore think that the unmodified demonstratives are neutral or unspecified with respect to proximity, cf. French *ce, ceci, cela*).

The correlatives of Sen:esepera are generally considerably longer than their Esperanto counterparts, although both consist of two parts: Henning (1995a) says, "Esperanto's correlatives are concise but hard to remember. ***Sen:esepera*** instead uses compound words, which provide greater clues for remembering". In the following tables (based on Henning (ibid.)) are compared the first and second components of the correlatives of both languages.

| Esperanto | ki- | | ti- | i- | neni- | ĉi- |
|---|---|---|---|---|---|---|
| Sen:esepera | caim | tin | dem | sum | an | omin |
| | 'which, what' | 'this' | 'that' | 'some' | 'no' | each, every, all |

Table 4.31: *First Components of Esperanto and Sen:esepera Correlatives*

| Esperanto | -u | -o | -a | -e | -el |
|---|---|---|---|---|---|
| Sen:esepera | uno | obico | sepeco | loco | emodo |
| | 'one' | 'thing' | 'kind' | 'place' | 'way' |

| -al | -am | -om | -es |
|---|---|---|---|
| cuso | tempo | enumo | unon |
| 'reason' | 'time' | 'quantity' | 'one's' |

Table 4.32: *Second Components of Esperanto and Sen:espera Correlatives*

Among the examples of correlatives that Henning (ibid.) gives are *tin:obico* 'this thing' and *omin:cuso* 'for every reason'. However, it seems that the first component of Sen:esepera correlatives can appear without the other, playing the role of a (full) correlative of Esperanto (unless Henning (ibid.) has made errors in his "Sample text"):

(24a)　o　tino　hu　comenci　o　fari
　　　　and　this　they　begin　and　do
　　　　'and this is only the start of what they may do'

(24b)　ureba　o　tura,　caimo　dimin:homa　codo　　homa　conseteri
　　　　town　and　tower　which　child　　of　man　build
　　　　'the town and the tower which the children of men were building'

In Esperanto *tino* and *caimo* would be *ĉi tio* (or *tio ĉi*) and *kiujn* respectively. While both Sen:esepera *tino* and Esperanto *tio* end in -o, the function of this element is different in the two words: in the latter it is the second component of the correlative construction, meaning 'thing', while in the former it is apparently the correlative class suffix and there is no second component. What is more, some of the correlatives in the sample text do not end in -o or -on. For example, *dem:loca* 'there' occurs four times; we would expect *\*dem:loco*, especially since one of the examples of correlatives in Henning (ibid.) is *sum:loco* 'somewhere'.

ARG (2005) does not use the term *correlative*, but one could say that the indefinite, demonstrative, interrogative, universal, and negative pronouns, adjectives, and adverbs form the same type of system, as can be seen in the table below (which combines tables (with minor changes) in ARG (2005:18, 19, 20); the interrogatives will be treated separately in section 4.2.3.2):

| Indef. | *Ti-* Demonst. | *Ta-* Demonst. | Univ. | Neg. |
|---|---|---|---|---|
| **Pronouns** | | | | |
| byo 'somebody, someone' | tibyo 'this somebody' | tabyo 'that somebody | omnibyo 'everybody' | nobyo 'nobody' |
| bwo 'something' | tibwo 'this something' | tabwo 'that something' | omnibwo 'everything' | nobwo 'nothing' |
| **Adjectives** | | | | |
| bya 'some kind of' (attributive) | tibya 'this kind of' (att.) | tabya 'that kind of' (att.) | omnibya 'every kind of' (att.) | nobya 'no kind of' (att.) |
| byai 'some kind of' (relational, category)' | tibyai 'this kind of' (rel., cat.) | tabyai 'that kind of' (rel., cat.) | omnibyai 'every kind of' (rel., cat.) | nobyai 'no kind of' (rel., cat.) |
| bwa 'some' | tibwa 'this' | tabwa 'that' | omnibwa 'every one of' | nobwa (= nula) 'none of' |
| **Adverbs** | | | | |
| bwerve 'somewhere, someplace' | tibwerve 'this place' | tabwerve 'that place' | omnibwerve 'everywhere' | nobwerve 'nowhere' |
| bwande 'sometimes, ever' | tibwande 'this time' | tabwande 'that time' | omnibwande 'always' | nobwande 'never' |
| bye 'somehow, in some manner' | tibye 'in this manner' | tabye 'in that manner' | omnibye 'in every manner' | nobye 'in no manner' |
| bewe 'somehow, by some method' | tibewe 'by this method' | tabewe 'by that method' | omnibewe 'by every method' | nobewe 'by no method, no way' |
| bwe 'somehow, to some degree' | tibwe 'this, to this degree; | tabwe 'that, to that degree' | omnibwe 'to every degree' | nobwe 'to no degree, not at all' |

Table 4.33: *Aiola Correlative-Type Words*

As indicated by the glosses, the *ti-* and *ta-* words have proximal and distal meanings respectively. For the difference between "attributive" and "relational" adjectives v. section 4.4; I do know what is meant by "category" here.

The correlative system of Perio is the same as that of Esperanto in some ways (e.g. interrogatives/relatives begin with *k*, and demonstratives with *t*), but there are also differences: the endings of many words are different, and new members have been added to the system. Below are the correlatives as given (with minor changes, and without the glosses) in Couturat and Leau (1907/1979:5):

| pronouns | | | adjectives | | adverbs | | | | | |
|---|---|---|---|---|---|---|---|---|---|---|
| pers. | thing | possess. | adj. | mann. | mann. | quant. | time | place | direct. | reason |
| ku, ky | ko | kul, kyl, kol, | ka | kea | ke | kar | ker | kan | ken | kur |
| tu, ty | to | tul, tyl, tol | ta | tea | te | tar | ter | tan, tin | ten | tur |
| cu | co | cul | ca | cea | ce | co | cer | can | cen | cur |
| nu | no | nul | na | nea | ne | no | ner | nan | nen | nur |
| iu, iy | io | iul | ia | ia | ie | iar | ier | ian | ien | iur |
| samu | samo | samul | sama | samea | same | samar | samer | saman | samen | samur |
| simu | simo | simul | sima | simea | sime | simar | simer | siman | simen | simur |
| simku | simko | simkul | simka | simkea | simke | simkar | simker | simkan | simken | simkur |

Table 4.34: *Correlatives of Perio*

The last three rows contain the words not present in the Esperanto system. Those starting with *sam-* mean 'same', e.g. *samo* 'same thing', *samer* 'at the same time'. The ones in the series beginning *sim-* mean 'other', e.g. *simur* 'for another reason'. The words in the final seem to be interrogatives (note that they contain *k*), and also involve the meaning 'other', e.g. *simker* 'at what other time'. Some of the words in the first column indicate gender, e.g. *ku* 'who' (M) and *ky* 'who' (F).[52] As Couturat and Leau (ibid.:6) note, in general there are not separate proximal and distal demonstratives, the exception being the demonstratives indicating location: *tan* means 'here' while *tin* means 'there'.

Atlango's system of correlative words shows a fair number of differences from that of Esperanto. For example, words of the indefinite series begin with *alg-*, e.g. *alge* 'somehow, in some way', and there are two series of demonstratives, proximal ones and distal ones, which start with *t-* and *tr-* respectively, e.g. *tey* 'here, in this place', *trey* 'there, in that place'.

Alfandari (1961:6-7) presents a large table of what he calls "adjectifs démonstratifs et des pronoms et adverbs en dérivants" of Neo. However, some of the words in the table are not demonstratives as the term is usually understood, but have the meaning of some other type of correlative in e.g. the system of Esperanto, or some other meaning. On the other hand, the table does not include counterparts of all of the Esperanto correlatives, as the interrogatives/relatives are not there. The table (with superficial changes) is below:

---

[52] I do not know whether the fact that the absence of feminine variants of some words in the first column is an inadvertent omission by Couturat and Leau (or Talundberg); certainly one could imagine such words, e.g. *ny* 'no woman'. However, I suspect that it is not an error, especially since the words of the third column also differ in whether they indicate gender.

| ADJECTIF | PRONOM INDIVIDU | PRONOM DE CHOSE | ADVERBE DE MODE | ADVERBE DE LIEU | ADVERBE DE FRÉQUENCE | POSSESSIF ADJ. ET PRONOM | ADVERBE DE CAUSE |
|---|---|---|---|---|---|---|---|
| *eta* (*et*) 'ce, cette' | *etun* 'celui-ci' | *eto* 'ceci' | *ete* 'ainsi, de cette façon' | *etye* 'en ce lieu-ci' | *etyes* 'cette fois-ci' | *etia* 'de celui-ci' | *etie* 'pour ceci, pour cette raison' |
| *yena* (*yen*) 'ce …-là' | *yenun* 'celui-là' | *yeno* 'cela' | *yene* 'de cette façon-là' | *yenye* 'en ce lieu-là' | *yenyes* 'cette fois-là' | *yenia* 'de celui-là' | *yenie* 'pour cela, pour cette raison-là' |
| *osa* (*os*) 'autre' | *osun* 'un autre, autrui' | *oso* 'autre chose' | *ose* 'autre-ment' | *osye* 'ailleurs' | *osyes* 'une autre fois' | *osia* 'd'un autre, d'autrui' | *osie* 'pour une autre raison' |
| *soma* (*som*) 'quelque' | *somun* quelqu'un | *somun* 'quelque chose' | *some* 'de quelque façon' | *somye* 'quelque part' | *somyes* 'parfois, quelquefois' | *somia* 'de quel-qu'un' | *somie* 'pour quelque raison' |
| *shaka* (*shak*) 'chaque' | *shakun* 'chacun' | *shako* 'chaque chose' | *shake* 'de chaque façon' | *shakye* 'en tout lieu' | *shakyes* 'chaque fois' | *shakia* 'de chacun' | |
| *totas* (*tot*) 'tous les' | *totun* 'chacun' | *toto* (*to*) 'tout' | *tote* 'de toutes façons' | *totye* 'partout' | *totyes* 'toutes les fois' | *totia* 'de tous' | *totie* 'pour toutes les raisons' |
| *nila* (*nil*) 'aucun' | *nilun* 'per-sonne, aucun, nul' | *nilo* 'rien' | *nile* 'nulle-ment' | *nilye* 'nulle part' | *nilyes* 'pas une fois' | *nilia* 'de personne' | *nilie* 'pour aucune raison' |
| *kela* (*kel*) 'n'im-porte quel, tout, chaque' | *kelun* 'qui-conque, n'importe qui' | *kelo* 'quoi que ce soit' | *kele* 'n'im-porte com-ment' | *kelye* 'n'im-porte où' | *kelyes* 'n'importe quand' | *kelia* 'de qui que ce soit' | *kelie* 'pour quelque raison que ce soit' |
| *certa* (*cert*) 'certain' | *certun* 'certain' | *certo* 'certaine chose' | *certe* 'd'un certaine façon' | | | | |
| *tala* (*tal*) 'tel' | *talun* 'un tel' | *talo* 'telle chose' | *tale* 'de telle façon' | *talye* 'en tel lieu' | | *talia* 'd'un tel' | *talie* 'pour telle raison' |
| *etosa* 'cet autre' | *etosun* 'cet autre' | *etoso* 'cette autre chose' | *etose* 'de cette autre façon' | | *etosyes* 'cette autre fois' | *etosia* 'de cette autre-ci' | |
| *yenosa* 'cet autre …-là' | *yenosun* 'cet autre …-là' | *yenoso* 'cette autre chose-là' | *yenose* 'de cette autre façon-là' | | *yenosyes* 'cette autre fois-là' | *yenosia* 'de cette autre-là' | |
| *somosa* 'quelque autre' | *somosun* 'quel-qu'un d'autre' | *somoso* 'quelque chose d'autre' | *somose* 'de quelque autre façon' | *somosye* 'quelque part d'autre' | *somosyes* 'quelque autre fois' | *somosia* 'de quel-qu'un d'autre' | *somosie* 'pour quelque autre raison' |

| | | | | | | | |
|---|---|---|---|---|---|---|---|
| *shakosa* 'chaque autre' | *shakosun* 'chacun d'autre' | *shakoso* 'chaque autre chose' | *shakose* 'de chaque autre façon' | *shakosye* 'en chaque autre endroit' | *shakosyes* 'chaque autre fois' | | |
| *totosas* 'tous les autres' | *totosunos* 'tous les autres' | *totoso* 'tout la reste' | *totose* 'de toutes les autres façons' | *totosye* 'partout ailleurs' | *totosyes* 'toutes les autres fois' | *totosia* 'de tous les autres' | *totosie* 'pour toutes les autres raisons' |
| *ailosa* 'aucun autre' | *ailosun* 'personne d'autre' auncun autre' | *ailoso* 'rien d'autre' | *ailose* 'd'au- cune autre façon' | *ailosye* 'nulle part ailleurs' | *ailosyes* 'aucune autre fois' | *ailosia* 'de personne d'autre' | *ailosie* 'pour aucune autre raison' |
| *kelosa* 'n'im- porte quel autre' | *kelosun* 'n'im- porte qui d'autre' | *keloso* 'n'im- porte quoi d'autre' | *kelose* 'de n'im- porte quelle autre façon' | *kelosye* 'n'im- porte où ailleurs' | *kelosyes* n'importe quelle autre fois' | *kelosia* 'de qui que ce soit d'autre' | *kelosie* 'pour quelque autre raison que ce soit' |

Table 4.35: *"Demonstratives" and Related Words of Neo (Alfandari 1961:36-7)*

Intero has a series of words beginning with *ali-* which look like additions to the Esperanto set of correlatives,[53] including *alia* 'another kind', *aliu* 'another',[54] *aliam* 'another time', *alie* 'another place',[55] and *aliel* 'another manner'. Thompson (2007a) says that "each of the original [Esperanto] correlatives now has a long form"; his three examples of this are "tial = al tiu kialo", "kien = en kiu kieno", and "iom = om iu kiomo" (ibid.). These long forms, or at least these examples of them, consist of a preposition which has the same form as a correlative ending, a correlative of the *-u* series, and a noun formed from the *k-* series of correlatives, e.g. *kiomo* 'amount' (such nouns also exist in Esperanto).

In their description of Reformed Esperanto Couturat and Leau (1907/1979:30) say that Zamenhof "supprimait le tableau des particules, et les remplaçait par des particules *a posteriori* (latines ou romaines)". Below (with very minor changes) is the table which they give (ibid.:31) of these words (with the Esperanto equivalents in italics under the Reformed Esperanto words); one can see that much of the regularity of the Esperanto system has disappeared and that many of the words are indeed different from their counterparts in Esperanto:

---

[53] In fact, such words do occur in Esperanto, but their use is frowned on; Wennergren (2005:319) says, "Iafoje oni renkontas la neoficialajn tabelvortojn *alio\*°, \*aliu\*°, \*alia\*°, \*aliel\** ... Ili estas eraraj kaj nepre evitendaj:" (The asterisk before and after the words means "erara aŭ tre malrekomendinda" (ibid.:18); to my knowledge Wennergren (2005) does not say what the small circle means.)

[54] Thompson (2007a) says, "The Esperanto *alia* becomes the Interu *aliu*. The Esperanto *alio* becomes the Intero *aliu* only when *alio* refers to a person".

[55] Thompson (2007a) states, "The Esperanto *alie* becomes the Intero *aliel*".

| alikve *ia* | alikvu *iu* | alikvo *io* | de alikvi *ies* | in alikve loco *ie* | alikvam *iam* | por alivko *ial* | in alikve maniero *iel* | alivkantu *iom* |
|---|---|---|---|---|---|---|---|---|
| kvale *kia* | kvu *kiu* | kvo *kio* | de kvu *kies* | ubu *kie* | kvandu *kiam* | por kvo *kial* | kom *kiel* | kvantu *kiom* |
| tale *tia* | is, hik *tiu (ĉi)* | id, ho *tio (ĉi)* | | ibu, ic *tie (ĉi)* | tum *tiam* | por ho *tial* | sik *tiel* | tantu *tiom* |
| omne *ĉia* | omnu *ĉiu* | omno *ĉio* | | partutu *ĉie* | semper *ĉiam* | | omne-maniere *ĉiel* | |
| nule *nenia* | nemo *neniu* | nulo *nenio* | de nemo *nenies* | nuskvam *nenie* | nunkvam *neniam* | | nule-maniere *neniel* | |

Table 4.36: *Reformed Esperanto Equivalents of Esperanto Correlatives (Couturat and Leau 1907/1979:31)*

Ido has also done away with some (but not all) of the regularity of the Esperanto correlative system, which was seen as a liability by some. Thus, for example, the temporal interrogative and relative word is *kande* 'when' while its locative counterpart is *ube* 'where', and while the distal locative demonstrative, *ibe* 'there' is rather similar to the latter, this is not true of the proximal locative demonstrative, *hike* 'here'.

### 4.2.3.1 Demonstratives

The Olingo words for 'this' and 'that' are *ta* and *to* respectively, and they take the same plural ending as nouns, *-n*, e.g. *ton* 'those'. The proximal demonstrative correlatives of Mondezo are single orthographic words, unlike their counterparts in Esperanto, and they begin with *z*, e.g. *zio* 'this thing' (cf. Esperanto *ĉi tio*), *zie* 'here' (cf. Esperanto *ĉi tie*). Modern Esperanto's proximal demonstrative correlatives are formed with *mal-*, e.g. *mal-tie* 'there'. Esperanto has the prefix *mal-*, but it is not used for this purpose.

Proximal demonstratives in the DLT Intermediate Language must have a hyphen between their two parts, e.g. *ĉi-tiu* 'this (one/person)', and apparently *ĉi* always precedes the word of the *ti-* series.

The demonstratives of Romániço were not taken from Esperanto; they are *ecuista* 'this' and *ecuila* 'that'. These forms serve as both demonstrative adjectives and demonstrative pronouns, e.g. *ecuista parva porcuço* 'this little piggy' (Morales n.d. g), *Ecuista has vaden ad mercato* 'This one went to market' (ibid.). They can take the nominal suffix *-o*, in which case "they mean not only 'this/that thing' but 'this/that business or fact'" (ibid.), e.g. *Ecuista has vaden ad mercato, et ecuisto placen ad mi* 'This one went to market, and this pleases me' (ibid.).

As with the 3rd person personal pronouns, Ido has more demonstratives than Esperanto. The proximal and neutral/distal demonstrative adjectives are *(i)ca* and *(i)ta* respectively. They also serve as the corresponding singular demonstrative pronouns; their plural forms are *(i)ci* and *(i)ti*. *Il, el,* and *ol* are attached to *ca, ta, ci,* and *ti* to create specifically masculine, feminine, and neuter demonstrative pronouns, e.g. *ilca* 'this man', *elci* 'these women'.

It can be seen from table 4.31 that Sen:esepera has different roots for 'this' and 'that', while in Esperanto the root *ti-* has roughly the same meaning as 'that',[56] with *ci* added before or after it (as a separate word) to form the equivalent of 'this'.

Hom-idyomo has three series of demonstratives whose deictic use depends on proximity to the speaker and hearer; Cardenas (1923:I:40) states that those beginning with *ti-* (e.g. *tiu* 'this one/person') "show the person or thing which is nearer in time or space, to the person who speaks than to the person spoken to", those starting with *ci-* (e.g. *cio* 'that (thing)', *cien* 'that person's') "show the person or thing which is nearer to the person to whom one is speaking than to the person who speaks", and those starting with *kwel-* (e.g. *kwelu* 'that one/person', *kwela* 'that' (adjective)) "show the person or thing which is distant from both interlocutors".[57] On the anaphoric use of these words Cárdenas (1923:I:40-1) says the following: "*Tiu, tio, tia, tien* indicate only the person or thing of which the first person is speaking or has spoken; and *ciu, cio, cia, cien* every other person or thing mentioned by the second person, a third person or by both interlocutors. In such case *kwelu* [and] *kwelo* are not used, except if it is necessary to distinguish a third person or thing."[58]

### 4.2.3.2  Interrogatives and Relatives

The Hom-idyomo words *ki* 'who(m)' and *kio* 'what, which, that' act as both interrogative and relative pronouns, while *kia* 'which, what' serves as an interrogative and relative adjective. *Kien* 'whose' also has both interrogative and relative functions. *Ke* is equivalent to the English conjunction *that*, and like *that*, it can also appear in relative clauses; Cárdenas (1923:I:39) says, "**ke** ... is sometimes used as a relative pronoun replacing kio when preced by another pronoun having the same ending. Thus, *tio ke mi di∂ay te*, 'this which I tell thee', instead of *tio kio mi di∂ay te*. However, this substitution is optional, not necessary".

The interrogatives of Virgoranto are *kvis* 'who', *kvod* 'what', *kvo* 'where', *kvam* 'when', *kvi* 'how', *for kvod* 'why', and *kvand* 'how much'. In her section on "Relative Clauses", Winkelhofer (2007b) states, "The relative pronoun is 'kvile' (who, what). Kvile is never changed". However, a different (form of the) relative pronoun appears in a sentence in Winkelhofer (2007c):

---

[56] According to Wennergren (2005:231), "Simpla TI-vorto ĉiam montras ion ne tute proksiman al la parolanto".

[57] Earlier on the page, in the list of demonstratives, Cárdenas raises the issue of visibility, saying that *ciu* is "for persons in sight" and that *cio* is "for things in sight"; he does not say this about the two other members of the *ci-* series, or about any members of the *ti-* series.

[58] *Ciu* ('that one/person'), *cio*, and *cia* ('that' (adjective)) can be used in another way, which Cárdenas mistakenly labels as use as a relative word; he also misidentifies *tal* as a relative word, as the following passage (1923:I:39) comes from his list of relative words:

> ***tal,*** (such) which refers to the person or thing just mentioned and which is not in sight. Ex: *Mi no knonoskay tal pe∂sono,* "I do not know such a person". In this same meaning the demonstrative pronouns *ciu, cio, cia* can used instead of *tal*. In such cases. of course, they are no longer demonstratives but relatives. Ex: *La ki∂u∂gisto voluntay ope∂acyoni∂ le, sed lia f∂at∂o no aceptay cio.* "The surgeon wishes to operate him [sic], but his brother does not accept it".

(25)  Godeo kom-ir    desu vidi      cito  un  turmo,  kvilken
      God   come-PST down see-INFN city  and tower   which

kindos   of  manos  kontrukt-ir.
children of  men    build-PST
'The Lord came down to see the town and the tower which the children of
the men were making.'

Further, in both Winkelhofer (2008a) and (2008b) *kvilken* is given as the equivalent of
*which/welcher*. In another sentence in Winkelhofer (2007c) there seems to be a null
relative pronoun (which may well be due to influence from English, as Winkelhofer
states that the source text for the translation was in English):

(26)  me ne  kan-ar    stop-i      hi-s  fran jeda ago   his
      I  not can-PRES stop-INFIN he-PL from any  action he-PL

vol-ar     mek-i
want-PRES do-INFIN
'I can not keep them from any action they wish to pursue'

Interrogative pronouns and adverbs in Olingo begin with *w-*: *wa* 'what', *wir*
'where', *wen* 'when', *wol* 'how, and *we* 'why'. The same form, *wir*, can apparently be
used for both location and direction (cf. Esperanto *kie* and *kien*):

(27)  Wir   ur-i     vi   al-ata?
      Where be-PRES you  go-PRESPARTIC
      'Where are you going?' (Jaque 1944:35, MT)

I do not know how much overlap of forms of interrogative and relative words there is
in Olingo; I suspect that *wir* could also be a relative word since *wireve* means
'wherever'.[59] In the texts in Jaque (1944) *wo* 'who' only occurs as a relative pronoun
so I cannot determine whether it can also be an interrogative pronoun. The objective
and possessive forms of *wo* are *wou* and *woa* respectively. Esperanto does not allow
relative clauses without relative pronouns. Jaque (1944) does not explicitly say
whether they are permitted in Olingo, but there is one such clause in one of his texts:

(28)  La  junega ... urita eqale  zela    en  removata cha   gra
      The younger was  equally zealous in  removing every grey

harero shi  povuta trovi.
hair   she could  find
'The younger [woman] ... was equally zealous in removing every grey hair
she could find.' (Jaque 1944:28)

---

[59] There is only one instance in texts in Jaque (1944) of 'where' occurring as a relative word, and it is
*wer* in the Olingo version, but I believe this may be an error for *wir*.

Perhaps this is an error; if so, it might well have been a result of influence from the English version of the text. It appears that the word *to* 'that' can introduce relative clauses in Olingo, given the following example:

(29)    I   uri   la    trabo   to    subteni        via    domo.
        I   am    the   beam    that  support-PRES   your   house
        'I am the beam that supports your house.' (ibid.:35, MT)

Esperanto, like some natural languages, uses the same words as relatives and interrogatives. In UTL, for which ambiguity is a major concern, the two types of word are slightly different, with the relatives having *j* where the interrogatives have *i*, e.g. *kju* 'who, which' (cf. Esperanto *kiu*), *kje* 'where' (cf. Esperanto *kie*). In the DLT Intermediate Language as well relatives and interrogatives are not the same in form, as the latter end in    *-do* (while the former remain as they are in Esperanto), e.g. *kiu-do* 'who' (interrogative), *kiu* 'who' (relative).

The first segment of Aiola interrogatives is *h*:

| Pronouns | |
|---|---|
| hyo | 'who[?]' |
| hwo | 'what[?]' |
| **Adjectives** | |
| hya | 'what kind of (att.)?' |
| hyai | 'what kind of (rel.) (cat.)?' |
| hwa | 'which one(s)?' |
| **Adverbs** | |
| hwerve | 'where?' |
| hwande | 'when?' |
| hye | 'how? in what manner?' |
| hewe | 'how? by what method?' |
| hwe | 'how? to what degree?' |
| hoe | 'why?[60]' |

Table 4.37: *Interrogatives of Aiola (from ARG 2005:20-1)*

There are only two relatives in Aiola, one pronoun, *kio* 'who, what, which', and one adverb, *kie* 'when, where, why, how, etc.'. They are both equivalent to more than one word or phrase in many languages, including English; the following sentences show this with respect to *kie*:

(30a)   Ya,   mi   sab-as        la    lwoko   kie   dea   stud-is.
        yes   I    know-PRES     the   place   *kie*   she   study-PST
        'Yes, I know the place where she studied.' (ibid.:66)

(30b)   La   metodo   kie   deo   nadj-is       est-is     ekstraordinera.
        the   method   *kie*   he    swim-PST      be-PST     extraordinary
        'The method by which he swam was extraordinary.' (ibid.:67)

---

[60] *Hoe* is left out of ARG's table of interrogatives here, but it appears in another table of interrogatives (ibid.: 51).

One derives some Aiola "clausal words" (v. section 4.8), namely clausal pronouns, clausal adjectives, and clausal adverbs, from interrogatives by means of the prefix *ki-*, e.g. *kihyo* 'who', *kihwande* 'when'. Word of this type, rather than interrogatives or relatives, are used in headless relative clauses and indirect questions, e.g.:

(31a)  Kihyo   rid-as         finte,   rid-as          pluste   bone.
       who     laugh-PRES     last     laugh-PRES      most     well
       'Who laughs last, laughs best.'

(31b)  Mi   no   sab-as         kihyo   rid-as          finte.
       I    not  know-PRES      who     laugh-PRES      last
       'I don't know who laughs last.' (ibid.:66)

### 4.2.3.3   Indefinite Pronouns and Related Words

The Romániço words for 'some', 'someone', 'something', and 'somehow' are *álica*, *áliqui*, *álico*, and *álique* respectively.

### 4.2.3.4   Negative Pronouns and Related Words

The series of Esperanto correlatives starting with *n* is changed in Modern Esperanto by the removal of the initial *ne*; thus Esperanto *neniu* 'no one' becomes Modern Esperanto *niu*. Likewise *neniam* 'never', *nenio* 'nothing', and *nenia* 'no kind of' become *niam*, *nio*, and *nia*. In Esperanto *nia* is 'our', but there is no homonymy involving this word in Modern Esperanto, since 'our' is *wia*.

This set of words was also altered by Trischen in the creation of Mondlingvo, the original *e* of the first syllable being replaced by *o*, e.g. *noniu* 'no one'.

Ido's negative pronouns, adjective, and adverbs begin with *nul-* e.g. *nulu* 'no one (SG)', *nulo* 'nothing', *nula* 'no' (adjective), *nultempe* 'never'. The negative words of Romániço generally begin in the same way, e.g. *nuli* 'no one', *nulo* 'nothing', and *nule* 'nohow, in no way'. However, the Romániço word for 'never' is *jamás*.

### 4.3       Numerals

The numerals from 'zero' to 'ten' in some daughters of Esperanto are shown in the table below:

| | 0 | 1 | 2 | 3 | 4 | 5 | 6 | 7 | 8 | 9 | 10 |
|---|---|---|---|---|---|---|---|---|---|---|---|
| Esperanto | nul | unu | du | tri | kvar | kvin | ses | sep | ok | naŭ | dek |
| Aiola[61] | nulo | uno | duso | trio | kwaro | kwino | seso | sepo | oko | naufo | deko |
| Arlipo | zero | un | duj | tri | kvar | kvin | sis | spe | ok | nau | dek |
| Farlingo | zero | un | du | tri | fir | fin | ses | ses | ok | nok | dek |
| Hom-id. | zeʑo | uni | du | tʑi | kwatʑi | cinki | sesi | septi | okti | noni | deko |
| Ido | zero | un | du | tri | quar | kin | sis | sep | ok | non | dek |
| Linguna | null(o) | unu | du | tri | qvar | qvin | sess | sep | oc | naun | dec |
| Mod. Esp. | nulo | uno | duo | trio | kvaro | kvino | seso | sep | oko | nawo | deko |
| Mond-lango | zero | un | bi | tri | kwar | kwin | siks | sep | ok | nef | dek |
| Neo | zero | un | du | tre | kuar | kuin | sit | sep | ot | non | is |
| Olingo | nil | unu | du | tri | qar | qin | ses | sep | oq | non | deq |
| Perio | | un | tem | tir | vor | kin | zek | zip | ok | nop | us |
| Romániço | zero | un | du | tri | cuar | cuin | sex | sep | oc | non | dec |
| Sen:-esepera[62] | | unin | duin[63] | tirin | forin | fifin | sesin | sepin | ocin | enin | decin |
| Virgor. | | en | du | tre | fir | fem | six | sev | ok | nin | ten |

Table 4.38: *Lower Cardinal Numerals of Esperanto and Some of its Daughters*

The Ido suffixes for ordinal and fractional numerals are *-esm-* and *-im-* respectively (to which one attaches the word class suffix for nouns, adjectives, or adverbs), e.g. *unesma* 'first' (adjective), *duimo* 'a half'.

The Novesperant word for 'one' is *un*; Cartier (p.c.) indicates that this is because *unu* resembles imperatives. In Intero as well *un* is 'one'. Several of Ido's cardinal numerals differ from their Esperanto counterparts and some of these differences cannot be explained by changes to Esperanto orthography and sounds.[64] The Reformed Esperanto words for 'one' and 'nine' are *un* and *novu*.

In Virgoranto ordinal numerals consist of a cardinal numeral and *-te*, e.g. *dute* 'second'.

Farlingo ordinal numerals are made up of a cardinal numeral and *-e*, which is the adjectival class marker of the language, e.g. *due* 'second'. There is one exception (that I know of) to this: the word for 'first' is irregular, being *prime*.[65]

Romániço ordinal numerals are made up of a cardinal numeral, the suffix *-ésim-*, and a word class suffix, e.g. *unésima* 'first' (as an adjective), *unésime* 'first' (as an adverb). Fractional numerals are derived by means of the suffix *-av-*, e.g. *duavo* '(a) half'.

---

[61] These are the Aiola forms of '[n]umbers as [n]ouns" (ARG 2005), which occur e.g. when one counts. Numbers which state a quantity of entities/things have the adjectival suffix *-a* rather than *-o*, e.g. *dusa libroi* 'two books' (ibid.).

[62] Henning (1995a) gives these as "The first 10 ordinal numerals … when used as adjectives". He probably means "cardinal" rather than "ordinal", since *unin* is used to translate 'one' in the sample text (ibid.), e.g. *O tutan tera eseti codo unin lingifa* 'And all the earth had one language'; v. also note 3.

[63] In Henning (1995b) *din* is given as 'two'.

[64] Collinson (1924) states, "The Ido habit of intercalating the conjunction *e* (=and) between the units and tens, hundreds, etc., does not appeal to Esperantists, especially when it results in the perpetration of such objectionable conglomerates as *mil-e-oka-cent-e-dua-dek-e-tr*".

[65] The word for '21st' is follows the general pattern: *dudek une*.

Modern Esperanto's (cardinal) numerals "are all nouns" (Lahago n.d.:44), and therefore end in -o. In most cases this -o is simply added onto the Esperanto numeral (with the word for 'nine' having <w> instead of <ŭ>), but in the case of the word for 'one' the u which would have been before -o. There have been two changes to higher numerals: '1000' is *kilo* (instead of Esperanto *mil*) and 'million' is *milo* (instead of Esperanto *miliono*). "Repetitives" (Lahago n.d.:45) consist of a cardinal numeral (without -o) and tempe, e.g. *dutempe* 'twice' (cf. Esperanto *dufoje*).

The Olingo names for numbers from 11 to 19, and for other numbers ending with a digit other than 0, are formed with a hyphen, unlike those of Esperanto, e.g. *deq-unu* '11', *dudeq-unu* '21', sent-unu '101'. As seen in the last example, the word for '100' is *sent*, while that for '1,000,000' is *milion*. The names of multiples of 1000 and 1,000,000 are written as single words, e.g. *dumil* '2000', *dumilion* '2,000,000'. The suffix meaning '-fold' is -opl-, e.g. *oqopla* 'eightfold' (cf. Esperanto -obl-).

The Perio words for '11' to '19' contain the prefix, s-, e.g. *sun* '11', *stem* '12'. Apparently the derivation of the numerals for multiples of 10 from 20 to 90 involves replacing the last consonant of the words for 'one' to 'nine' with -s, e.g. *tes* '20', *tis* '30', *vos* '40'. In the following table are the higher numerals given in Couturat and Leau (1907/1979:4):

| '100' uq | '1000' ul | '10,000' uns | '100,000' uqs | '1,000,000' uls |
|----------|-----------|--------------|---------------|-----------------|
|          | '1100' suq |             |               |                 |
| '200' teq | '2000' tel |             |               |                 |
| '300' tiq | '3000' til |             |               |                 |

Table 4.39: *Some Cardinal Numerals of Perio*

Ordinal numerals in Perio end in -o, -u, -y, -a, and -e, depending on what type of word they are (noun, noun denoting a male, etc.).

Linguna's words for '11' and '12', *ilf* and *das*, are quite different from those of Esperanto. Also, its first three ordinal numbers are irregular: *prima, segonda, tércia*. Most ordinals are consist of a cardinal numeral and -ta or -ata, e.g. *qvarta* 'fourth', *naunta* 'ninth', *décata* 'tenth', *dásata* 'twelfth'. The word for 'sixth' is as given in Goeres (2004a) is slightly irregular, since the second s of the cardinal numeral is dropped in its formation: *sesta*. However, this word is *sessta* in Goeres (2004b).

The ordinal numerals of Mondlango are formed by means of the suffix -u, e.g. *unu* 'first', *biu* 'second' (cf. Esperanto *unua, dua*).

The words for 'one' in 1919 Esperantida, 1923 Esperantida, and Nov-Esperanto are *un, uni*, and *unu* respectively. De Saussure (1923:6) states that *uni* can function pronominally, but de Saussure (1926) rules this out for *unu*, saying "La formo *unu* esprimas nur numbru. En senco ajektiva (or pronoma) oni uzas la formu *una* (or: *unay*), ex.: parolante *unay* kun aliay" ('The form unu expresses only a number. In an adjectival (or pronominal) sense one uses the form *una* (or *unay*) …'). In both 1919 and 1923 Esperantida the word for 'nine' is *noy*, while in Nov-Esperanto it is *neùn*. Ordinal numerals in 1923 Esperantida and Nov-Esperanto contain the suffix -m-, e.g. the adjective *sepma* 'seventh' (in both languages) and the adverb *unime* 'first' (1923 Esperantida). In 1919 and 1923 Esperantida fractional numerals are derived by means of -f.

The Sen:esepera words for 'thousand' and 'million' are *decentin* and *emililin* respectively.

## 4.4    Adjectives

There are two adjectival endings in Aiola: -*a* and -*ai* mark what are called in ARG (2005) "attributive adjectives" and "relational adjectives", that is, a relational adjective is derived from an attributive adjective by means of the suffix -*i*. ARG (ibid.:10) defines these as follows: "An attributive adjective describes a property or characteristic belonging to a noun. Attributive adjectives occur in English noun phrases such as, 'the blue house,' 'happy baby,' or 'human observer'. A relational adjective describes a noun as being of or pertaining to something else. Relational adjectives occur in English noun phrases such as, 'sports magazine,' 'dining room,' and 'human observer'." ARG (ibid.) continues to explain the distinction using the example *human obverver*:

> The *observer* <noun> is characterized as being *human* <adjective>.
> → the observer is human
> → THE ADJECTIVE IS AN ATTRIBUTIVE ADJECTIVE
>
> The *observer* <noun> is of or pertaining to *humans* <relational adjective>.
> → the observer is one who observes humans
> → THE ADJECTIVE IS A RELATIONAL ADJECTIVE

In Aiola the former idea would be expressed as *humana observo* and the latter as *humanai observo*. Another example in ARG (2005) is piska nutro and *piskai nutro*, both translated into English as 'fish food', but the former means 'food consisting of fish' while the latter means 'food for fish to eat'. (Note also that in both cases the equivalent of the English noun *fish* is an adjective, not a noun; v. section 4.0.3.)

### 4.4.1    Agreement Marking on Adjectives

In Modern Esperanto adjectives are not marked for agreement with their nouns in plural or accusative marking. Lahago (n.d.:29) gives an aesthetic reason for the lack of plurality marking on adjectives: "To prevent Esperanto from becoming a monotonous sound [sic], because all similar '-j' endings after nouns, its adjectives or its possessive pronouns [sic], do we have eliminated these '-j' endings after the adjectives or the possessive pronouns." He indicates (ibid.:31) that word order will show the relationship between an adjective and a noun: "The adjectives are distinctive by their placing in a sentence. For example: He painted the blue door – li pentras la bluA pordoN. He painted the door blue – li pentras la pordoN bluaA."[66] However, on p. 26 he allows for attributive adjectives to be placed after their nouns, which seems to undermine this.

There is also no adjectival agreement in Mondezo, which "makes it so much easier" (Medrano 2002). The same is true of Aiola, Atlango, Intero, Mondlango, Novesperant,[67] Olingo, Perio, Reformed Esperanto, Virgoranto, and Ido.[68] Hoover

---

[66] Lahago has made an error in these sentences: *pentras* should be *pentris* (or the English sentences should be in the present tense rather than the past).

[67] According to Cartier (n.d.), "An adjective placed next to the noun it modifies is quite understandable, rendering adjective/noun agreement unnecessary".

(n.d.) states that adjectives (and adverbs!) in Baza "do not have to agree with the direct object". He says nothing about whether adjectives are marked for number agreement.

In 1923 Esperantida adjectives are marked for number agreement with the nouns that they modify (taking the same plural suffix as nouns, -n), but not for case agreement, even though nouns bear accusative marking. This is shown in (32):

(32)    la     patro   havas  bona   fil-u ...
        the    father  has    good   son-ACC
        'the father has a good son ...'  (de Saussure 1923:6, MT)

However, if there is no overt nominal head of an NP, but only an adjective, that adjective will take the accusative ending, which becomes -w (i.e. [w]) after the -a of the adjective.[69]

(33)    mi    ne    volas   ti     libr-u,      mi    volas   alia-w
        I     not   want    that   book-ACC   I     want    other-ACC
        'I do not want that book, I want another' (ibid., MT)

Neo adjectives agree in number with the nouns that they modify, taking the same plural suffix as them, -s. However, since adjectives in prenominal position can appear without the adjectival suffix, and without this plural marker (I assume that if the former is absent the latter must also be, and vice versa, when a plural noun is being modified), sometimes they will not bear (overt) agreement marking.

As in Esperanto, Linguna adjectives agree with their nouns in number and case, but since Linguna has more cases than Esperanto, it also has more forms of adjectives. V. Table 4.14 for a paradigm showing both nominal and adjectival case forms.

### 4.4.2    Comparatives and Superlatives

Intero uses the same forms as Esperanto for marking comparatives and superlatives, except that in Intero they are prefixes rather than being separate words, i.e. *pli-* and *pley-*. The words that mark comparatives and superlatives in Sen:esepera are *pelo* and *supelo* respectively, and *olo* is placed before the object of comparison in comparative constructions. In Henning (1995a) *olo* is called a conjunction, but in Henning (1995b) it is labelled as a preposition, as in fact are *pelo* and *supelo*.

---

[68] Collinson (1924), after stating that "most of the European languages" have obligatory adjectival agreement, expresses the following opinion:

> While it is perfectly true that, from the point of view of strict logic, there would not seem to be any necessity to repeat in the adjective the expression of grammatical function already embodied in the noun, cases may easily arise where adjectival inflection is the best means of avoiding ambiguity. The English phrase, *"The French* (sing. or plural) *and German* (sing. or plural) *handbooks, approved by the Academy,"* may be taken as typical of such ambiguities, which in Esperanto are removed by the use of a singular or plural adjective to express the idea intended. In spite of its vaunted precision Ido is helpless here
> ...

[69] The same thing happens in Nov-Esperanto, but with the accusative ending in this context being written <ù> by de Saussure (1926).

Olingo has synthetic comparative and superlative forms of adjectives, the suffixes for them being *-eg-* and *-az-* respectively; Jaque (1944:33) gives the examples *alta* 'high', *altega* 'higher', and *altaza* 'highest'.

In Ekselsioro comparatives are formed with *ple* rather than with the *plej* of Esperanto, e.g. *la ple sperta homo* 'the most clever man' (Greenwood 1906b:18).

Hom-idyomo has the irregular comparative adjectives *melyora* 'better', *pejora* 'worse', *superyora* 'superior (in place)' and *inferiora* 'inferior (in place)', as well as the corresponding adverbs, e.g. *melyore*. Cárdenas (1923:I:50) states, "These ... special forms, although irregular, are adopted here because they are international, but they do not by any means exclude the regular forms *plus bona, plus mala, plus alta, plus abasa*". There are two irregular superlative adjectives, *optima* 'best' and *pesima* 'worst', but again one can use regular forms for these meanings.

Virgoranto has analytic comparatives and superlatives, the words involved being *mer* and *mest* respectively, e.g. *Anne esar mer bela kvi Claudia* 'Anne is more beautiful than Claudia' (Winkelhofer 2007b).

Ido comparatives and superlatives are analytic, marked by *plu* and *maxim* respectively. Romániço comparatives and superlatives involve the same words, but the latter word is written with an acute accent over the vowel of the first syllable, i.e. as *máxim*.[70] The comparatives and superlatives of Mondlango are also analytic, and are constructed with the words *mor* and *most*.

Linguna has both analytic and synthetic comparatives and superlatives, the former constructed as in Esperanto (i.e. with *pli* and *plej*), the latter using *-ior-* and *-íssim-* respectively.

## 4.5     Adverbs

The suffix of derived adverbs in many of the languages dealt with here, e.g. Perio, is the same as that of Esperanto, *-e*. As already indicated (Table 4.2), the word class suffix *-ai* marks both adjectives and adverbs in Esperloja, while most Farlingo adverbs end in *-en*. Among the adverbs of Hom-idyomo which do not come from Esperanto are *alore* 'then, at that time', *bisayde* 'besides', *ergo* 'therefore', *ofkowrse* 'of course', *perhapse* 'perhaps', *rader* 'rather', *so* 'so', and *veri* 'very'. It will be noticed that most of these come from English.

Apparently all adverbs, both derived and non-derived, bear a characteristic suffix in Intero.[71] However, there are several of these, depending on the kind of adverb: *-e* is the suffix for locative adverbs, while directional, temporal, and instrumental adverbs end with     *-en, -am,* and *-el* respectively. It is not stated how other types of adverbs, such as manner adverbs, are marked, but the following passage from Thompson (2007a) indicates that the group of instrumental adverbs includes more than one might think (as well as giving information on how some adverbs are constructed, presumably starting from an Esperanto adverb): "Above I note that primitive adverbs take new endings. First, they may or may not drop their old endings according to this rule: one by one each letter is dropped from the end of the word until the last letter is a

---

[70] *Máxim* has this accent mark, even though it presumably follows the typical stress pattern of Romániço of having penultimate stress. This accent mark was perhaps "inherited" from *máxima* 'most' (as an adjective), from which it may have been derived by deletion of the final vowel.

[71] I was led to this conclusion by the following sentence from Thompson (2007a): "Even primitive adverbs end in **-el, -en, -am,** or **-e** as appropriate."

letter other than *a, e, i, j, o, u,* or *ŭ.* If the word is like *nur,* then it loses no letters and just becomes *nurel.* Most importantly, note that *ne* becomes *nel.*"

## 4.6 Verbs

Aiola has what ARG (2005:84) calls *verb substitutes,* although they are actually substitutes for larger components of sentences, including verb phrases. There are two of these, *duyare* and *huyare.* The former is somewhat like English *do* when it stands for a verb phrase, but it occurs in a wider range of contexts: ARG (ibid.) says, "It translates in English as 'do/does' in the present, 'did' in the past, 'will' in the future, 'would' in the conditional present or future, 'would have' in the conditional past, 'have/has/had' in the perfect tenses, and 'to' in the infinitive". It can be a substitute for all verb phrases except those whose head is *estare* 'to be'. Among the examples given in ARG (ibid.:84-5) are the following:

(34a) Ei vu fondas Boston?    Ya. Mi duyas.
'Do you like Boston'    Yes. I do.'

(34b) Ei vu andos alu la konserto?    Mi duyos.
'Will you go to the concert?    I will.'

(34c) Ei vu kukos dineato?    Mi povos duyare.
'Will you cook some dinner?    I will be able to.'

*Huyare* is the interrogative equivalent of *duyare.*

(35a) Mi atcetis nuva komputero.    Vu huyis?
'I bought a new computer.    You what?'

(35b) Mi volas vendare miza tcaro.    Vu volas huyare?
'I want to sell my car.    You want to what?' (ibid.:85)

All verbs in Esperanto are regular, and this is true of almost all of its daughters. In Linguna the verb *esti* 'to be' is irregular, as can be seen in Table 4.40 (compare the regular verb forms in Table 4.41 below):

|  | present | imperfect | perfect |
|---|---|---|---|
| 1SG | szum | eram | fuvym |
| 2SG | est | eras | fuvas |
| 3SG | est | era | fuvas |
| 1PL | szoms/aro | erams | fuvams |
| 2PL | staz/aro | eraz | fuvaz |
| 3PL | szon/aro | eran | fuvaz |

Table 4.40: *Some Forms of the Linguna Verb* Esti *'To Be' (after Goeres 2004a)*

The verb *iri* 'to go' is also irregular in the present tense.
The Perio verb *sasi* is unusual and slightly irregular. It means both 'être' and 'devoir', and unlike most verbs meaning 'to be', it can be put into the passive voice,

and then changes its meaning: *sasih* 'devenir'. Most of its active forms consist only of verbal endings, i.e.there is no overt root, e.g. *it* and *at*, which I believe are the present and past indicative forms. Its present active participle is *sasa*.

Atlango has a contracted version of *esta*, the present of its verb *esti* 'to be', *-s*. Two of the examples that Antonius (2008b) gives of its use are *Mi-s felica* 'I'm lucky' and *Lu ne-s rica* 'They are not rich'. Antonius then states, "*It would be interesting to use -s after nouns in more advanced Atlango:* My car is very big. Ma auto-**s** molte grana". [72] The roots *vad-* 'go' and *fer-* 'make' can be shortened to *v-* and *f-*, yielding e.g. in the present tense *va* and *fa*.

In Romániço there is a short form of *esen* 'is/am/are', *es*.

### 4.6.1 Person/Number Agreement

Not surprisingly, with the exception of Linguna, Farlingo, and Perio,[73] to my knowledge no modification of Esperanto has introduced person/number agreement marking on finite verbs.[74] In the following table person/number agreement marking in Linguna is illustrated:

|      | present | perfect  |
|------|---------|----------|
| 1SG  | lavym   | lavuvym  |
| 2SG  | lavas   | lavuvas  |
| 3SG  | lavas   | lavuvas  |
| 1PL  | lavams  | lavuvams |
| 2PL  | lavaz   | lavuvaz  |
| 3PL  | lavaz   | lavuvaz  |

Table 4.41: *Some Forms of the Linguna Verb* Lavi *'To Wash'*

It can be seen that the 2nd and 3rd person forms are identical, as generally the case (but cf. the imperfect forms of *esti* 'to be' in Table 4.40). Possibly related to the presence of person/number agreement is the fact that to at least some extent Linguna allows the omission of subject pronouns (i.e. pro-drop); there may be a rule restricting when this omission can occur, but it is not entirely clear to me what the rule is.

### 4.6.2 Tense and Aspect

Sen:esepera does not have morphologically distinct tense forms; Henning (1995a) states, "The verb undergoes no change with regard to person or number or tense, which is instead conveyed as necessary through context".

---

[72] One might be surprised at these examples, since according to Antonius (ibid.) predicate adjectives "behave like verbs", and thus a form of 'to be' is not necessary, e.g. *Mi (te) foma* 'I am so hungry' (ibid.). Antonius then says, "Instead of: *Mi estas (te) foma*", but it is not clear when or whether 'to be' must be omitted, as shortly after this he gives the following sentence among examples illustrating the use of the infinitive: *Mi glada Tun vidi. = Mi esta glada, ke mi Tun vida.* 'I am happy to see you'.

[73] Farlingo and Perio have singular and plural imperatives (v. section 4.6.3), but their other finite verb forms are not marked for person/number agreement.

[74] I say "on finite verbs" because in Esperanto and some daughter languages participles can take plural marking.

The past, present, and future tense suffixes of E-speranto are identical to those of Esperanto, and there is also a "perpetual" (Holmes 2008:6) suffix, -es.[75] Ido also has the same past, present, future tense suffixes as Esperanto, and, as in Esperanto, constructs periphrastic active progressive and perfect forms with a form of the verb 'to be' and an active participle. In addition (and unlike Esperanto), Ido has synthetic perfect forms, which involve the suffix -ab-, e.g. for 'had written' one can say skribabis or esis skribinta and for 'will have loved' amabos or esos aminta. Originally -ab- (once it had been adopted into the language) was not to be used in the present tense, but since 1947 this has been permitted, e.g. vidabas 'have seen'.

Arlipo's tense suffixes have the same vowel as their Esperanto equivalents, but a different consonant, t replacing s. Thus the present, past, and future endings of this language are -at, -it, and -ot respectively. The tense suffixes of Reformed Esperanto are different from those of Esperanto: the past, present, and future tenses are marked by -in, -en, and -on respectively. EsF does not have the Esperanto suffixes for past, present, and future tense: the infinitive is used instead of forms with these endings. Harrison (2004) states that "Adverbs and context indicate the time of an occurrence". The tense suffixes of Mondezo end with -n instead of -s; thus the past, present, and future endings are -in, -an, and -on respectively. The use of tense suffixes is not required in Mondezo (this is also true of the conditional suffix): "an infinitive may be the main verb in a phrase when time is not important or is known from context" (Medrano 2002). Mondlango's tense suffixes are identical to those of Mondezo.

Present tense forms in Novesperant have no endings, e.g. est 'is'. (On the other hand, the Esperanto infinitive ending -i is retained in Novesperanto, as shown by the sentence mi ne pov trovi mi automobil 'I cannot find my car' (Cartier n.d., MT).)

Neo has synthetic present, imperfect/(simple) past, and future forms, created by means of the suffixes -ar, -ir, and -or respectively. [76] Alfandari (1961:38) gives examples of "temps composés" forms, involving the verb i (= avi) 'to have', e.g.:

(36a)   mi   ar          s-at
        I    have.PRES   be-PSTPARTIC
        'j'ai été'

(36b)   nos   or          v-at
        we    have.FUT    want-PSTPARTIC
        'nous aurons voulu'

There is a suffix -ens- meaning 'begin', e.g. verdensi 'begin to become green'.

The present, past and suffixes of Virgoranto are also -ar, -ir, and -or. In Farlingo -a, -i, -u, -ari, and -aru are the endings for the present, completed past, completed future, incomplete past, and incomplete future respectively.[77]

---

[75] Holmes (ibid.) says, "Verb endings use the five vowels for a kind of temporal placement. Thus a signals here and now, o signals ahead or the future, i behind or the past, u conditional or propositional, and e perpetual or definitional". This appears to be a part of the vowel-meaning correspondence of E-speranto brought up in section 3.1.

[76] Alfandari was attached to the imperfect and the subjunctive, although Neo does not have (distinct) forms for them, as the following passage (1961:39) shows: "C'est bien à contre-cœur que nous avons renonce à l'imparfait proprement dit ... et au subjonctif, si riche en nuances. Nous avons dû y résigner parce que beaucoup de peoples, qui n'ont pas ces formes dans leur langue, auraient eu du mal à les saisir. Nous avions cependant établit une desinence (-iar) pour l'imparfait et une autre pour le subjonctif (-u). Si un jour on jugeait devoir les réintroduire dans la langue, elles sont donc toutes prêtes."

In Olingo the present tense forms, infinitives and imperatives all have the same form, ending in *-i* (although the infinitive is often preceded by *al* 'to'). The past and future tenses (what Jaque 1944:33) refers to as "discontinued action" and "expected action") are marked by *-ita* and *-ota* respectively, e.g. *urita* 'was' *brinota* 'will bring'. (The past/passive participle also ends in *-ita*.) Olingo seems to have analytic tense/aspect forms, though they are not called such by Jaque (1944), who says (p. 33), "When two or three action words are used to describe a single action, the word ending sign is dropped from the first or first two words, and they are united by hyphens to the last word of the group. Examples: ur-provota—are trying, dev-ur-uzita—must be used". The first of these examples indicates how progressive aspect forms are created, with *uri* 'to be' and a form in *-ata* (which is a present participle). The second example shows that modal auxiliaries and *uri* when used as a passive auxiliary are also connected to other verbs with a hyphen. The following sentence indicates that there is no formal distinction between the (present) perfect and the pluperfect when no words intervene between the auxiliary and the main verb, perhaps due to this hyphenation (since an auxiliary verb will not have its own tense ending):

(37)  Un mezeldida    viro,   woa   haro   av-qomens-ita              al  turni
      A  middle-aged  man   whose hair    have-begin-PSTPARTIC   to  turn

      gra,  qort-ita    du   virino-n    be   la    simla tempo.
      gray  court-PST   two  woman-PL    at   the   same  time
      'A middle-aged man, whose hair had begun to turn gray, courted two women
      at the same time.' (Jaque 1944:28)

Although Olingo has a future tense suffix, there is a verb *voli*, which Jaque (1944:46) glosses as 'will' in the "Olingo-English Glossary" and which he (ibid.:58) gives as the equivalent of *will* in the "English-Olingo Glossary". Further, in one of the texts in Jaque (1944) it is used as a future marker:

(38)  Wol  ofte   herepos    lev-ata                voli   shi   vizeni
      How  often  hereafter  rise-PRESPARTIC        will   she   look
      'How oft hereafter rising shall she look' (ibid.:27, "Excerpts from the
      Rubáiyát of Omar Khayyám")

Further, on the same page *devi*, glossed (ibid.:37) as 'must, shall', is used this way:

(39)  E    wen    Viego    qun    brilada    Piedo  dev-pasi
      and  when   yourself  with   shining    foot   *dev*-pass
      'And when Thyself with shining Foot shall pass' (ibid.)

*Devi* also appears with this function in another text (ibid.:51). In two texts Jaque may make an error in marking tense; consider the following example:

---

[77] I have used "completed" and "incomplete" for Farber and Farber's (2005) "законченное" and "незаконченное".

(40)  La    respondon  al   tan    quiron    brin-ota    om   qonajo,     e
      The   answers    to   these  questions bring-FUT    all  knowledge   and

quond-i     be   laste   al   perfa     qomprado
lead-PRES   at   last    to   perfect   understanding
'The answers to these simple questions will bring all knowledge, and lead at
last to perfect understanding' (ibid.:32, "The Socratic Aim")

What this sentence probably means is 'The answers to these simple questions will
bring all knowledge, and **will** lead at last to perfect understanding', i.e. one could say
that there was an instance of *will* in the second verb phrase which has been deleted.
Thus *quondi* should be in the future tense: it should be *\*quonota*. Jaque might have
been misled into using the present by the fact that in the English version the infinitive
*lead* appears, which is identical to the finite present tense form, because it is preceded
by (a deleted occurrence of) *will*. It is possible that this is not an error, and that there
is a rule in the language (which has not been stated by Jaque) requiring or allowing
present/infinitive forms in such contexts, but I think it is unlikely.

Perio has five tenses/aspects in the indicative mood; example forms are below,
accompanied by the 1st person singular pronoun:

| present          | mi vidit 'je vois'       |
|------------------|--------------------------|
| past             | mi vidat 'j'ai vu'       |
| pluperfect       | mi vidaat 'j'avais vu'   |
| future           | mi vidut 'je verrai'     |
| future anterior  | mi vidaut 'j'aurai vu'   |

Table 4.42: *Indicative Tense/Aspect Forms of Perio (from Couturat and Leau
1907/1979:5)*

There are six tense/aspect forms in Mondlingvo: the "temps simples" (Couturat
and Leau 1907/1979:87), the imperfect, present, and future, whose markers are the
suffixes *-as*, *-es*, and *-os* respectively, and perfect forms which consist of these and the
prefix *e-* (apparently borrowed from Ancient Greek). Couturat and Leau (ibid.) give
the following examples of these forms:

| mi laŭdas 'je louais'   | mi elaŭdas 'j'avais loué' |
|-------------------------|---------------------------|
| mi laŭdes 'je loue'     | mi elaŭdes 'j'ai loué'     |
| mi laŭdos 'je louerais' | me elaŭdos 'j'aurai loué   |

Table 4.43: *Tense/Aspect Forms in Mondlingvo*

It is perhaps worth noting that while both Esperanto and Mondlingvo have a suffix *-as*
which marks a tense/aspect, but its meaning is different in the two languages, present
in Esperanto and imperfect in Mondlingvo.

The Atlango past, present, and future tense markers are *-i*, *-a*, and *-u* respectively;
thus the same suffix is used to mark past tense and the infinitive. Atlango also has
perfect endings, *-is* and *-os*. The latter is the future perfect marker; Antonius (2008b)
indicates that the former is a past perfect suffix, but in fact it can have a present

perfect meaning also.[78] One of the examples which Antonius (ibid.) gives for the suffix is *mi skribis*, which he translates as 'I have (already) written, I had written'. Another of his examples *is Mi vidis hi* 'I have seen him'. What is more, Antonius (ibid.) sometimes translates verbs ending in *-is* with English simple past forms, e.g. *Mi alportis le buko* 'I brought the book'.[79] He (ibid.) indicates that the perfect can mark "sudden and momentary action". Atlango has a suffix *fre-* meaning 'frequently, habitual, customary', e.g. *freviziti* 'frequently visit'.

There are no tense/aspect affixes in Esperloja; there is a set of (optional) "time modifiers" (Sulky n.d.) which give the same sort of information. Below we see a verb with these modifiers, from the vocabulary list in Sulky (ibid.):

| paliu | 'speak' |
|---|---|
| paliu pai | 'spoke' |
| paliu fai | 'will speak' |
| paliu dai | 'speak now'[80] |
| paliu papai | 'had spoken' |
| paliu fapai | 'will have spoken' |
| paliu dapai | 'has spoken' |
| paliu pafai | 'had been about to speak' |
| paliu fafai | 'will be about to speak; |
| paliu padai | 'was speaking' |
| paliu fadai | 'will be speaking' |
| paliu rai | 'speak repeatedly' |
| paliu bai | 'speak continuously' |

Table 4.44: *Esperloja "Time Modifiers"*

The tense endings of Aiola are the same as those of Esperanto. However, different aspects can (but do not have to) be marked with each of these tenses: the progressive, perfective, and inceptive suffixes are *-ant-*, *-int-*, and *-ont-* respectively and they appear between the root and the tense suffix. The progressive and the perfect suffixes can co-occur in a verb form, with the former preceding the latter. Example forms are given below:

---

[78] In addition there is a perfect conditional ending, *-us*. (The Atlango conditional suffix is *-u*)

[79] Perhaps (some of) the occurrences of *-is* in such cases are errors, under Esperanto influence.

[80] The word *dai* is also listed separately in Sulky's vocabulary list and is defined as "that (definitive)", which probably means the demonstrative 'that'.

| present progressive | moi ludantas 'we are playing' |
|---|---|
| past progressive | moi ludantis 'we were playing' |
| future progressive | moi ludantos 'we will be playing' |
| present perfective | moi ludintas 'we have played' |
| past perfective | moi ludintis 'we had played' |
| future perfective | moi ludintos 'we will have played' |
| present inceptive | moi ludontas 'we are going to play' |
| past inceptive | moi ludontis 'we were going to play' |
| future inceptive | moi ludontos 'we will be going to play' |
| present perfect progressive | moi ludantintas 'we have been playing' |
| past perfect progressive | moi ludantintis 'we had been playing' |
| future perfect progressive | moi ludantintos 'we will have been playing' |

Table 4.45: *Indicative Active Verb Forms of Aiola in Different Aspects (from ARG 2005:40-1)*

Linguna has a relatively large number of tenses/aspects, including the present, preterite, imperfect present, imperfect preterite, future, aorist, perfect, and pluperfefct.

There are four synthetic tenses in Hom-idyomo. The suffixes marking these are shown below, along with example forms:

| present | -ay | mi doʑmay 'I sleep' |
|---|---|---|
| preterite | -ey | mi doʑmey 'I slept' |
| copreterite | -avit | mi doʑmavit 'I was sleeping' |
| future | -oy | mi doʑmoy 'I shall sleep' |

Table 4.46: *Synthetic Tenses of Hom-Idyomo*

The following remarks by Cárdenas (1923:I:71) apparently are about the copreterite, even though he uses the term "imperfect":

> The imperfect tense has two significations:
>
> 1st. That the action was taking place at the time another action had already taken place, as *la bʑigando abigeey la heʑdo dum ke mi doʑmavit* (the rascal stole the herd while I was sleeping).
>
> 2nd. That the past action or being was prolonged or not yet finished, as *mia fem-filyo no estay nun tante salubʑa kwante si estavit* (My daughter is not now so healthy as she used to be).
>
> In the last case the tense is not a simultaneous preterit, but only a prolonged preterit.

In addition to these tenses Hom-idyomo has a considerable number of analytic indicative tense/aspect forms. The largest group of these involve estiʑ 'to be' as an auxiliary. The table below shows how they are constructed and gives examples (from Cárdenas 1923:I:89-93), with the 1st person singular pronoun:

| present | pres. indic. of *estiɀ* + pres. act. partic. | mi estay maɿčante 'I am walking' |
|---|---|---|
| immediate preterite | pres. indic. of *estiɀ* + pret. act. partic. | mi estay maɿčinte 'I have just walked (am having walked)' |
| present future | pres. indic. of *estiɀ* + fut. active partic. | mi estay maɿčonte 'I must walk' |
| ante-present | pret. indic. of *estiɀ* + pres. act. partic. | mi estey maɿčante 'I was walking' |
| double past | pret. indic. of *estiɀ* + pret. act. partic. | mi estey maɿčinte 'I had just walked' |
| anterior fut. | pret. indic. of *estiɀ* + fut. act. partic. | mi estey maɿčonte 'I had to walk' |
| copreterite | copret. indic. of *estiɀ* + pres. act. partic. | mi estavit maɿčante 'I was walking' |
| copreterite-preterite | copret. indic. of *estiɀ* + pret. act. partic. | mi estavit maɿčinte 'I had just walked' |
| undefinable copreterite | copret. indic. of *estiɀ* + fut. act. partic. | mi estavit maɿčonte 'I was to walk' |
| future | fut. indic. of *estiɀ* + pres. act. partic. | mi estoy maɿčante 'I shall be walking' |
| undefinable future | fut. indic. of *estiɀ* + pret. act. partic. | mi estoy maɿčinte 'I shall have just walked' |
| double future | fut. indic. of *estiɀ* + fut. act. partic. | mi estoy maɿčonte 'I shall have to walk' |

Table 4.47: *Hom-Idyomo Analytic Indicative Tenses/Aspects formed with* Estiɀ

The auxiliary *haviɀ* 'to have' is used in the formation of some other analytic tenses/aspects (examples from Cárdenas 1923:I:110-111):

| imm. pret. | pres. indic. of *haviɀ* + pass. partic. in *-ite* | mi havay mandukite 'I have eaten' |
|---|---|---|
| pret. | pret. indic. of *haviɀ* + pass. partic. in *-ite* | mi havey mandukite 'I had eaten' |
| copret. | copret. indic. of *haviɀ* + pass. partic. in *-ite* | mi havavit mandukite 'I had eaten' |
| fut. | fut. indic. of *haviɀ* + pass. partic. in *-ite* | mi havoy mandukite 'I shall have eaten' |

Table 4.48: *Hom-Idyomo Analytic Indicative Tenses/Aspects formed with Haviɀ*

Cárdenas (1923:I:113) gives some examples illustrating the "Compound conjugation with the auxiliary 'mustíɀ'", including *Mi mustay eskɿibiɀ* 'I must/have to write'. There is also a "compound conjungation" involving the verb *iviɀ* 'to go' and an infinitive, e.g. in *Bia fɿatɿo ivey diɀiɀ io* 'Your brother was going to say something' (ibid.:I:77). One might hesitate to agree with Cárdenas that "compound tenses" (ibid.) include sequences of mustíɀ or iviɀ and an infinitive. Although he provided his language with such a large array of analytic tense/aspect forms, Cárdenas (ibid.:I:74) says, "Simple tenses should be preferred to compound, except where clearness or construction makes the compound form indispensable".

With the exception of the present tense, which is marked by the suffix *-en,*[81] all the tenses and aspects of Románico are analytic. Past forms consist of *has* 'did' (which Morales (2008b) labels as an adverb) and a present tense form. However, it is not necessary to use *has* in describing past events or states; one can use instead an adverb referring to past time, e.g.:

(41)   Here       dingo manj-en   elia bebo.
       yesterday  dingo eat-PRES  her  baby
       'Yesterday a dingo ate her baby.'  (Morales n.d. n)

The future tense is constructed with *van* 'will' (which also is considered to be an adverb by Morales) and a present tense form, but *van* need not occur in clauses describing future events/states if there is an adverb referring to future time.[82] Concerning progressive aspect, Morales (ibid.) says, "In the present tense, action is often 'in progress' by default, and needs no special marker … When the unfinished nature of an action is not otherwise clear, one can use the particle **ta**". The example that he gives (which is in the future tense) is below:

(42)   mi van    ta     lecten li     demane.
       I  will   PROG   read   3SG    tomorrow
       'I'll be reading it tomorrow (and may or may not finish).'

Románico also has "compound verbs" (ibid.), involving sequences of *es(en)* 'is/am/are'[83] and a participle. Morales (ibid.) says about them, "With compound verbs, one can express *any* degree of completion in any tense". His examples include the following sentences:

(43a)   La dingo  has  es  manj-inta          je   la   bebo  cuande  mi
        the dingo did  is  eat- PSTPARTIC     *je*[84] the  baby  when    I

        has    envaden.
        did    enter-PRES
        'The dingo had (already) eaten the baby when I walked in.'

---

[81] One might prefer to see forms ending in *-en* as general finite forms (rather than being marked for present tense), with the default interpretation of sentences being present tense (i.e. in the absence of words indicating the past or future nature of an event/state).

[82] Unlike most designers of artificial languages, Morales (ibid.) discusses the issue of sequence of tenses: "In English, when one reports what someone else says or feels, the tense of the quoted action changes depending on the tense of the main verb … In Románico, the tense of the quoted material stays the same as if it were quoted directly".

[83] There are also sequences in which a participle is preceded by another verb; I do not know whether Morales considers these to be compound verbs as well, although he discusses them in the section "Compound Verbs" (ibid.), saying, "Note that **eser** followed by a participle expresses a *pre-existing state* in Románico, just as it would if followed by any other adjective. To say, for example, **la dingo has es manjinta ye 3:00** means that the dingo had finished eating at *or before* 3:00. To indicate that the dingo finished at 3:00 and not before, use **devencioner** ("to become") or **fer** ("to be rendered") instead of **eser**". The example he then gives is *La dingo has fen manjinta je la bebo cuande mi has envaden* 'The dingo finished eating the baby when I walked in'.

[84] V. section 4.7 for the function of *je*.

116

(43b)  La  dingo  has  es  manjanta        je  la   bebo  cuande  mi
      the dingo did  is  eat- PRESPARTIC  je the  baby  when    I

      has  envaden.
      did  enter-PRES

'The dingo was eating the baby when I walked in.'

### 4.6.3  Mood and Modality

The conditional and imperative suffixes of Reformed Esperanto are *-un* and *-an* respectively. Mondezo's conditional suffix is *-us* while that of Arlipo is *-ut*. Mondlingvo's conditional and imperative suffixes are *-eb-* and *-ib-* respectively. They precede the tense/aspect suffixes (i.e. unlike the conditional suffix of Esperanto, the conditional suffix of Mondlingvo can, and apparently has to, co-occur with a tense/aspect suffix.) Mondlango's conditional and imperative markers are *-uz* and *-ez* respectively; however, anon. (n.d. b) states, "The conditional and imperative endings are optional".[85] The conditional suffix of Virgoranto is *-ur*; imperatives consist simply of stems of verbs, e.g. *sing!* 'sing!' (cf. *singi* 'to sing'). In Neo the conditional suffix is also *-ur*, while the infinitive (which ends in *-i*) serves as the imperative. The imperative ending of 1923 Esperantida and of Nov-Esperanto is *-oy*, while that of Ido is *-ez*.

    Farlingo has past, present, and future conditional forms, ending in *-ei*, *-ai*, and *-ui* respectively, and singular and plural imperatives, marked by *-ez* and *-au*.

    Conditional forms of Romániço are analytic, containing *volde* (which is an adverb according to Morales (2008b), although the English gloss given for it is "would") and a present tense form of a verb; they can also contain the past tense marker *has*,[86] e.g.:

(44)  Dingo  volde   has  manj-en  elia  bebo
      dingo  would  did  eat-PRES  her   baby
      'A dingo would have eaten her baby'  (Morales n.d. n)

The word *fay* (for which an English equivalent is not given in Morales (2008a), (2008b), or (n.d. n)) occurs in some, but not all, imperative sentences; Morales (n.d. n) says, "When expressing a request, the verb by itself will usually suffice as long as there's no subject; otherwise, one can add **fay** to make the request clear". Some examples of imperative sentences with and without *fay* are below:

(45a)  Ne   reguard-en   mi!
      not  look.at-PRES  me
      Don't look at me!

(45b)  Vi      fay  ne   reguard-en    mi!
      you.SG  *fay* not  look.at-PRES  me
      Don't you look at me!

---

[85] It is not clear to me what this means, perhaps that one can use indicative forms as conditional or imperative forms.
[86] I do not know whether they could contain the future tense marker *van* 'will'; Morales (n.d. n) says nothing on this question and does not have any relevant examples.

(45c)   Los   fay   manj-en   cuco!
         they  *fay*  eat-PRES  cake
         'Let them eat cake!'  (Morales n.d. n)

In Morales' webpages *fay* also appears in some sentences that do not contain imperatives, including the following:

(46a)   mi   prefer-en      que  ili  ne   fay   ven-en
         I    prefer-PRES    that  he   not  *fay*  come-PRES
         'I'd rather he didn't come'  (Morales 2008b)

(46b)   Mi   volicion-en   que  vi      fay   colp-en   mi   tam  fort-e
         I    want-PRES     that  you.SG  *fay*  hit-PRES  me   as   strong-ADV

         cam   posíbile.
         as    possible
         'I want you to hit me as hard as you can.'  (Morales n.d. m)

(46c)   mi   fay   remplaciif-en   la    trapiquita   neumático …
         I    *fay*  replace-PRES    the   punctured    tire
         'I must replace the punctured tire …'  (Morales 2008b)

(46d)   Mi   van  sorg-en           que  eli   fay   recept-en      li.
         I    will  see.to.it-PRES   that  she   *fay*  receive-PRES   3SG
         'I'll see that she gets it.'  (Morales n.d. m)

(46e)   17,  mi   fay   dic-en        18
         17   I    *fay*  say-PRES      18
         '17, I mean 18'  (Morales 2008b)

Note that some of these sentences involve a wish or desire or similar meaning, and thus are semantically similar to imperatives.

Perio has conditional and imperative forms marked by the suffixes *-o-* and *-e-* respectively. Below are example forms from Couturat and Leau (1907/1979:6):

| pres.indic.    | mi vidit 'je vois'       |
| -------------- | ------------------------ |
| past indic.    | mi vidat 'j'ai vu'       |
| pres. condit.  | mi vidot 'je verrais'    |
| past condit.   | mi vidaot 'j'avais vu'   |
| sing. imper.   | videt 'vois'             |
| pl. imper.     | videts 'voyez'           |

Table 4.49: *Mood Forms of Perio*

The imperative of Aiola is marked by *-au*, e.g. *ludau* 'play!'. The language has present past, and future conditional forms, ending in *-uas*, *-uis*, and *-uos* respectively (i.e. *-u-* is the marker of the conditional mood), and these can be preceded by any of the aspect suffixes of the language. A few example forms are below:

| present conditional | moi luduas 'we would play' |
|---|---|
| past conditional | moi luduis 'we would have played' |
| future conditional | moi luduos 'we would play (future)' |
| present progressive conditional | moi ludantuas 'we would be playing' |
| present perfective conditional | moi ludintuas 'we would be having played' |
| past perfective conditional | moi ludintuis 'we would have been having played' |
| future inceptive conditional | moi ludontuos 'we would be going to play (future)' |

Table 4.50: *Some Conditional Forms of Aiola (from ARG 2005:40-1)*

In Hom-idyomo there are more moods than in Esperanto: indicative, conditional, suggestive, hypothetic, and imperative. The suffixes for the non-indicative moods and example forms (Cárdenas 1923:I:72-3) are given below with the 1st person singular pronoun except for the imperative, with which the 2nd person singular pronoun is given, since it apparently does not occur in the 1st person singular:

| conditional | -uy | mi dozmuy 'I should sleep' |
|---|---|---|
| suggestive | -in | mi dozmin '(that) I sleep' |
| hypothetical | -il | mi dozmil 'I slept' |
| imperative | -ivi | dozmivi tu 'sleep (thou)' |

Table 4.51: *Non-Indicative Moods in Hom-Idyomo*

Although in the paradigms in Cárdenas (1923) imperative forms appear with an overt subject, as seen in the table above, it seems that they do not have to have one, given sentences such as *No akusivi ile* 'do not blame them' (ibid.:I:136).

Beyond indicating that the suggestive mood is equivalent to the "English subjunctive, etc." (Cárdenas 1913:I:72) and that the hypothetic mood is the "English subjunctive with implied hypothesis" (ibid.), to my knowledge Cárdenas does not give information on when particular moods should be used. We can get some idea about this by looking at when they occur in texts.

The verb 'to doubt' can (or must) take a clause with a suggestive verb form:

(47)  Mi dub-ay       ke   la   retazdo ag-il              je  plus  justa.
      I   doubt-PRES  that  the  delay   make-SUGGEST  it   more  just
      'I doubt whether the delay would make it more just.' (ibid.:I:61)

Likewise, when *prefezir* 'to prefer' takes a finite clause, the verb of that clause can or must be in the suggestive. In the following example *a fin ke* 'in order that' takes a clause with its verb in the suggestive mood:

(48)  a fin ke        mia    decido     est-in          juzidika.
      in.order.that  my     decision   be-SUGGEST       legal
      '... in order that my decision be legal' (ibid.:I:18)

The conjunction *kondicyone ke* 'provided that' takes verbs in the suggestive:

(49)   kondicyone ke   esi   est-in              fɾitatas  *entɾe*  la   kaseɾolo
       provided.that   they  be-SUGGEST          fried     in       the  casserole

       pɾevie …
       first
       'provided they are first fried in the pan …' (ibid.:I:85)

*Kwanke* 'although' also takes the suggestive, e.g.:

(50)   kwanke  li   pɾaktik-in              tutas  las  ceteɾas
       although he   practice-SUGGEST       all    the  others
       'even if he possesses all others' (ibid.:I:41, tr. I:42)

The noun *espeɾo* 'hope' can (must?) take a clause whose verb is in the suggestive:

(51)   Oni  toleɾ-ay       ile        pacyente,  kun  espeɾo  ke   maɾdo
       one  tolerate-PRES  them       patiently  with hope    that Tuesday

       est-in               re-establis-ata                 la   noɾmalo.
       be-SUGGEST           re-establish-PASSPARTIC          the  normalcy
       'They are patiently tolerated, in the hope that by Tuesday normal conditions
       will be restored.' (ibid.:I:35, tr. I:36)

Below we see a clause introduced by *kwande* 'when' containing a verb in the
suggestive:

(52)   Memoɾ-ivi          tia  aksyomo  kwande  oni  demand-in
       remember-IMPER     this axiom    when    one  ask.for-SUGGEST

       bia   sufɾago …
       your  vote
       'Remember this axiom when they ask you for your vote …' (ibid.:I:30)

   As its name might suggest, the hypothetic mood occurs in contrafactual statements
and conditions:

(53a)  La   socyeto sine   riĉals     est-il          tante  im-perfecte,  ke
       The  society without rich.men  be-HYPOTH       so     imperfect     that

       ji   no   posibl-uy      pɾogres-iɾ.
       it   not  can-CONDIT     advance-INFIN
       'Without wealthy men, society would be so imperfect that it could not
       advance.' (ibid.:I:76)

(53b)  … si  no  eksist-il          ričals,        ki  pag-uy        las
         if  not  exist-HYPOTH  wealthy.men  who  pay-CONDIT  the

taksos …?
taxes
'… if there were no wealthy men, who would pay the taxes …?'  (ibid.:I:77)

However, not all contrafactual sentences contain a hypothetic form; compare (53a) with (54), which has instead a conditional verb, although it is similar, and occurs on the same page:

(54)   Jes,  sine     ričo    la    homo  est-uy        fama,   nuda,  sula …
         Yes  without  wealth  the  man    be-CONDIT  hungry  naked  unclean
         'Yes; without wealth, man would be hungry, naked, unclean …'

On the other hand, the hypothetic mood is not limited to contrafactual sentences; consider the following examples:

(55a)  La    reklamato  diɹ-ay    ke  li  no  sab-ey        … ke    la
         The  defendant    say-PRES  that  he  not  know-PRET      that    the

vendanto  est-il              una  abigeisto
seller        be-HYPOTH      a      thief
'The defendant says that he did not know that the seller was a thief'
(Cárdenas 1923:I:18)

(55b)  La    dio  ventuɹa  en  kio    la-s      homo-s  posed-il              una
         The  day  happy    in  which  the-PL  man-PL  possess-HYPOTH  a

idyoma      komuma,  la    haɹmonia  en  la    mundo  est-oy    multe
language    common    the  harmony    in  the  world    be-FUT  much

minus  difikulta.
less    difficult
'In the happy day when men shall have a common language, harmony in the world will be much far less difficult.'  (ibid.:I:32)

I do not know why the verb 'be' is in the hypothetical mood in (55a); the reason might be that the clause containing it states a fact that the reported speaker of the larger clause (i.e. the defendant) did not have first-hand knowledge of or had been (according to him) unaware of.

We saw in the previous section that Hom-idyomo has a large array of analytic tense forms in the indicative mood; it also has analytic forms in other moods. Below are some forms involving *estiɹ* 'to be' (from Cárdenas 1923:I:93-96):

| condit. | pres. | pres. condit. of *estiʑ* + pres. act. particip. | mi estuy maɾčante 'I should be walking' |
| | imm. pret. | pres. condit. of *estiʑ* + pret. act. particip. | mi estuy maɾčinte 'I should have just walked' |
| | fut. | pres. condit. of *estiʑ* + fut. act. particip. | mi estuy maɾčonte 'I should have to walk' |
| suggest. | pres. | pres. suggest. of *estiʑ* + pres. act. particip. | mi estin maɾčante '(that) I be walking' |
| | imm. pret. | pres. suggest. of *estiʑ* + pret. act. particip. | mi estin maɾčinte '(that) I have just walked' |
| | fut. | pres. suggest. of *estiʑ* + fut. act. particip. | mi estin maɾčonte '(that) I have to walk' |
| hypoth. | pres. | pres. hypoth. of *estiʑ* + pres. act. particip. | mi estil maɾčante 'I were walking' |
| | imm. pret. | pres. hypoth. of *estiʑ* + pret. act. particip. | mi estil maɾčinte 'I had just walked' |
| | fut. | pres. hypoth. of *estiʑ* + fut. act. particip. | mi estil maɾčonte 'I had to walk' |
| imper. | pres. | pres. imper. of *estiʑ* + pres. act. particip. | estivi tu maɾčante 'be (thou) walking' |
| | fut. | pres. imper. of *estiʑ* + fut. act. particip. | estivi tu maɾčonte 'be (thou) ready to walk' |

Table 4.52: *Hom-Idyomo Non-Indicative Analytic Tenses/Aspects formed with* Estiʑ

There are also analytic forms which contain *haviʑ* 'to have'.

Linguna has a conditional and imperative mood, as well as a "Subjunctivo (Eventuálissa)" (Goeres 2004a) [87] and a "[c]onjunctivo (de opinión forana)" ('subjunctive of foreign [i.e. someone other that the speaker's?] opinion', Goeres 2004a).

### 4.6.4 Infinitives

Esperanto has a single synthetic infinitive, ending in *-i*, e.g. *ami* 'to love'. Some of its daughters, although they also have only one synthetic infinitive, differ with respect to the form of its suffix. For example, Reformed Esperanto's infinitive suffix is *-a*. The infinitive suffix of Arlipo is *-on*, e.g. *siegon* 'to besiege', while that of Romániço is *-er*, e.g. *creder* 'to believe'.

In Ido there are three infinitive forms (in the active voice), the past, present and future infinitives, marked by the suffixes *-ir*, *-ar*, and *-or* respectively, e.g. *amir*, *amar*, *amor* from *am-* 'love'). Farlingo also has past, present, and future infinitives, ending in *-ir*, *-ar*, and *-ur* respectively. Mondlingvo has a (synthetic) infinitive for each of the "simple tenses", e.g. *amenti*, *amanti*, and *amonti* are, I believe, the present,

---

[87] Goeres (2004b) states, "eventuáliss = Subjunktiv des Zweifels, der Unsicherheit über etwas, der unbestimmten Eventualität und potentiellen Möglichkeit".

imperfect, and future infinitives of the verb meaning 'to love'.[88] There are present and past infinitives in Perio, e.g. *vidi* 'to see', *vidati* 'to have seen'. These can be substantivized, e.g. *il viki* 'the victory', *il vikihs* 'the defeats' (Couturat and Leau 1907/1979:7).

Aiola active infinitives are marked by -*are*. They can contain one or two aspect suffixes:

| infinitive | ludare 'to play' |
|---|---|
| progressive infinitive | ludantare 'to be playing' |
| perfective infinitive | ludintare 'to have played' |
| inceptive infinitive | ludontare 'to be going to play' |
| perfect progressive infinitive | ludantintare 'to have been playing' |

Table 4.53: *Active Infinitives of Aiola (from ARG 2005:40-1)*

The first form (i.e. the one with no aspect suffixes) is not said to have any tense in the paradigm in ARG (2005:40); the perfective and inceptive infinitives seem to be equivalent to the perfect and future infinitives respectively of Latin.

Hom-idyomo has one synthetic active infinitive, marked by -*iʑ*, e.g. *amiʑ* 'to love', and several analytic active infinitives, e.g. *estiʑ maʑčante* 'to be walking', *estiʑ maʑčinte* 'having walked',[89] *estiʑ maʑčonte* 'having to walk'. Apparently there is only a single analytic active infinitive involving *haviʑ*, e.g. *haviʑ mandukite* 'to have eaten'. Given the following example, it seems that infinitives can be used in indirect statements:

(56) La reklamanto diʑ-ay est-iʑ ownisto de uni
    the plaintiff say-PRES be-INFIN owner of one

    bovin- estalyono ...
    bull
    'The plaintiff says that he is the owner of a bull ...' (Cárdenas 1923:I:16)

One would not have an infinitive in this context in Esperanto. The next sentence of this text also has an indirect statement, and it is introduced by *ke* 'that' and contains a finite verb, i.e. it has the same structure as the equivalent Esperanto sentence would have.

In Atlango the word *a* can introduce infinitives (57a-b);[90] apparently this is optional, as there are infinitives in various contexts occurring without it in Antonius (2008b), e.g. (57c); Antonius (ibid.) says it appears "Spesyale qem talba infinitivo komensa senenso!" ('Especially when such an infinitive begins a sentence!'):

---

[88] Couturat and Leau (1907/1979:87) give these forms without glosses.

[89] This might appear to be an unusual translation for an infinitive form, but it is the gloss which Cárdenas (1923:I:89) gives. The same is true of the next form.

[90] This word is not homophonous with the preposition that marks indirect objects (*ka*), unlike the equivalent word in e.g. English.

(57a)    Mi  dez-i      a    manj-i[91]    to
             I      want-PST  *a*   eat-INFIN   it
             'I wanted to eat it'

(57b)    A   xanti         lo-s  ne    facil-e
             a   sing-INFIN   it-is  not   easy-ADV
             'It is not easy to sing'

(57c)    To-s  facil-e     kritik-i
             it-is  easy-ADV  criticize-INFIN
             'It is easy to criticize' (ibid.)

### 4.6.5    Participles

Reformed Esperanto has fewer participles than Esperanto: an active participle ending in *-ente*, and a passive participle ending in *-ate*. Only one Aiola participle is mentioned in ARG (2005), the passive participle, which ends in *-ata*. In Mondlingvo the present, imperfect, and future participles, like their infinitive counterparts, contain *-ent-*, *-ant-*, and *-ont-* respectively, but end in *-a* rather than the *-i* of the infinitives, e.g. *amenta, amanta, amonta*. Perio has present and past participles, e.g. *vida* 'seeing', *vidata* 'having seen'.

The past participle of Neo, ending in *-at*, also serves as the passive participle, e.g. *el sar amat* 'she is loved' (Alfandari 1961:39). Alfandari (ibid.:38) gives *-ande* as the suffix for the present participle (apparently the only other participle of the language), e.g. *dande* 'en donnant'; he (ibid.) states, "Du PARTICIPE PRÉSENT dérive l'adjectif en *anda*: **los viros fartandas** les hommes qui partent; **los fartandas** les partants".

In Olingo past tense forms and past participles have the same ending, *-ita*, and this form is also the passive participle. The present participle ending is *-ata*. These participles are converted into adjectives by replacing the *t* of these endings with *d*, e.g. *pirsata* 'piercing' (participle), *pirsada* 'piercing' (adjective) (Jaque 1944:34). Nouns derived from participles have *do* as their last two segments instead of the sequence *ta* of the participles, e.g. *qolpata* 'beating' (participle), *qolpado* 'beating' (noun) (ibid.).

In Farlingo the past, present, and future active participles have the endings *-ine*, *-ane*, and *-une* respectively, while the suffixes for the past, present, and future participles are *-ite*, *-ate*, and *-ute*. There is also an adverbial form (i.e. "деепричастие" (Farber and Farber 2005)) corresponding to each of the active participles; these end in *-in*, *-an*, and *-un*.

There are many participial forms in Hom-idyomo. The three synthetic active participles are the preterite, present, and future, marked by the suffixes *-inte*, *-ante*, and *-onte* respectively, e.g. *do₂minte* 'having just slept', *do₂mante* 'sleeping', and *do₂monte* 'having to sleep'. As for passive participles, on the one hand Cárdenas (1923:I:74) states that "The passive participle ends in *áta*, as in *do₂máta*, 'slept', 'asleep'", but on the other hand three lines below on the same page he says, "In the compound conjugation, the passive participle has two endings: *ata*, with the auxiliary *esti₂* and *ite*, with the auxiliary *havi₂*. The former takes the plural form, but the latter

---

[91] Recall that the past tense suffix and the infinitive suffix are homophonous.

does not".[92] In the tables below are some analytic active participial forms of Hom-idyomo (examples from Cárdenas 1923:I:96-7, I:112):

| pres. | pres. partic. of *esti2* + pres. act. particip. | estante ma2čante 'being walking' |
|---|---|---|
| imm. pret. | pres. partic. of *esti2* + pret. act. particip. | estante ma2činte 'having just walked' |
| fut. | pres. partic. of *esti2* + fut. act. particip. | estante ma2čonte 'being ready to walk' |
| antepres. | pret. partic. of *esti2* + pres. act. particip. | estinte ma2čante 'having been walking' |
| double pret. | pret. partic. of *esti2* + pret. act. particip. | estinte ma2činte 'having just walked' |
| undefinable pret. | pret. partic. of *esti2* + fut. act. particip. | estinte ma2čonte 'having just been ready to walk' |

Table 4.54: *Hom-Idyomo Analytic Active Participles Formed with* Esti2

| imm. pret. | pres. (act.) partic. of *havi2* + pass. partic. in *-ite* | havante mandukite 'having walked' |
|---|---|---|
| double pret. | pret. (act.) partic. of *havi2* + pass. partic. in *-ite* | havinte mandukite 'having had eaten' |
| undefinable fut. | fut. (act.) partic. of *havi2* + pass. partic. in *-ite* | havonte mandukite 'having to have eaten' |

Table 4.55: *Hom-Idyomo Analytic Active Participles Formed with* Havi2

One might take the following statement to mean that in Arlipo adverbial forms of participles can have subjects which are not clausal subjects (unlike in Esperanto): "gerundio (kaptante, kaptinte, ktp.) esat uzebla ech por neekvala subjekti" ('a "gerundio" (kaptante, kaptinte, etc.) is usable even for different [?] subjects', Vitek (n.d. b)).

### 4.6.6   Voice

The passive of Mondlingvo, unlike that of Esperanto, is synthetic: one makes passive forms from active ones by means of the prefix *p-/pa-* (the former variant being used with vowel-initial stems, the latter with consonant initial ones). (The passive marker of Volapük is also *p-*, and so one might think that it was borrowed into Mondolingvo.)

Passives in the DLT Intermediate Language are synthetic, involving the suffix *-ajt-*. For example, the past, present, and future passive forms of *skrib'i* 'to write' are *skrib'ajt'is*, *skrib'ajt'as*, and *skrib'ajt'os* respectively.

---

[92] One might think it odd to call participles ending in *-ite* "passive participles" since they often (if not always) are found in active forms, e.g. in the analytic indicative forms in Table 4.48 above. Cárdenas (1923) does not present any paradigms of passive forms in which they occur, although one might expect that such forms could exist in the language.

Ido has both synthetic and analytic passive forms. The latter are created with a form of the verb *esar* 'to be' and a passive participle (as in Esperanto) while the former involve the affixation of forms of *esar* to the root. Some of these passive forms are below:

| | | |
|---|---|---|
| past indicative | esis amata | amesis |
| present indicative | esas amata | amesas |
| future indicative | esos amata | amesos |
| conditional | esus amata | amesus |
| present infinitive | esar amata | amesar |

Table 4.56: *Some Passive Forms of Ido*

Perio also has synthetic passive forms, and they are not constructed in a uniform manner:

| | active | passive |
|---|---|---|
| present infinitive | vidi 'to see' | vidih 'to be seen' |
| past infinitive | vidati 'to have seen' | vidai 'to have been seen' |
| present indicative | mi vidit 'I see' | viditt 'I am seen' |
| imperative plural | videts 'see' | videtts 'be seen' |
| present participle | vida 'seeing' | viditah 'seen' ("in the present") |
| past participle | vidata 'having seen' | vidah '("who has been") seen' |

Table 4.57: *Active and Passive Forms of Perio (after Couturat and Leau 1907/1979:6)*

Atlango has a reciprocal prefix, *bi-*, as in e.g. *biami* 'to love each other', while in Neo there is a reciprocal suffix, *-uc-*, as in e.g. *amuci* 'to love each other'.

## 4.7    Prepositions

Ido has some prepositions which do not come from Esperanto, including *alonge* 'along(side)', *segun* 'according to', and *til* 'until, up to'. *An* "expresas relato di kontigueso o di apogo, tale ke la kozo kontaktas o preske" ('expresses a relation of contiguity or support such that the thing is in contact or almost so', de Beaufront 1925/2005:58). The semantic range of *de* is narrower in Ido than in Esperanto since in Ido *di* has the meaning of possession and of "la relato generala di ul objekto" ('the general relation of some object', ibid.:61). While Esperanto *antaŭ* 'before' is used in a locative or a temporal sense, Ido has different prepositions for these meanings, *avan* and *ante* respectively.

In Arlipo one may omit a preposition "se la signifo esat tute klara ech sen il" ('if the meaning is completely clear even without it', Vitek (n.d. b)).

The sequence *er* occurs at the end of all Nov-Esperanto prepositions of more than one syllable. De Saussure (1926:8) states that this sequence "ne estas gramatika finajo" ('is not a grammatical ending') and apparently he does not consider it a suffix of any kind, as he says (ibid.) that "ji estas nedisigebla parto de la radiko" ('it is an inseparable part of the root').

There are several Mondlingvo prepositions which are not of Esperanto origin, including *to*, which Couturat and Leau (1907/1979:88) gloss as 'à'. Among the prepositions of Farlingo are *on* 'about' and *from* 'from, out of'.The prepositions of Mondlango include *alen* 'into', *escept* 'except', *konter* 'against', and *spite* 'in spite of'.

Virgoranto uses the prepositions *of* and *an* to express the genitive and dative cases respectively, e.g. *Buko of Claudia* 'Claudia's book' (Winkelhofer 2007b), *Me givar an Claudia buko* 'I give Claudia the book' (ibid.). *Per* 'by, through' introduces agents in passive constructions.

Olingo prepositions, unlike those of Esperanto, apparently always take accusative pronominal objects, a.g. *qun mi* 'with me' (Jaque 1944:31), *unu de linu* 'one of them' (ibid.:28).

Intero replaces the Esperanto accusative suffix appearing after prepositions with the meaning of movement to(wards) with *en-* attached to the preposition. This language has some prepositions which are identical to endings forming words of different correlative series:

| am | ' at (time)' |
| e | 'in (place)' |
| el | 'by (instrumental)' |
| en | 'to (place)' |
| es | 'of (possession)' |
| om | 'of (quantity)' |

Table 4.58: *Some Prepositions of Intero (after Thompson2007a)*

The preposition *en* seems to have more than just a literal directional meaning, given the following examples, from the "Babel Text" (Thompson 2007b):

(58a)  Kay  loy   diris   un   en aliu
       and  they  said  one  en another

(58b)  moy  konstru-u     en  moy   urbo
       we   build-IMPER  *en*  we     city

One might think that the preposition *es* is unncessary, since there is a genitive case suffix. Thompson (2007a) says about this preposition, "it does not completely replace the Esperanto *de*. The word **de** is still used in descriptions, e.g. **bildo de Johano** means 'picture of John'[,] which does not indicate that John owns the picture, but only that he is in it". *Om* corresponds to the Esperanto preposition *da*, but there is a difference between them: as Thompson (ibid.) says, "*om* reverses the syntax", i.e. in Intero the phrase stating the quantity follows this word (and perhaps one could argue that it is a postposition rather than a preposition; otherwise one might have to say that the quantity phrase is the object of the preposition). Thompson's (ibid.) example is *libroy om dekduo*, which is equivalent to *dekduo da libroj* in Esperanto.

As already mentioned, in Sen:espera prepositions are indicated by the suffix *-o*, but this ending is not unique to prepositions, since it is also found on correlatives. Examples of Sen:esepera prepositions are *anto* 'before', *caso* 'because of', and *emelanto* 'behind'; *lo* is the equivalent of *je* in Esperanto. Henning either conflates or confuses the classes of prepositions and conjunctions since the following words are labelled in his dictionary (1995b) as prepositions (as well as being -*o* final): *anco* 'also', *o* 'and', *ro* 'or', *sedo* 'but', and *seo* 'if'. *Ceo* 'that' is also labelled as a preposition; I assume that this is the conjunction 'that' rather than the demonstrative 'that'. In Henning (ibid.) two words, *do* and *codo*, are both glossed 'of', but the difference between their meanings (if there is one) is not explained; the latter seems to be made up of *co* 'with' and *do*. For that matter, there are two words for 'with', *co* and *cono*, and again there is no statement about any differences that there might be between them.

Couturat and Leau (1907/1979:7) say of the prepositions of Perio that they "offrent des formes corrélative du sens", but based on the examples which they give the meaning relationships among similar forms does not seem to be as regular as in the correlative system:

| | | | |
|---|---|---|---|
| an 'hors de' | | | in 'dans' |
| aq 'avant' | | eq 'entre' | iq 'after' |
| par 'pour' | | per 'au moyen de' | pir 'contre' |
| sar 'sous' | sur 'sur' | | sir 'au-dessus de' |
| za 'depuis' | | | zi 'jusqu'à' |

Table 4.59: *Some Perio Prepositions*

Nouns, verbs, and adjectives can be derived from them by the attachment of the appropriate suffix, e.g. *paru* 'friend (M)'. The name of the language itself is due in part to such a process: *peri* 'être intermédiaire' (from *per*), *perio* 'l'intermédiaire'. Adverbs can be derived from prepositions by zero derivation, i.e. the adverbial suffix -*e* is not attached, e.g. *sir* 'more than', *in* 'inclusively'.

Atlango allows its definite article (*le*) to be contracted and attached to at least some prepositions, "I pronunso, literaturo kay poezyo" ('in speaking, literature, and poetry', Antonius 2008b), e.g. *dil* (from *di* 'of'), *sul* (from *su* 'on'), *sobrel* (from *sobre* 'above').[93] The preposition *ka* is the marker of dative case, e.g. *ka purto* 'to/for the harbor' (ibid.). It can also appear as an affix (without its vowel), at least with some personal pronouns, e.g. *mik* 'to me' (from *mi* 'I/me').

In Neo there is a relatively large number of contractions of prepositions and definite articles. All of them involve the deletion of the vowel of the article, as well as of its final -*s* if it is plural, and of the final consonants of the preposition, if it ends in one or two consonants, with the exception that *in* loses its vowel instead and has a vowel inserted before *l*. For example, *al* is the contraction of both *a* + *lo* and *a* + *los*. Below is a list of these forms, along with the prepositions from which they are made:

---

[93] Antonius (2008b) says, "aw simple ne uzili ta artiklo!" ('or simply do not use this article!'); one of the examples which he then gives is *di popol* 'of the people' (MT).

| prep. | prep. + art. | meaning | prep. | prep. + art. | meaning |
|---|---|---|---|---|---|
| a | al | 'à, vers, en' | pe | prel | 'par' |
| da | dal | 'de (provenance)' | po | pol | 'pour' |
| de | del | 'de' | pre | prel | 'avant' |
| do | dol | 'apres' | pri | pril | 'au sujet de' |
| dre | drel | 'derrière' | pro | prol | 'pour, en faveur de' |
| dun | dul | 'pendant' | she | shel | 'chez' |
| gre | grel | 'malgré' | su | sul | 'sous' |
| in | nel | 'dans, en' | tra, trans | tral | 'au-delà' |
| kon | kol | 'avec' | tru | trul | 'à travers' |
| on | ol | 'sur' | um | ul | 'autour' |
| | | | ver | vel | 'vers' |

Table 4.60: *Prepositions and Contractions of Preposition + Article in Neo (after Alfandari 1961:45)*

Other prepositions of Neo include *ab* 'a partir de, depuis, de (*orig[ine]*)', *dep* 'depuis', *fra* '*dans* (temps)', e.g. *fra un mes* 'dans un mois' (Alfandari 1961:460),[94] *inte(r)* 'entre', *les* 'selon', e.g. *Les lo korispondent del A.F.P in Kayro* 'selon le correspondent de l'A.F.P. au Caire' (ibid.:189, tr. 188), and *us* 'jusqu'a'. In addition to functioning as a preposition *gre* is used as a conjunction:

(59)  … gre   it   sar   sem   lo   plu   dufa
      although it   is   always the   more   difficult
'… bien qu'elle est toujours la plus difficile' (ibid.:48)

There is no accusative suffix in Romániço; the preposition *je* precedes direct objects of clauses whose word order is not SVO:

(60a)  Brutus   has   pugnalijen   Julius.
       Brutus   did   stab          Julius
       'Brutus stabbed Julius.'

(60b)  Je Julius Brutus has pugnalijen.
       (same meaning)

(60c)  Je Julius has pugnalijen Brutus.
       (same meaning)  (Morales n.d. c)

In addition *je* introduces direct objects of nouns[95] (i.e. it corresponds to an objective genitive marker), e.g. *amo je Deo* 'love of (for) God' (ibid.), participles, e.g. *amanta je patro* 'loving a father' (ibid., cf. *amanta patro* 'a loving father' (ibid.)), and adverbs, e.g. *concerne je via létero* 'concerning your letter' (Morales n.d. m).

Concerning Esperloja Sulky (n.d.) says (apparently contradicting himself), "Every subject and object is marked with a preceding preposition. The preposition can be omitted if the meaning is clear without it and the utterance follows the normal subject-

---

[94] There is a single word meaning 'in a month' *frames*, as well as words meaning 'in a week' and 'in a year', *fravek* and *fraanyo*.
[95] or rather, NPs which would be direct objects if they were arguments of a verb.

verb-object word order". He does not give the form of these prepositions. Also about prepositions is the following rather confusing statement (ibid.): "A set of modifier prepositions is provided to mark a modifier as modifying a preceding modifier." The Esperloja word for possessive 'of' is *dua*.

The DLT Intermediate Language distinguishes among locative (including directional), temporal, and other senses of prepositions by attaching *ie-* to them when the first of these is involved and *iam-* for the second (and nothing for other senses), e.g. *ie-en Nederlando* 'in the Netherlands' (Schubert 1986, MT), *iam-en la venonta jaro* 'in the coming year' (ibid., MT), *en tiu signifo* 'in that meaning' (ibid., MT). In Esperanto several prepositions, e.g. *en*, *sub*, take nominative or accusative complements (depending on whether they mean location in/at or movement towards). In the DLT Intermediate Language *da*, *de*, and *je* also have this property. For example, when *de* marks the objective genitive its complement is in the accusative (e.g. *La acêtado de librojn* 'The buying of books', ibid., MT), otherwise it is nominative. *Je* has its complement in the nominative when it marks location in time (with times and dates), e.g. *Je la dudeksepa de februaro* 'On the 27th of February' (ibid., MT), and when it "enkodukas mezurindikon" (ibid.) its complement bears accusative marking, e.g. *La dua eldono estas je dudek guldenojn pli kosta ol la unua* 'The second edition costs 29 guilders more than the first' (ibid., MT). *Pe* rather than *je* is the "indefinite prep[ositio]n" (Wells 1969:91) of the DLT Intermediate Language.

Hom-idyomo does not have an accusative case suffix for nouns (although there are accusative forms of some pronouns). The preposition *a* marks NPs which are direct objects (among other things), although it is sometimes optional, and in fact sometimes is not supposed to be used. Cárdenas (1923:I:128) says about this preposition:

> It serves to indicate the objective case and also to express cause, the end of a period of time or the terminus or goal of a movement. *Maria dilektay a Julio.* If we said, *Maria dilektay a Julio*, it would not be plain whether Julius was the lover or the person loved. When this preposition governs the dative or the accusative case, it may be omitted if there is no danger of ambiguity; otherwise it should be used.

Shortly after this (pp. I:128-9), he gives more instructions:

> Keep the preposition *a* (to) in the regimen of complements before any proper noun, or designating a person. [...] If there are several complements governed by the preposition *a* keep the first one and change the second for another preposition if possibly [sic].
>
> In case the direct complement is followed by another complement governed by the preposition *a* the first *a* is omitted. Ex.: Li invitey lia maritino *a* dineri; mi liveray Eduard *a* lia patro.
>
> In case the complement is not a proper noun, every body [sic] is free to put there the preposition *a* or not, according to his own judgment, but avoiding amphibiology.

In the following sentence there is both a direct and an indirect object, and neither is preceded by *a*, i.e. the pattern is the same as in English:

(61)  Bi  ofeɾ-ay  me  una  veɾa  banketo.
      you  offer-PRES  me  *a*  true  banquet
      'You offer me a real banquet.'  (ibid.:I:11)

The verb *plačiɾ* 'to please' sometimes, but not always, occurs with complements governed by *a.*:

(62a)  Perhapse  plač-ay  a  bi  una  angleza  kolacyono
       perhaps  please-PRES  *a*  you  an  English  breakfast
       'Perhaps you would like an English breakfast'  (ibid.:I:11)

(62b)  Tio  no  plač-ey  a  la  señoɾino
       this  not  please-PST  *a*  the  lady
       'This did not please the lady'  (ibid.:I:59, tr. I:60)

(62c)  Cio  no  plač-ay  me
       that  not  please-PRES  me
       'I do not like that'  (ibid.:I:40)

Aside from marking "the end of a period of time" *a* apparently can also be used for location in time, given the following example:

(63)  La  pɾofesoɾo  iɾ-oy  a  medicin-iɾ  a  cia  señoɾo
      The  professor  go-FUT  *a*  see-INFIN[96]  *a*  that  gentleman

      a  la  14ª.  hoɾo.
      *a*  the  14th  hour
      'The professor will call to see that gentleman at two o'clock in the afternoon.'  (ibid.:I:139, tr. I:141)

There are three prepositions which Cárdenas (1923:I:129) glosses as 'of' in his list of prepositions, *da*, *de*, and *di*. *Da* "indicates quantity, contents, measure, substance of which a thing is made" (ibid.) while *de* "denotes possession, an event, the person or thing that performs an act, or the prompting motive or reason of the act: *libɾo de Tomas*, 'Tomas' book'; *la dio de pluvyo*, 'the rainy day (day of rain)'; *pasyono de Kɾisto*; *vojajo de nupcyo* 'we[d]ding trip'; *fabɾiko de gantos*" (ibid.). Cárdenas (ibid.) says the following about *di*: "In all cases in which 'of' cannot be logically rendered by *da*, *de*, *from*, *pɾi* or *en*, it should be rendered by *di*: *la pɾovincyo di Salto*, 'the province of Salta'."

Below are two instances of *di* in texts in Cárdenas (1923):

---

[96] Given the translation, *mediciniɾ* means something like 'to see' in the sense of a doctor seeing (i.e. examining) a patient.

(64a)  sinon  anke  libeɾ-iɾ  le  di  multas eɾoɾos, defektos  kay

but  also  free-INFIN  them  *di*  many  mistakes defects  and

vicyos …
vices
'but also to free them from many mistakes, defects and vices …' (ibid.:I:7)

(64b)  Pawlo  absten-ay  se  di  komodo,  familyo,  patɾyo

Paul  abstain-PRES  him-/herself  *di* comfort  family  country

kay  homa  gloɾyo
and  human  glory
'Paul forsakes comfort, family, country and human glory' (ibid.:I:46)

At least in (64a) one might have expected *fɾom* to appear, which according to Cárdenas (ibid.:I:130), "indicates extraction or starting point in time or space, and also the person who sends one something or whom one has just seen". It might be difficult for a user of Hom-idyomo to choose correctly between *de* and *di*; Cárdenas (ibid.:I:131) states, "Care should be exercised in the use of the prepositions *de* and *di*. In doubtful cases, however, there is no serious objection to interchanging them". The objective genitive is sometimes indicated by *de*, e.g. la ekpɾeseso de mia gɾato 'the expression of my gratitude' (ibid.:I:18), but *da* also sometimes has this meaning, e.g. la fabɾikado kay vendo da beveɾajos alkoholas 'the making and sale of alcoholic drinks' (ibid.:I:35, tr. I:37). The example below shows Cárdenas' inconsistency in a different context, with the verb *dependiɾ* 'to depend'; interestingly he is also inconsistent in the preposition that he uses in the English version of it:

(65)  Cio  depend-ay  di  las  resuɾsos[97]  ke  la  lekso

That  depend-PRES  *di*  the  resources  that  the  law

pɾoukuɾ-in  kay  da  la  kapablo  de la  Judico
provide- SUGGEST  and  *da*  the  capability  of the  judge
'That depends upon the means provided by law and on the ability of the Judge' (ibid.:I:47)

There are also several prepositions which correspond to the English preposition *for* in one of its meanings. To convey the meaning 'for the sake of' *pɾo* is used, while *tɾoke* means 'in exchange/return for', *poɾ* is used for "destination, purpose or desire" (ibid.:I:131), and *foɾ* "indicates supposition, exchance [sic], cause or time" (ibid.:I:130). Cárdanas (ibid.) says further of this last preposition, "Whenever the English 'for' cannot be logically rendered by *poɾ, peɾ, paɾ, pɾo, puɾ, a fin di*, it should be rendered by *foɾ*". Below is an example of the use of *poɾ* which might not fit the function that Cárdenas gave it:

---

[97] I believe that this spelling may be an error and should be "resuɾcos".

(66)     Mi pens-ay    cia no est-ay     laboʑo poʑ mensos
        I   think-PRES  that not be- PRES work   poʑ months
        'I think that ought not to be a work of months'  (ibid.:61)

The Hom-idyomo preposition *at* 'at' (apparently from English) "denotes location, place or position" (ibid.:129). Cárdenas (ibid.) states, "In case of hesitation between *en* and *a*, use *at*". The verb 'to enter' takes *at* (ibid.:I:68, I:76) which one might find suprising. Another preposition which fairly clearly was borrowed from English is *intu* 'into', although its use may be more restricted than that of *into*: Cárdenas (ibid.:I:130) says that it "denotes the change from one condition into another", giving the example *Tʑansfoʑmivi tias petʑos intu panos* 'Change these stones into bread loaves'. Cárdenas (ibid.:I:129) states that *en* ('in, at') "denotes location, a thing, time, form, manner, and circumstances, but never the terminus of a movement". Below are some sentences in which it occurs:

(67a)    En longa tempo mi  no  hav-ay       mandukite  una  kolacyono
        in   long  time  I    no  have-PRES   eaten        a      breakfast

        tante   savoʑa  kiel tia.
        as      tasty    as    this
        "It is a long time since I have tasted a breakfast as this.'  (ibid.:I:11)

(67b)    …  principalc  kwandc  csc  kulmin-ay       cn  la    bono
             prinicipally  when    they  culminate-PRES  in  the   good
        '…specially when culminating in the good'  (ibid.:I:11-12, tr. I:12)

(67c)    En kaso  de asalto,  robo,     rikso,         etc., ki   vokay a  la
        in   case   of assault  robbery quarreling  etc.  who calls  *a*   the

        Policio?
        police
        'in case of assault, robbery, quarreling, etc., who calls the police?'
        (ibid.:I:42)

(67b) may seem to go against what Cárdenas says about *en*, since arguably *la bono* is the terminus of a metaphorical movement.

ARG (2005:53-4) lists the "commonly used" prepositions of Aiola, including *atu* 'at', *enu* 'in', *frentu* 'in front of', *hintru* 'behind', *underu* 'below', *apudu* 'beside', *parmu* 'among', *delu* 'from', *deru* 'away from', *toru* 'toward', *lengu* 'along', *gansu* 'throughout (a region)', *kausu* 'because of', *trotsu* 'in spite of', and *naku* 'according to'. It will be seen that many of these do not seem to come from Esperanto; some apparently were borrowed from English. There are also "compound prepositions" (ibid.) in Aiola, consisting of two prepositions (with -*u* being deleted from the first one). Among these are *alunderu* 'to under', *delfrentu* 'from in front of', *sinsanteu* 'since before', and *djispostu* 'until after'.

The Aiola preposition *vau* is called "The Additional Object Preposition" by ARG (2005:55). ARG (ibid.:55-6) says of it:

In addition to their direct object, some verbs take an additional object to complete their meaning which is not in one of the categories covered by the common prepositions given above such as source, recipient, origin, destination, etc. The general preposition **vau** exists in Aiola to cover the large number of these cases since the use of a special preposition for each case would be cumbersome. Thus, **vau** is translated in a variety of ways in English, but there is no ambiguity because the meaning is clearly indicated by the particular verb used.

The following examples (ibid.:56) give an idea of the range of verbs appearing with *vau*:

(68a)    Dea  kompar-ant-as        albergoi  vau  moteloi.
             she    compare-PROG-PRES  inns      vau    motels
             'She is comparing inns <u>and/to/with</u> motels.'

(68b)    Dea  miks-iz-is         la     faruno  vau    la     sukero.
             she    mix-CAUS-PST   the    flour   *vau*   the    sugar
             'She mixed the flour <u>and/with</u> sugar.'

(68c)    Plea  separ-[a]u         la     magazinoi  vau  la     jurnaloi.
             please  separate-IMPER  the    magazines  *vau* the    newspapers
             'Please separate the magazines <u>from</u> the newspapers.'

(68d)    La    profesoro plenizis      la     balono  vau  heliumo.
             the    professor fill-CAUS-PST the    balloon *vau* helium
             'The professor filled the balloon <u>with</u> helium.'

(68e)    Plea  help-au      mi  vau  lern-are     Aiola.
             please  help-IMPER  mi  *vau*  learn-INFIN  Aiola
             'Please help me <u>to</u> learn Aiola.'

(68f)    Deo  est-is    akuz-ata            vau  rabato   ce    murdajo.
             he    be-PST  accuse-PASSPARTIC  *vau*  robbery  and  murder
             'He was accused <u>of</u> robbery and murder.'

(68g)    Deo  est[i]s   absolv-ata          vau   murdajo.
             'he   be-PST  acquit-PASSPARTIC  *vau*   murder
             'He was acquitted <u>of</u> murder.'

In Aiola verbs can be derived from prepositions other than *vau* and *kyu* by deleting the prepositional suffix *-u* and attaching verbal suffixes to them; as ARG (2005:57) puts it, "prepositions … may be verbified". The resulting verbs have the meaning of the verb 'to be' and the preposition from which they are derived:

(69a)    La    floro-i      on-is     la    tablo.
             the    flower-PL  on-PST  the    table
             'The flowers <u>were on</u> the table.'

(69b)    Tibwo  proh-as    vuza  helpajo.
            this     for-PRES  your  help
            'This is for your help.'  (ibid.)

ARG (ibid.) states that "Verbification results in a more compact form which is sometimes stylistically preferable".

    Aiola prepositions can only be heads of phrases which are constituents of verb phrases; the corresponding words which are heads of phrases inside noun phrases are "links" (ARG 2005:4) and are different in form from prepositions, being derived from them by the attachment of *ji-* and *jy-* to consonant- and vowel-initial stems respectively. For example, from the prepositions *postu* 'after' and *anteu* 'before' are derived the links *jipostu* and *jyanteu*. The following sentences (ibid.:59) contain links:

(70a)    Plea   don-au         alu  mi    libro  jipartu  lingwo-i.
            please  give-IMPER  to   me   book  about    language-PL
            'Please give me a book about languages.'

(70b)    Dea  far-is     la     komparajo  je  pomo-i    jivau   orango-i.
            she  do-PST    the   comparison  of apple-PL  jivau   orange-PL
            'She did the comparison of apples and/to/with oranges.'

(70c)    Mi  atcet-os   la    libro  skribata          jikyu  la     autoro.
            I   buy-FUT    the   book   write-PASSPARTIC  by     the    author
            'I will buy the book written by the author.'

(70c) is interesting (if there is not an error in it) because it shows that even if a participle takes what would be a prepositional phrase in e.g. English, the phrase is headed by a link and not a preposition if that participle modifies a noun.[98] In any case, the formal distinction between prepositions and links eliminates a potential source of ambiguity: as ARG (ibid.) points out, there are two interpretations associated with sentences such as *He read the book in the room* due to the fact that the prepositional phrase can be a constituent of the verb phrase headed by *read* or the noun phrase headed by *book*. These two interpretations are expressed by different sentences in Aiola (ibid.:59):

(71a)    Deo  leg-is     la    libro  enu  la     tcambro.
            he   read-PST  the   book   in   the   room
            'He read the book (while he was) in the room.'

(71b)    Deo  leg-is     la    libro  jyenu  la     tcambro.
            he   read-PST  the   book   in    the   room
            'He read the book (that was) in the room.'

---

[98] Thus the difference between prepositions and links as set out in ARG (2005:59) is not accurate (again assuming there is no error, and assuming that participles count as verbs), since *jikiyu la auotoro* 'by the author' is modifying *skribata* 'written', although the latter is in turn modifying the head noun *libro* 'book': "When a preposition occurs in a prepositional phrase which modifies a verb, it is called a preposition in Aiola; when a preposition occurs in a prepositional phrase which modifies a noun, it is called a link."

The Aiola links *je* and *ye* do not have prepositional derivational sources, although they both correspond to some meanings of the English preposition *of*. ARG (2005:60) calls the former "the general purpose link" and the latter "the possessive link". As its name indicates, *ye* marks possession, e.g.:[99]

(72a)  la      tcaro   ye    miza    frato
       the     car     of    my      brother
       'the car of (owned by) my brother'

(72b)  la      fotografuro  ye    Maik
       the     photograph   of    Mike
       'the photograph of (used by) Mike.' (ibid.:62)

*Je* has a variety of meanings, including that of the objective genitive of Latin, e.g. *la skribajo je la libro* 'the writing of the book' (ARG 2005:61). The other meanings listed for it in ARG (ibid.:61-2), and some of the examples given there, are: "a state/property-subject or degree-subject relation for an abstract noun derived from a noun or adjective", e.g. *la celsenso je la edificio* 'the height of the building', "a part-whole relation", e.g. *la kapo je la tcevalo* 'the head of the horse', "a kinship relation", e.g. *la matro je Dik* 'the mother of Dick', "a superordinate-subordinate or subordinate-superordinate relation, e.g. la redjo je la fransanoi *'the king of the French'*, la padjio je le redjo *'the page of the king'*, "a group-member or member-group relation", e.g. *komiteo je* profesoroi 'a committee of professors', *membro je la komiteo* 'a member of the committee', "a representation-object relation", e.g. *la fotografuro je Maik* 'the photograph of Mike', "a container-contents relation" e.g. *taso je kafo* 'a cup of coffee', "an object-environment relation", e.g. *la personoi je Frans* 'the people of France', *la insketoi je la somero* 'the insects of the summer', "an origin relation", e.g. *An je Verdain Gabloin* 'Anne of Green Gables', "an including-set relation", e.g. la pluste-bono je la libroi 'the best of the books'. The subjective genitive is not marked by *je*, but with the link *jikyu* 'by', e.g. *la amajo jikyu Helen* 'the loving of (by) Helen' (ibid.:62).

It may not come as a surprise that Linguna has a large inventory of prepositions, many of which do not come from Esperanto, or which are different in form from their Esperanto equivalents, as can be seen in the following table. The definitions are from Goeres (2007); I have modified some of them:

---

[99] ARG (2005:62) states, "English 'of' is translated as **ye** when it expresses a possessive relation, i.e. one of ownership or usership and is equivalent to 'owned by' or 'used by' in English". One might point out that "usership" does not fall under possession in a strict sense, so the range of meaning of *ye* is slightly broader than just possession, though much narrower than that of English *of* or the genitive case of e.g. Latin.

| amfi | 'to/from both sides of, taking/taken from both sides of, gripping/seizing both sides of s.th.' |
|---|---|
| antílocau | 'in place of, instead of, in default of' |
| arribau | 'farther above' |
| congré | 'in conjunction with, in harmony with, aided by, in accordance with' |
| dal | 'as to, at, from the viewpoint of, when dealing with, concerning' |
| diá | 'owing to, in consequence of, as a result of' |
| dra | 'by (as author)' |
| dre | 'sailing close-hauled, hard a-starboard, close to/by the wind, against the wind' |
| dysau | 'at a distance from, standing away from, refraining from, desisting from, keeping one's distance from, "to say nothing of", "let alone", taken away from, alienated from, enticed away from' |
| garau | 'almost, about, roughly, round about, around, approximately' |
| hamá | 'simultaneously with, at the same time as' |
| im | 'alongside with, in conformity with, compliantly to, conformably to, according to, in the degree of, as to, along' |
| isclu | 'except, but, not counting, save, excluding' |
| meth | 'made of' |
| parau | 'sideways of, (passing) by, sideways, abeam, askance, askew, aside, far apart from' |
| piedau | 'at the foot of' |
| piera | 'made for, meant for' |
| qvau | 'in favour of, preferring' |
| salvau | 'save, except, irrespective of, without prejudice to, notwithstanding, with reservation as to, subject to' |
| sequum | 'according to' |
| spreau | 'in front of, in view of, frightened before, with fears against or in anguish before, before a person's very eyes, worrying very much in the presence of, confronting, warding off, face to face with' |
| syn | 'together (with), in concert, jointly, in company unitedly' |
| usque | 'up to, until, till' |
| versau | 'towards, in direction to' |
| versus | 'versus (in a lawsuit against)' |
| via | 'by way of, via' |

Table 4.61: *Some Prepositions of Linguna*

There are two synonymous prepositions in Linguna which assign dative to their objects, *ob* and *objase* 'thanks to, owing to'. (However, there is another preposition *ob* meaning 'somehow opposite, encountering, towards, opposing, coming to meet, running to meet, meeting halfway, brought against, met on the way, lying opposite to'.) As in Esperanto, some prepositions take a nominative complement with a meaning of location and an accusative one with a meaning of motion towards. This set includes *arrier* 'behind, at the back, abaft, aft, astern of' and *migau* 'among(st), amidst'.

## 4.8    Conjunctions

Several of Esperanto's daughters have some conjunctions which are rather different from their equivalents in Esperanto, as the following table shows:

| Esperanto | Reformed Esperanto | Ido | Olingo | Romániço |
|-----------|-------------------|-----|--------|----------|
| aŭ 'or' | u | o, od [100] | or | aut |
| ĉar 'for, because' | nam | nam | por, pro [101] | nam |
| kaj 'and' | e | e, ed | e | et |
| sed 'but' | sed | ma | sed | mas |

Table 4.62: *Some Conjunctions in Esperanto and Daughter Languages*

The Farlingo equivalents of the English conjunctions 'and', 'but', and 'or' are *ve*, *bat*, and *o*. The Hom-idyomo word for 'or' is *oẑ*.

The Perilo word for 'and' is *ka*. Although the word for 'and' in 1919 Esperantida, 1923 Esperantida, and Nov-Esperanto as presented in de Saussure (1926) is *kay* (and thus phonetically identical to Esperanto *kaj*), this is not true of all of the languages created by de Saussure; in Lingwo Internaciona it is *e* and in Esperanto II it is *ey*. The Mondlingvo words *aŭt*, *kar*, and *parĉe* are glossed by Couturat and Leau (1907:88) as 'ou', 'car', and 'parce que' respectively; *parĉe* appears to have come from French. At least some of the conjunctions of Perio are derived from prepositions by means of the suffix *-s*, e.g. *aqs* 'before' (from *aq* 'before'). The Mondlango words for 'and', 'if', and 'or' are *ay*, *if*, and *or*. The Esperloja conjunctions *pue*, *txarue*, and *kue* mean 'and', 'because', and 'that' respectively.

In Olingo, unlike in Esperanto, but as in English, the demonstrative 'that' and the conjunction 'that' have the same form:

(73a)  to    ur-i        sufiqa
       that  be-PRES  sufficient
       'that is sufficient' (Jaque 1944:29)

(73b)  hi  tre  sonte  trovita  to    hi  avita  ne    una  hareno  sur  hia  qapo
       he  very  soon  found   that  he  had    not   a    hair    on   his  head
       he very soon found that he had not a hair on his head' (ibid.:28)

As we have seen (section 4.2.3.2), *to* can also appear at the beginning of relative clauses.

In addition to having two classes of words that correspond to prepositions of e.g. English (v. sec. 4.7), Aiola has two parts of speech corresponding to conjunctions, *connectives* and *conjunctions*. The latter are used only to join clauses; if smaller units (phrases, words) are to be joined, the former are employed. What is more, there are three words for 'and' and two for 'or', as the following table shows:

---

[100] In the case of both *o/od* and *e/ed*, "on uzas prefere la formo sen *d*, kande l'eufonio permisas" ('one preferably uses the form without *d*, when euphony permits' (de Beaufront 1925/2005:78).
[101] *Por* is equivalent to English 'for' and like it is both a preposition and a conjunction, while *pro* is equivalent to 'because'.

| ce | 'and' |
|---|---|
| cwe | 'and (jointly)' |
| cai | 'and (sequentially)' |
| ca | 'or (inclusive), and/or' |
| co | 'or (exclusive)' |
| mau | 'but' |

Table 4.63: *Aiola Connectives (from ARG 2005:68-9)*

The use of some of these is shown in the examples below (ibid.:69):

(74a)   Cirli    cwe  mi  mandj-os pomo-i   ce   pirno-i.
         Shirley  and  I    eat-FUT  apple-PL  and  pear-PL
         'Shirley and I will eat apples and pears.'

(74b)   Deoi  lud-is    cai  dorm-is.
         they  play-PST  and  sleep-PST
         'They played and then slept.'

(74c)   Tinokte moi pov-as     and-are   alu  teatro ca alu   restoranto.
         tonight  we  can-PRES  go-INFIN  to    theatre or to   restaurant
         'Tonight we can go to a theater or to a restaurant.'

(74d)   Pren-au      la  libro-i   co  la    cinemo-i.
         take-IMPER  the  book-PL  or  the   movie-PL
         'Take the books or the movies.'

ARG (2005:69) says, "Use **cwe** to denote that the people or things referred to by two terms or phrases are acting simultaneously or jointly". This seems to mean that only noun phrases could be joined with *cwe*, and not all noun phrases, e.g. it might be hard to see how direct objects could be joined with it.

    There are several sources of Aiola conjunctions. Coordinating conjunctions consist of the prefix *i-* and a connective. For examples, there are conjunctions corresponding to each of the connectives meaning 'and':

(75a)   Dea  kur-is    ice  dea  lud-is.
         she  run-PST  and  she  play-PST
         'She ran and she played.'

(75b)   Dea  kur-is    icai  dea  lud-is.
         she  run-PST  and  she  play-PST
         'She ran and then she played.'

(75c)   Mai  ovid-is    icwe  dai   dans-is.
         we  watch-PST  as    they  dance-PST
         'We watched as they danced.' (ibid.:70)

Some subordinating conjunctions consist of a connective and the suffix *-ke*, and some are made up of a preposition (without its prepositional marker *-u*) and *-ke*. The conjunctions of the former type are: *ceke* 'in addition to', *cweke* 'as', *coke* 'unless', and *mauke* 'although'. (The connectives *cai* and *ca* cannot be bases for conjunctions.) Among the latter type are *dumke* 'during', *metke* '(by means of that)', *trotske* '(in spite of that)', *proke* '(in return for that)', *anstatke* '(instead of that)', *pertke* 'about that'.[102] [103] Below are sentences containing some of these (ibid.:70, tr. subordinate clauses p. 71, main clauses MT):

(76a)  Metke          mi   uzis   komputero, mi   faris   la    laborato
       by.means.of.that  I    used   computer   I    did    the   work

       mutce  pluse  rapide.
       much   more   quickly
       'By using a computer I did the work much more quickly.'

(76b)  Trotske          da   nivetcis,  mi   andis.
       in.spite.of.that  it   snowed     I    went
       'In spite of the fact that it snow[ed] I went.'

(76c)  Mi   felitcas    pertke      dea   lernantas   Aiola.
       I    am.happy    about.that   she   is.learning   Aiola
       'I am happy that she is learning Aiola.'

Coordinating conjunctions can appear as the first word of a sentence; ARG (2005:71) states, "In this initial position a coordinate conjunction conjoins the immediately following clause with *what has been stated previously*". The following examples are then given (ibid.):

(77a)  Lwav-au      la   geciroi. Icai   zorg-au      la    kato.
       wash-IMPER   the   dishes.  and    take.care.of   the   cat
       'Wash the dishes. And then take care of the cat.'

(77b)  Mi studis   la   libro. Imau  mi aune   no   kompren[a]s la   topiko.
       I  studied  the  book   but   I  still   not  understand   the   topic
       'I studied the book. However I still do not understand the topic.'

Aiola has two underived conjunctions, *ci* 'if' and *cu* 'whether or not', which ARG (ibid.:71) calls *dependence* and *independence conjunctions*. An example containing the latter is below:

---

[102] ARG's (ibid.:70) instructions on the derivation of these words is "drop the **-u** ending [of the preposition] and apply the **-ke** suffix to the root". However, in the case of *metke* an additional change has been made: the second of the preposition (*medu*) has become voiceless. Another change has also occurred in the derivation of *proke* – the third consonant of the preposition (*prohu*) has been deleted.

[103] The glosses here are those in ARG (ibid.:70); on the next page is the statement "The English translations given in parenthesis are a literal translation of the Aiola but would not be used in correct grammatical English. Instead, a gerundive construction [i.e. a construction containing a gerund] or some other paraphrase would be used". Examples of grammatical translations of clauses introduced by these conjunctions are then given, and I shall use some of them in the translations of the sentences just below. The gloss 'about that' should also be in parentheses, but it is not. In fact, 'during' is also not a grammatical gloss (for *dumke*) since *during* does not introduce finite clauses; I would have given 'while' as a gloss here.

(78)   Mi and-os    cu              da    pluv-os.
       I   go-FUT   whether.or.not  it    rain-FUT
       'I will go whether-or-not it rains.' (ibid.)

There is another underived word *ke*, which to some extent is equivalent to the English conjunction *that*; however, it apparently is not classified as a conjunction by ARG (2005) but as a "clausal word" (ibid.:64). ARG (ibid.) gives the following description of this type of word: "A clausal word occurs at the beginning of a clause which is used as the subject or object of a larger main sentence." In particular, *ke* is called "the declarative clausal word" (ibid.). The following sentences (ibid.:65) illustrate its use:[104]

(79a)  Ke    dea  kompren-is       la    satso      surpriz-is    mi.
       that  she  understand-PST   the   sentence   surprise-PST  me.
       'That she understood the sentence surprised me.'

(79b)  Deo  no   sab-is      ke    dea  kompren-is      la    satso.
       he   not  know-PST    that  she  understand-PST  the   sentence
       'He didn't know that she understood the sentence.'

*Ke* is not used to introduce result clauses, as English *that* is; rather *ake* (the "consequence conjunction" (ibid.:72)) fulfills this role, e.g.:

(80)   La cinemo  est-is    sowa tedo     ake mi  depart-is.
       the movie   be-PST    such.a bore   that I  leave-PST
       'The movie was such a bore that I left.' (ibid.:72)

*Ake* is classified as a conjunction by ARG (2005), unlike *ke*.[105]

### 4.9   Particles

Baza apparently lacks the interrogative particle *ĉu* of Esperanto since, according to Hoover (n.d.), "Simple questions (requiring 'yes/no' response) will be formed simply by adding 'Jes' or 'No'[106] at the end of the senten[c]e, and adding a question mark. 'Vi amas mi, jes?'".

Hom-idyomo has the same interrogative particle as Esperanto, spelled *ĉu*. The word *an* sometimes seems to have the same function as *ĉu* (although Cárdenas (1923) does not explicitly say this), e.g.:

---

[104] ARG (ibid.:64) states, "The use of **ke** indicates that the speaker/writer is affirming the truth of the sentence which follows it". However, this is not the case, given the following sentences:

(ia)   Mi esperas ke <u>voi</u> gozos la bela sablo.
       'I hope that you will enjoy the beautiful sand' (ibid.:45)

(ib)   Tsi estas importenta ke vu komprenas tibwo.
       'It is important that you understand this.' (ibid.:86)

[105] ARG (ibid.:72) says, "Note that a true conjunction and not just the clausal word **ke** is necessary for this function. The use of ke alone following any verb such as **sabare, esperare, dirare** which can take a **ke**-clause as object would lead to ambiguities".

[106] Presumably this is an error and "Ne" was meant here.

(81a)  An  iŕay  bi  poŕ  negoyos?
      Q[?]  go  you  for  business
      'Do you go there for business?' (Cárdenas 1923:I:97, tr. I:99)

(81b)  Kay  an  estay  justas  las  sentencos?
      and  Q[?]  are  just  the  sentences
      'And are the sentences just?' (ibid.:I:47)

Note the different word order in these two examples: the former has subject-verb inversion, while in the latter the subject is at the end of the sentence.

Ido has an interrogative particle but a different one than Esperanto, namely *kad* (or *ka*) rather than *ĉu*. The interrogative particle of Perilo is *ku*. The equivalent particle of Arlipo is *cha*, while that of Mondlango is *cu*.

The Aiola word *ei*, one of two "head words" (as they are called in ARG (2005)) is roughly equivalent to Esperanto *ĉu*, but it does not occur in all the contexts in which *ĉu* does. It is placed before statements to create *yes-no* questions from them, as *ĉu* is, e.g.:

(82)  Ei  voi  vol-as  lern-are  Aiola?
     Q  you.PL  want-PRES  learn-INFIN  Aiola
     'Do you want to learn Aiola?' (ARG 2005:51)

It is not used in alternative questions; rather, the head word *ea* appears as their first word:

(83)  Ea  moi  and-as  enu  Sabadon  co  Dimantcon?
     Q  we  go-PRES  in  Saturday  or  Sunday?
     'Do we go on Saturday or on Sunday?' (ARG 2005:51)

In Esperanto *ĉu* can also occur after a statement, creating a tag question, but this is not true of *ei* or *ea*; in this situation one of the two "tail words" (ARG 2005:51) appears, *einou* if the statement is affirmative, *eiya* if it is negative, e.g.:

(84a)  Dai  kis-ant-is,  einou?
      they  kiss-PROG-PST  Q
      'They were kissing, weren't they?'

(84b)  Voi  no  trink-as  vino,  eiya?
      you-PL  not  drink-PRES  wine  Q
      You don't drink wine, do you? (ARG 2005:51)

Further, *ei* and *ea* do not appear in indirect *yes-no* questions, as *ĉu* does; instead clausal words derived from them, *kwei* and *kwea*, are used, e.g.:

(85a)  Mi  demand-is  kwei  dea  ven-is.
      I  ask-PST  whether  she  come-PST
      'I asked whether she came.'

(85b)   Mi demandis kwea     deo trinkas       lo     teho co   lo
          I   ask-PST  whether  he   drink-PRES  GART  tea   or    GART

          kafo.
          coffee
          'I asked whether he drinks tea or coffee.' (ibid.:65)

There is a "[f]ocus [p]article" (Medrano 2002:sec. 11) in Mondezo, *ya*, which precedes the constituent to be focussed. Presumably because of its presence in the language, "Word order changes, as in Esperanto, are not required [to show focus]" (ibid.). Medrano (ibid.) gives the following examples:

(86a)   Ya   ni   parol-an     Svedezo.
          FOC  we   speak-PRES  Swedish
          '*We* speak Swedish'

(86b)   Ni ya parolan Svedezo.
          'We *speak* Swedish' (cf. Esperanto *Parolas ni la Svedan*)

(86c)   Ni parolan ya Svedezo.
          'We speak Swedish' (cf. Esperanto *La Svedan ni parolas*)

## 4.10    Interjections

The interjections of Ido include *psit!*, the function of which is to attract someone's attention, and *sus!*, which serves "por ecitar al defenso, al persequo" ('to arouse to defence, to pursuit', de Beaufront 1925/2005:80). Among the words in Cárdenas' (1923:I:145-6) list of interjections of Hom-idyomo are *alas!* 'alas!', *asee!* 'enough', *ea!* 'up, go ahead!', *magaƶi* 'would that, God grant', and *retƶe!* 'go back!'. Linguna has the interjection *ach* 'ah, alas', which was probably taken from German.

## 5    Syntax

In general those who write descriptions of artificial languages do not devote much space to syntax, and much or most of what they say about it concerns word order. This chapter will only deal with word order; some other syntactic issues come up briefly in Chapter 4.

### 5.1    Word Order

Esperanto's "baza ordo" (Wennergren 2005:493) is SVO and this is true of most, if not all, languages based on it. However, some of these languages differ from Esperanto in the degree of freedom of word order they have, as we shall now see.

Mondezo's "standard word order" (Medrano 2002) is SVO. This is also true of *wh*-questions, i.e. *wh*-phrases stay *in situ* (1a). However, there is *wh*-movement in relative clauses (1b):

(1a)    Kato    kapt-an       kio?
        cat     catch-PRES    what
        'What does the cat catch?'  (MT)

(1b)    Hundo   vid-an     rato,   kiu     kato     kapt-in
        dog     see-PRES   rat     which   cat      catch-PST
        'The dog sees the rat, which the cat caught' (ibid., MT)

Mondlango's "basic word order" (anon. n.d. b) is SVO and "There is no inversion" (ibid.): one marks a *yes-no* question by placing *cu* in sentence-initial position. However, there is subject-verb inversion in some, but not all, Mondlango *wh*-questions:

(2a)    Kiel    far-an     yia    famil-an-o-s?
        How     do-PRES    your   family-member-NN-PL
        'How is your family?'

(2b)    Kiel yi    faran?
        How  you   do-PRES
        'How do you do?'

(2c)    Kio    es-an      yia    nomo?
        What   be-PRES    your   name
        'What is your name?'

(2d)    Kiel   la    aferos    ir-an?
        how    the   affair-PL  go-PRES
        'How are things going?'  (anon. n.d. d)

Both prenominal and postnominal positions are allowed for attributive adjectives, e.g. *guda libro*, *libro guda* 'good book' (anon n.d. b, MT)

Ido is not as free in word order as Esperanto, although there is a fair degree of latitude, due largely to presence of the accusative suffix -*n*:[1] de Beaufront (1925/2005:86) states, "Sen esar fixigita rigoroze e neflexeble, l'ordino dil vorti esas submisata en Ido ad ula reguli, quin impozas logiko e klareso" ('Without being strictly and inflexibly fixed, the order of the words is governed by some rules, which logic and clarity impose'). The "normal ordino" (ibid.:87; 'normal order') of major clause constituents is SVO. In Esperanto nouns and their attributive adjectives do not have to be adjacent (although they usually are):

(3)    Ĉevalo-j-n      ili    tie  ĉi  havas  tre    bonajn
        horse-PL-ACC  they   here   have  very  good-PL-ACC
        'They have very good horses here' (Wennergren 2005:57, MT)

As Ido lacks adjectival agreement markers, it does not sanction such separation: de Beaufront (1925/2005:86) states, "L'*adjektivo* devas preirar o sequar nemediate la substantivo quan ol relatas" ('The *adjective* must immediately precede or follow the noun to which it relates'). De Beaufront (ibid.) says further that "tre longa" ('very long') adjectives or those with complements occur in post-nominal position. This sounds like a rule of the language, but earlier (p. 22) he says similar things as "konsili" ('advice') on adjectival position, so it appears that it is not an absolute requirement.[2]

Aiola *wh*-questions and relative clauses must involve *wh*-movement.[3] According to ARG (2005:51) subject-verb inversion does not take place in questions: "Unlike

---

[1] For issues of word order connected with the presence/absence of -*n*, v. section 4.14.
[2] These "konsili" are:

    1e Se l'adjektivo esas plu longa per du o tri silabi kam la substantivo, pozez lu dop ica ...
    2e Se uzesas plura adjektivi, pozez li dop la substantivo ...
    3e Se l'adjektivo havas komplemento, e precipue komplementi, pozez unesme la
        substantivo ...
    4e Se l'adjektivo esas tam longa kam la substantivo, o preske, konsultez l'eufonio, e
        nome evitez la hiati, se to esas posibla ...
    (' 1. If the adjective is longer than the noun by two or three syllables, put it after the latter
      2. If several adjectives are used, put them after the noun
      3. If the adjective has a complement, and especially more than one complement, put the
      noun first
      4. If the adjective is as long as the noun, or almost as long, consider the euphony,
      namely avoid hiatus, if that is possible')
[3] This is not true of *wh*-questions in Esperanto; Wennergren (2005:331) says, "La KI-vorto normale staras komence de la demanda frazo" and later (ibid.) states:

    Se oni iam metas demandan KI-vorton frazfine anstataŭ frazkomence, oni kreas tre fortan emfazon pro la malkutimeco. Tia demando estas ofte eĥa demando por rekonfirmo de io ĵus aŭdita:
    • *Mi volas, ke vi donu al mi vian novan aŭton!* — *Vi volas **kion**?!* Demando miksita kun forta surprizo.

The *ofte* here indicates that a question with a *wh*-word in situ does not have to be an echo question. ARG's (2005:51) actual words about *wh*-questions are, "The **h**- words [i.e. *wh*-words] in Aiola are either used by themselves or placed initially in a sentence." It is not clear to me what happens when there is more than one *wh*-word in a question -- must they all move?

English and many other languages the verb and the subject of an affirmative sentence in Aiola cannot invert places to form a question." However, on the same page are two *wh*-questions in which inversion has taken place, both containing the verb 'to be' (some language designers seem to have trouble analyzing *wh*-questions containing this verb), e.g. *Hwo estas vuza namo?* 'What is your name?'.

In Aiola, attributive adjectives can only occur in prenominal position, according to the following statement by (ARG 2005:37): "When using adjectives to modify a noun, always place them after the article and before the noun." Possessive adjectives are also placed prenominally. If what ARG (2005) calls a "relational adjective" (v. section 4.4) and an attributive adjective both modify a noun, the attributive adjective must occur before the relational adjective:

(4a)  veha  libr-a-i        vendo
      old   book-ADJ-RA   seller
      'old book seller (book seller who is old)'

(4b)  *librai veha vendo  (ibid.:12)

ARG (2005:81) gives directions about where one particular word can occur: "in Aiola **anku** ['aslo, too'] always *directly precedes* its modified word or phrase. In contrast, in English 'also' and 'too' usually follow it, although 'also' can precede verbs and adjectives. Therefore ... it is sometimes unclear which word 'also' is modifying [in English]."[4] The same rule applies to *nuru* 'only'. The following sentence (ARG 2005:8) indicates that Aiola has some freedom in word order: "Just as in English, in Aiola one can place emphasis or prominence on words or phrases by arranging their order in the sentence." ARG (2005) does not say what the possibilities are for this, but they may be limited by the fact that there is no case inflection in Aiola.

According to the following remark from Vitek (n.d. b), Arlipo has a quite free word order, although I doubt that "any" order would be approved of: "**Vortsekvo:** zhenerale irgala, ma on preferat meton adjektivo avan ila substantivo, kaj je frazo komencon per subjekto, sekvanta[5] per verbo kaj objekto" ('Word order: Generally any, but one prefers to put an adjective before its noun and for a sentence to begin with [the] subject, followed by verb and object').

One might think that Intero is strict with respect to word order, given that Thompson (2007a) says, "Intero mandates SVO syntax in order to eliminate the accusative *-n*". However, there is *wh*-movement in this language, meaning that objects can precede subjects and verbs, as shown by the following example from the "Babel Text":

(5)    ... por        vidi u    urbo  kay u    turo,  kiuy  u
       in.order.to  see  the  city  and the  tower  which the

---

Apparently in Esperanto even in relative clauses *wh*-movement is not absolutely obligatory; Wennergren (2005:463) says, "Rilata KI-vorto staras (normale) komence de la subfrazo kiel frazenkondukilo", the key word here being "normale".

[4] Compare the following remarks (Wennergren 2005:262) about Esperanto *ankaŭ*: "Tre ofte oni aŭdas, ke *ankaŭ* troviĝu ĝuste antaŭ tio, al kio ĝi rilatas. Tio estas tre bona ĝenerala konsilo por klara stilo, sed ĝi tute ne estas deviga regulo, kiel oni ofte ŝajnigas. [...] Kiam *ankaŭ* koncernas KI-vorton, estas eĉ regulo, ke oni metu *ankaŭ* poste."

[5] I believe that this is an error for *\*sekvata*, the present passive participle.

homidoy    konstru-is
men        build-PST
(Thompson 2007b)

In fact, although real-world knowledge will tell us that *kiuy* is the object of the relative clause here, one can easily imagine examples in which it would not be clear whether *kiuy* was the subject or the object.

Cárdenas (1923:I:153) says of Hom-idyomo, "The general rule is to place first the subject, then the verb, and then the complements". Later on the same page he states, "In the position of the adjectives there is freedom of choice within the limits of clearness and euphony". With respect to personal and reflexive pronouns he states (ibid.:I:30), "The pronouns ending in *e* [i.e. accusative forms] must be placed after the verb, when there are other pronouns; otherwise, they may either precede or follow the verb, at pleasure".

In Hom-idyomo it seems that generally *wh*-movement takes place in *wh*-questions and relative clauses, e.g.:

(6)    kiel    pas-ey    bi    la    nokton?
       how     pass-PRET you   the   night
       'How did you pass the night?'  (ibid.:I:10)

Note that subject-verb inversion has taken place in this example, which also generally seems to occur in wh-questions. Cárdenas (ibid.:I:153) explicitly says that it takes place in *yes-no* questions if they do not begin with *ču*, giving the example *Estay bi maŗitata?* 'Are you married?' However, this does not always seem to be the case: consider the following question, which does not contain *ču* (or *an*, v. section 4.9) and in which subject-verb inversion has not taken place:

(7)    Una  gŗatifiko  da 20  fŗankos pŗo  la   konducisto  sufic-oy?
       A    tip        of 20 francs  for  the  chauffeur   suffice-FUT
       'Will a 20-franc tip to the chauffeur be enough?'  (ibid.:I:117, tr. I:118)

In the following example the *wh*-phrase is in an unusual position, between the subject and the verb:

(8)    Wel, kay cias sufŗagos kio repŗesentay?
       well and those votes what represent
       'Well, and what do those votes represent?'  (ibid.: I:158)

Since the Esperanto accusative affix is "not required" (Hoover n.d.) in Baza, and since the information that it would give is to be indicated by the SVO order of this language, one might think that word order might not be permitted to vary much (if at all) from SVO (aside from possibility of the change of order caused by *wh*-movement of direct objects, and Hoover (ibid.) does not give any indication about whether there is *wh*-movement in Baza).

However, Neo, which does not have an accusative marker for nouns, does apparently have a "une grande liberté" (Alfandari 1961:66) of word order. Alfandari (ibid.) states that "la préoccupation majeur" is "toujours de s'exprimer de façon claire et euphonique". The basic word order for statements is SVO, but pronominal objects usually are placed before the verb, as in French:

(9a)      Luis    kof-ir     lo dom
            Louis  buy-PST  the house
            'Louis acheta la maison'

(9b)      Mi   te          am-ar
            I    you.SG.ACC   love-PRES
            'je t'aime' (ibid.)

An emphasized pronoun follows the verb, e.g. *Mi amar te* 'c'est toi que j'aime' (ibid.). Further, the subject and the object can both occur before the verb ("*surtout en poésie*" (ibid.)) or after it, the permitted orders being OSV and VSO, i.e. the subject "est le plus près du verbe" (ibid.):

(10a)    lo  fel   Jan    vid-ir
           the girl  John   see-PST
            'Jean vit la jeune fille'

(10b)    Jan lo fel vidir
            'La jeune fille vit Jean' (ibid.)

(11a)    mir-ar        l     infan lo    matro
           look.at-PRES  the  child  the  mother
            'l'enfant regarde la mère'

(11b)    mirar lo matro l infan
            'la mère regarde l'enfant' (ibid.)

The position of an attributive adjective in relation to its noun is fairly free, both pre- and postnominal positions being permitted, "selon ce qu'on juge être plus harmonieux, ou selon le poids ou la nuance que l'on veut donner à l'adjectif même" (ibid.). The example that Alfandari (ibid.) gives is that *un gran klezo* and *un klezo grand* 'a big church'. However, if there is more than one attributive adjective modifying a noun, "il est préferable" (ibid.) for them to follow it.

    There is one area in which Alfandari specifies a strict order: if there are both indirect and direct object pronouns preceding a verb the order is IO DO:

(12a)    mi ve            le          prezent-or
           I   you.PL.DAT  him.DAT   present-FUT
           'je vous le présenterai'

(12b)    me  luy       ve        prezent-or
           I    her.DAT  you.PL.ACC  present-FUT
           'je vous présenterai à elle' (ibid.:34)

148

Ekselsioro has a fixed word order. Greenwood (1906a:5-6) explains the advantage of this:

> In languages other than English, many will have noticed, much to their annoyance, apparently the peculiar shuffling up of the words of very many sentences, not only in spoken phrases, but poetical license … The reader of such must perforce perform a feat of intellect, with many weary moments, in divining the inner meaning of the author of such phrasing, however beautiful, and from a general point of view is absolutely unnecessary to express our thoughts. […]
>
> All the above hindrances are at once swept away in EKSELSIORO, the words taking a straight forward [sic], invariable position of: –Subject, Verb, Object, (except Passive) with various qualifiying or modifying phrases in their normal place, but entire in themselves. No splitting up of the sequence in a prepositional or adverbal phrase, the qualifying adjective, always precedes the noun. These vital rules transcend all, and allow immense facility of expression and obviation of inflection.

Esperloja also has a fixed order with respect to some words: Sulky (n.d.) states: "Modifiers (adjectives and adverbs) always follow the noun or verb they modify". Sulky (ibid.) speaks of the "normal subject-verb-object word order"; this does not seem to be the only possible order.

Winkelhofer (2007a), writing about Virgoranto, also uses "normal" in describing word order: "In normalen Aussagesätze ist die Satzstellung Subjekt-Prädikat-Objekt." The English version of this sentence, in Winkelhofer (2007b), might give a slightly different impression, that SVO is the only order for statements, since the word "normal" does not appear in it: "The word order is Subject-Verb-Object in statements." What is more, earlier in this webpage, in the section on case, Winkelhofer says, "Acussative [sic] is identical to the nominative. So it is necessary to have a strict word order (S-V-O)". (No such statement appears in this section of Winkelhofer 2007a.)

With respect to questions Winkelhofer (2007a) says, "In Fragesätze ist die Wortstellung Prädikat-Subject-Object". However, the example she gives immediately after this has the subject after the verb: *Kvo esas balo* 'Where is the ball?' Further, several questions in Winkelhofer (2007a, b) and in her blog entries about Virgoranto have the subject before the verb, e.g.:

(13)　Kvod　ju　mek-ar?
　　　what　you　do-PRES
　　　'Was machst du?' (<http://pauker.at/VIP/Andoromeda/blog/326/>)

There apparently is *wh*-movement in relative clauses as well as in *wh*-questions. The following sentence in Winkelhofer (2007a, b) is intriguing as the *wh*-word itself has been moved but the other element of its phrase remains *in situ* (assuming an analysis in which *kvand jaros* is a constituent):

(14)　Kvand　　ju　havar　jaros?
　　　how.much　you　have　years
　　　'How old are you?'

Winkelhofer (2007b) makes the following statement about the word order of relative clauses: "To mark the different [sic] between subject and object relations in the relative clause, the word order is decisive."[6] She then gives the following examples:

(15a)    Girlo, kvile me vidir, esir bela.
        Girl who I/me saw was beautiful
        'The girl, who I saw, was beautiful.'

(15b)    Girlo, kvile vidir me, esir bela.
        Girl who saw I/me was beautiful
        'The girl, who saw me, was beautiful.'

As we have seen, Reformed Esperanto involved some grammatical changes from Esperanto, including the elimination of the accusative suffix and of the article. So that instances of ambiguity would not arise as a result of these, Zamenhof "recomandait" (Couturat and Leau 1907/1979:29) SVO order and "de placer l'adjectif de manière à le rattacher clairement à son substantif" (ibid.). He was not making strict prescriptions; Couturat and Leau (ibid.:30) say, "c'étaient là de simples conseils pour les commençants, non des règles obligatoires qui imposeraient une construction rigide et supprimeraient sans nécessité la liberté de l'ordre des mots". Thus Reformed Esperanto is different from Virgoranto (as it is described in Winkelhofer (2007b)).

Morales (n.d. d) describes Romániço word order in non-technical terms: "In Romániço, the way one determines who does what to whom in a sentence is by the order in which the words appear. In general, the person or thing appearing most immediately before the verb performs the action; the person or thing appearing after the verb is the object or complement." OSV and OVS orders (as well as other orders?) are permitted if the object is preceded by the preposition *je* (v. section 4.7). There is *wh*-movement in Romániço, including of objects; Morales (n.d. g) says, "Interrogative pronouns generally come first in a sentence, but beyond this the word order of Romániço sentences does not alter when made into questions, as it often does in English sentences". This also seems to be true of relative clauses. Below is a sentence containing a *wh*-moved object:

(16)    Cui mi volde moren nun?
        who I CONDIT love now
        'Whom could I love now?'

This sentence indicates that the preposition *je* is not required before objects which have undergone *wh*-movement and that there is no subject-aux inversion, in line with Morales' statement.[7] Subject-verb inversion has taken place in (R) below, contrary to the just quoted statement and the statement in Morales' (n.d. e) discussion of question formation, "One should bear in mind that, in Romániço, the subject of the sentence

---

[6] She does not make such a statement in the German version of this page, Winkelhofer (2007a).
[7] However, it is possible for je to precede an object that has undergone *wh*-movement:

(i)    Je cuo signífiquen ...?
      je what means
      'What does ... mean?' (Morales n.d. f)

(the person or thing performing the sentence's action) is whatever person or thing that most closely precedes the verb":

(17)     Cua coloro es la celo en via mundo?
         'What color is the sky in your world'

This may be due to confusion of subject and subject complement. Perhaps this only happens when the verb is *eser* 'to be', given the following sentences:

(18a)    Cuale   vi    standen?
         how     you   fare
         'How are you?'

(18b)    Cua     es via    nómino?
         what    is your   name
         'What is your name?'

(18c)    Cuale   vi    nòminijezen?
         how     you   are.named
         'What is your name?'  (Morales n.d. f)

It appears that there does not have to be inversion with *eser*:

(19)     De      ube      vi     es?
         from    where    you    are
         'Where are you from?' (ibid.)

Morales (n.d. c) explicitly rules out the possibility of stranding prepositions: "In Romániço, prepositions never end a sentence, as they often do in English".

Morales (n.d. h) discusses the positions of adjectives in Romániço, making the basic statement, "In general, one places adjectives before the people or things they describe unless one wishes to underscore their difference from other nouns of the same type". Among the examples that he gives to illustrate this are the following:

(20a)    Donen   li   ad   la    extrania    alumno-adiutanto.
         give    it   to   the   weird       intern
         'Give it to the weird intern (the only intern we have, who's a weirdo).'

(20b)    Donen li ad la alumno-adiutanto extrania.
         'Give it to the weird intern (not the normal one).'

This applies to demonstrative adjectives:

(21a)    Ecuista   parva   porcuçho
         this      little   piggy
         'This little piggy'

(21b)    parva porcuçho ecuista
         'This little piggy' (ibid.)

Morales (ibid.) continues, giving one firm restriction, "For simplicity's sake, one can almost always put the adjectives first; only the stylistically bold need think about altering that order. However, adjectives that have a complement *must* come after the person or thing being described in order to make sense".

The following statement in Holmes (n.d) indicates that E-speranto is not very free in the order of constituents of phrases: "Word sequence within phrases is quite narrowly specified by rules that in effect require the words that relate directly to the same entity to be as close together as possible." However, Holmes does not give the actual word order rules in his webpages on E-speranto, or to my knowledge, anywhere in publically available materials. The language allows more freedom in the construction of clauses and sentences; Holmes (ibid.) states, "E-speranto has rules for composing clauses out of phrases, sentences out of clauses, paragraphs out of sentences, and so on. At this level of language construction the sequence is less strictly specified, but the main problem to be solved is to reduce as far as possible the ambiguity of references between phrases, between clauses, and between sentences". Again the rules in question are not given.

Jaque's (1944:34) remarks about word order in Olingo include the following: "Basic world syntax: (a) simple sentence–"What does what to what?" (b) complex sentence–"What what does what and how to what what and why?" Place modifying words close to, and either directly before or after, the things and actions they are intended to affect." The "(a)" part of this means that the basic word order is S V DO IO; the "(b)" part is more difficult to interpret but perhaps indicates the order S V O adv./PP IO adjunct,[8] with the adjunct (which could be a prepositional phrase or a subordinate clause) giving the reason for the action; "what what" perhaps means 'adjective noun'. In any case, these orders do not hold for *wh*-questions and relative clauses (although this fact is not explicitly stated by Jaque), e.g.:

(22)    Wir    povi  I  pursi   una  bileta  al ..
        where  can   I  buy     a    ticket  to
        'Where can I buy a ticket to …' (ibid.;35, MT)

Olingo has the same word for 'not' as Esperanto, *ne*. However, the position of this word is sometimes different. Wennergren (2005:327) says of this word in Esperanto, "Normale *ne* staras antaŭ la ĉefverbo"; one of the examples that he then gives (ibid.) is *Mi ne dormas* 'I do not sleep'. Consider then the following Olingo sentences:

(23a)   I   qompri    ne!
        I   understand not
        I do not understand!' (Jaque 1944:35, MT)

(23b)   I   wanti  ne   la    qonstelon      ze    proxega
        I   want   not  the   constellations any   nearer
        'I do not want the constellations any nearer' (ibid.:29, "Excerpt from 'Song

---

[8] However, one might think the adv./PP should precede the direct object, given the next sentence in the passage just quoted; Jaque (1944) uses the term "action" for 'verb', and manner adverb or prepositional phrase with the same kind of meaning would modify the verb, if it were thought to modify any single word, and therefore should be adjacent to it.

of the Open Road' by Walt Whitman"[9])

(23c) I   devi   ne   wanti
     I   shall  not  want
     'I shall not want' (ibid.:31, "The Shepherd Psalm")

(23d) La   junega ... ne   dezirata  al   urkomi la   andrino
     the   younger  not  wishing  to  become the   wife

     de  una  elda viro
     of  an   old man
     'The younger ... not wishing to become the wife of an old man' (ibid.:28,
     "Excerpt from 'Aesop's Fables': 'The Man and his Two Sweethearts'")

In (23a-b) *ne* follows the verb while in (23c-d) it precedes the (main) verb. These latter sentences are different since the former contains a modal verb and in the latter the negated verb is a participle; they are the only relevant examples of these types in the texts in Jaque (1944) and so one could not confidently make any generalizations about the position of *ne* in relation to the main verb in Olingo. One might however note that in all the clauses containing *ne* which do not involve a modal verb or participle (a total of five clauses) *ne* follows the verb.

In Modern Esperanto an adjective can either precede or follow its noun, as in Esperanto: Lahago (n.d.:26) states, "The '-a' ending of an adjective clearly differentiates the adjective from the noun, and for this reason there can be no confusion if it is placed 'after' the noun – a usage to which some non-English-speaking Esperantists are more accustomed than we". However, given that the difference between attributive adjectives and adjectives acting as secondary predicates is indicated by word order (v. section 4.4.1) there could sometimes be "confusion" if an attributive adjective follows the noun that it modifies.

According to Henning (1995a), in Sen:esepera, "Adjectives ... typically precede the noun they describe". However, this language has free word order (at least to the extent Esperanto does); Henning (ibid.) states, "Like Esperanto, **Sen:esepera** has no fixed word order". 1919 Esperantida is also said to have free word order, although not all orders would be seen as equally good: de Saussure (1919:9) says, "La ordo de la vorton en la frazo estas tute libera, se nur la signifo de la frazo restas klara. La pley bona vortordo estas tiu, kiu estas samtempe la pley klara, la pley logika k. la pley agrabla slo la stila vidpunkto" ('The order of the words in the sentence is completely free, provided that the meaning of the sentence remains clear. The best word order is that which is at the same time the most clear, the most logical, and the most agreeable from the point of view of style').[10]

Goeres's (2004a) "régula generella" ('general rule') concerning word order in Linguna, ('general rule') is for "czio qvi sense synappartenas" (everything which

---

[9] In this text there is one other instance of *ne* following the (main) verb: *Frotale I peti ne bonfortuno* 'Henceforth I ask not good-fortune' (ibid.) and as can be seen, in this case in the original English *not* also is after the verb. However, this is not true of (23b), and in any case *ne* occurs after the verb not only in poetry, but also in prose, as shown by (23a) and by *Ji materi ne* 'It does not matter' (ibid.:35, MT).

[10] V. section 4.7 for the use of the preposition *e* as an object and subject marker with certain word orders.

belongs together in sense') to be "qviomeble próxima unu cze ália" ('near one another as much as possible'). Adjectives usually occur in postnominal position; Goeres (2004b) makes the following (somewhat difficult to understand) statement: "Stellung der Adjektive: Normalerweise fast immer nach dem Substantiv (Nur sehr kleine Adjektive können gelegentlich voranstehen); ist jedoch das Adjektiv eine die normale innere Eigenschaft [sic] des Substantivs verstärkende, ergänzende oder bestätigende Aussage, dann kommt das Adjektiv vor das Substantiv (siehe den spanischen Gebrauch)".[11] Goeres (2004a) gives an additional rule about adjectives: "cze substantivoi feminai … stipulaz strictan postposícion las adjectives resp. las adjectivois" ('with feminine nouns strict postposition of the adjective or the adjectives is stipulated').

Goeres (ibid.) also says, "Praedicato praeferinde cai saepe cze proposícies fin apperas qviel en la Língua Latina; praedicativo post la verbo apperas", an approximate translation of which is, 'A predicate preferably and often appears at the end of a proposition, as in Latin; a predicative appears after the verb'. Goeres (ibid.) concludes his section on word order by stating, "Czio ália, praecipe las adverbes posício tute líbera est; posícioi daeaz occase czangjatir en plena liberitato!", which means roughly 'Everything else, especially the position of the adverb, is completely free; positions may on occasion [?][12] be changed in complete freedom!'

---

[11] Goeres' (ibid.) English version of this is: "position of adjectives: almost always behind the noun; only very small adjectives may sometimes be placed before the noun, and else - like in Spanish - adjectives can appear only then before the noun, where they stress and complete the noun in accordance with its meaning, not bearing any new aspect."

[12] I am uncertain of the meaning of *occase* here.

# 6 Semantics

Creators of artificial languages have usually not said much about the semantics of their languages. However, as we have seen, some designers of daughters of Esperanto have been concerned with ambiguity and reducing potential causes of it. In this chapter we shall see some more evidence of this, and look very briefly at some two other issues.

## 6.1 Homonymy and Ambiguity

Neo is not without homonyms although Alfandari (1961:19) states that they "sont beaucoup moins fréquent en Neo qu'en français". He then (ibid.) gives some examples of homonymy, including *kol* ('neck' and 'with the') and *ski* ('ski' and 'to ask'). However, most of the homonymy (and that in most of the examples given by Alfandari (ibid.)) is due to the possibilities for deletion of suffixes in the language, and this operation is optional; thus many instances of potential ambiguity resulting from homonymy can easily be eliminated if one desires.

Homonymy may be an undesirable feature of an artificial language in the view of Jeffrey Henning, since he says (1995a) of Sen:esepera, "The final version of the vocabulary will attempt to reduce the number of basic morphemes to 600. As part of this effort, all homonyms will be removed from the vocabuary". Teodoro Lahago apparently saw homonymy (and polysemy?) as something to be avoided, as he (n.d.:16) gave the following as one of the properties of Modern Esperanto: "Each word with only one meaning, instead of one word having more than one meaning as is [the case] now in the living languages."

UTL has no homographs: Sabarís et al. (2001) say, "Every word has only one meaning in Esperanto, and the few exceptions have been fixed in the UTL version". Esperanto has fewer potential sources of ambiguity than at least many natural languages, but UTL goes further in this regard. In e.g. English some ambiguity arises because a prepositional phrase could be a modifier of a noun phrase or of a verb phrase. E.g. *I saw a man with a telescope* (Sabarís et al. 2001). In UTL prepositional phrases which modify NPs are preceded by the preposition *de*. Thus the following sentences have only one meaning each:

(1a)  Mi   vidis   homo-n      de kun   teleskopo.
      I    saw     man-ACC   *de* with teleskopo
      'I saw a man with a telescope, i.e. who had a telescope.'

(1b)  Mi vidis homon  kun teleskopo.
      'I saw a man with, i.e. by means of, a telescope.'  (ibid.)

Also, in UTL one can make it clear what the antecedent of a pronoun is. Sabarís et al. (ibid.) give the follow example of a passage which is ambiguous because a pronoun (*it,* in this case) has two possible antecedents: *The garden has a tree. I saw it.* In UTL if such a word is "tagged" (ibid.) the intended reading will be known:

(2a)  La ĝardeno havas arbon. Mi vidis ĝin (>ĝardeno)
(2b)  La ĝardeno havas arbon. Mi vidis ĝin (> arbo)  (ibid.)

In Esperloja a possible source of ambiguity is removed by limiting the meaning of "modifiers":

> Modifiers describe attributes intrinsic to nouns or verbs; they must be expressible as predicate modifiers that follow the copula ("...is..."). For example, "wood box" can only mean a box that is wood; it cannot mean a box for holding wood or a box that happens to be full of wood regardless of its intended purpose. Extending the example, "green wood box" can only mean a box that is wood and is green, not a box full of green wood or a green box full of wood or a wood box full of green! There is a series of little words for expressing the more common complex attribute relationships ("a box for holding wood", "á society founded by masons"). (Sulky n.d.)

## 6.2 Synonymy

Hom-idyomo has a fair number of synonyms, according to Cárdenas (1923:I:159-160):

> ... the number of synonyms has been considerably increased, and with it the vocabulary of the new language. Fortunately the excess consists mainly of international words with which most Europeans and Americans are familiar.
>
> A language so concise as to have but one word to express each idea, would not be practicable as present; it might be convenient to the listener, but not for the speaker, who would find difficulty in remembering the one word in every case. Besides, definitions would be impossible in such a language.
>
> If, however, a common language were accepted and extensively used, the academy directing it could simplify it gradually.

Goeres (2004b) shows by the following statement concerning Linguna that he favors the presence of synonyms in a language:[1]

> Immer gibt es, im Grundwortschatz, auch gute Synonyme an Stelle oder neben den nur von einer Wurzel abgeleiteten Wörtern. Das Fehlen solcher war ein fürchterliches Handicap im Altesperanto. –
> Die Leute lernen in Wirklichkeit gerne ausreichend selbständige Grundwörter, sie sind nicht so blöd, wie sie von L. L. Zamenhof eingeschätzt wurden. Die Menschen haben ein gesundes Gedächtnis. Sie sind empört, wenn sie unterfordert werden. Sie wollen mit Fug und Recht nicht für beschränkt gehalten werden.

---

[1] His (ibid.) English version of this is: "But there are always alternatives by other words instead of the derivated [sic] ones of only one root. The lack of synonyms was a hard handicap of Old-Esperanto. People are not nearly as purblind and stupid as have obviously been estimated by L. L. Zamenhof (the author of obsolete former Old-Esperanto): they like learning, they like learning other expressions, too."

## 6.3    Idioms and Non-Literal Language

The designers of some daughters of Esperanto did not look favorably on idioms and non-literal language. Concerning E-speranto Holmes (n.d. a) says, "The use of idioms, though inevitable in practice, is always to be discouraged. E-speranto should be used as a literal language, and any expression should always be given its literal meaning, unless humour is intended or poetry is being translated". Jaque (1944:34) makes a similar remark with respect to Olingo: "The idiomatic use of words and phrases should be avoided by expressing each thought in direct words and according to the literal meaning of the words." UTL does not have idioms: Sabarís et al. (2001) say, "The UTL user writes being conscious [sic] that the text is going to be machine-translated".

Cárdenas (1923:153) states with respect to Hom-idyomo:

> Words should be used and interpreted in their natural meanings and not with the figurative meanings they may have in other languages. Thus, *pesto* ['pest'] should not be used in the sense of "invective", nor *mazo* ['sea'] in that of "abundance", nor *nigza* ['black'] in that of "sad" or "gloomy". The expression, *Gladyo sitya di sango* ['sword thirsty for blood'] may be very poetical, but it is not true. A language which has not come into general use should not be employed figuratively, at least for the translation of idioms and sayings. That will come later.

# References

Anonymous (no date a) *Mondlango*. At URL < http://www.mondlango.com/english/>.

Anonymous (no date b) *Basic Grammar of Mondlango*. At URL <http://www. mondlango.com/english/grammar.htm >

Anonymous (no date c) *Questions and Answers* [about Mondlango]. At URL <http:// www.mondlango.com/ english/FAQ.htm>.

Anonymous (no date d) *Mondlango 300* (translated by Oscar Mifsud). At URL <http://www.mondlango.com/ english/ml300.htm >.

Anonymous (no date e) *Alphabet* [of Mondlango]. At URL <http://www.mondlango. com/english/ alphabet.htm>.

Anonymous (no date g) *Mondlango Course*. At URL <http://www.mondlango.com/ course/>.

Anonymous (no date h) *The International Language Ido - Questions and Answers.* At URL <http://idolinguo.org.uk/idofaq.htm>.

Anonymous (n.d. i) *Basic Grammar of the International Language Ido*. At URL <http:// idolinguo.org.uk/bgrammar.htm>.

Aitai, P. (2006) "La nova planlingvo Snifferanto". Blog entry, available at URL <http://peeteraitai.blogspot.com/2006/11/la-nova-planlingvo-snifferanto.html>.

Albani, P. and B. Buonarroti (1994) *Aga Magéra Difúra*. Zanichelli, Bologna.

Alfandari, A. (1961) *Cours Pratique de Néo*. Éditions Brepols, Brussels.

Antonius, R. A. (2008a) *Beskribo koncerne stilistiko Atlanga kay otra spesyala formadoy langall*. At URL < http://vido.net/atlango/15puntoy.htm>.

Antonius, R. A. (2008b) *Atlango*. At URL <http://vido.net/atlango/>.

Antonius, R. A. (2008c) *Mikra Vortaryo Angla - Atlango*. At URL <http://vido.net/ atlango/vortajo.htm>.

ARG [Aiola Research Group] (2005) *Aiola Essential Grammar*. Formerly available on the world wide web.

ARG (2008) *Ayola*. At URL <http://www.aiola.org/>.

Barandovská-Frank, V. (1993) "Noto pri planlingvistikaj kriterioj kaj latina influo ". *Grundlagenstudien aus Kybernetik und Geisteswissenschaft* 34.2, 89-92.

Bergen, B. K. (2001) "Nativization Processes in L1 Esperanto". *Journal of Child Language* 28:575-595.

Bodmer, F. 1944. *The Loom of Language.* W. W. Norton, New York.

Cárdenas, C. (1923). *Hom-Idyomo* (second edition). Leipzig. (apparently self-published)

Carlevaro, T. (no date) "Recenzo de Tazio Carlevaro [of Albani and Buonarroti (1994)]". Available at URL <http://ling.cuc.edu.cn/htliu/amdrec.htm>.

Carlevaro, T. and R. Haupenthal (1999) *Bibliographio di Ido.* Hans Dubois, Bellinzona, Switzerland/Edition Iltis, Saarbrücken.

Cartier, M.[1] (no date). "Novesperant". Available at URL <http://www.geocities.com /mikeheavy/novesperant.html>.

Collinson, W. E. (1924) *Esperanto and Its Critics.* London. Online version (put on the internet by Don Harlow) available at URL <http://donh.best.vwh.net/Languages /ido.html>.

Corneilus, J. (2002) *Vivling.* Available at URL <http://www.geocities.com/ baalzephon999/vivling/>.

Couturat, L. and L. Leau (1903 and 1907/1979) *Histoire de la language universelle* bound with *Les nouvelles langues internationales.* Georg Olms Verlag, Hildesheim.

Cowan, J. (2004) "Re: CHAT: another new language to check out". Posting to the Conlang Mailing List, June 29, 2004. Available at URL <http://archives.conlang.info/ dhu/toenchoe/ birkhaelphoen.html>.

De Beaufront, L. (1925/2005) *Kompleta Gramatiko detaloza di la linguo internaciona Ido.* Krayono: Ponferrada, Spain. At URL <http://es.geocities.com/krayono/kgd.pdf>.

de Graaff, R. (1997) "The EXperanto Experiment". *Studies in Second Language Acquisition* 19.2:249-276.

de Saussure, R. (under the name Antido) (1919) *Fundamento de la internacia lingvo Esperantida.* Bern.

de Saussure, R. (under the name Antido) (1923) *Fundamenta krestomatio de la internacia lingvo "Esperantida".* Bern.

de Saussure, R. (under the name Antido) (1926) *Fundamenta krestomatio de la internacia lingvo Nov-Esperanto* (2nd edition). Bern.

---

[1] Cartier's name is not given on this webpage.

Farber, M. and Farber V. (2005) *Краткая грамматика языка Farlingo*. At URL
<http:// www. farlingo.narod.ru/f_grammar.html>.

Farber, M. and Farber V. (2006) *English - Farlingo Dictionary*. At URL <http://www.
farlingo.narod.ru/anglia/ev_englingo.htm>.

Gacond, C. and A. Gacond (1967) "Okdek jaroj de esperanta vivo, 10-a parto La
reformita dialekto" (radio program). Transcript at URL <www.esperanto-
gacond.ch/ Claude_Gacond_ Radioprelego_0188.pdf>.

Gant, N. M. (1997) "More on Poliespo and its creator". Letter to the *SSILA Bulletin*
58, available at URL
<http://www.linguistlist.org/ssila/Bulletins/Archive/bull58.pdf>.

Gobbo, F. (2005) "The European Union's Need for an International Auxiliary
Language". *Journal of Universal Language* 6.1: 1-28.

Goeres, H. D. W. (2004a) *Grammatik*. At URL <http://www.linguna.de/old/html/
grammatik.html >.

Goeres, H. D. W. (2004b) *Vokabeln*. At URL <http://www.linguna.de/old/html/
vokabeln.html >.

Goeres, H. D. W. (2007) "Linguna-Sprachreichtum/Affixe". Blog entry at URL
<http://linguna.blogspot.com/2007/05/linguna-sprachreichtum-affixe.html >

Goeres, H. D. W. (2008) *Germana-Angla LINGUNA glossaro*. Blog entry starting at
URL <http:// glossaro-linguna. blogspot.com/2008/06/blog-post.html >.

Goeres, H. D. W. (n. d.). *Linguna*. At URL <http://www.linguna.de/old/index.html>.

Greenwood, F. (1906a) *Ekselsioro, the New Universal Language for All Nations.
First Lesson*. Miller and Gill, London.

Greenwood, F. (1906b) *Ekselsioro the New Universal Language for All Nations.
Second Lesson*. The Universal Language Society, Bridlington.

Grimley Evans, E. et al. (1994) "Riisma Esperanto". Available at URL
<http://ftp.stack.nl/pub /esperanto/esperanto-texts.dir/riismo.txt>.

Harrison, R. (2004) Untitled Webpage (about Esperanto sen Fleksio) At URL <http://
www.rickharrison.com/language/esf.html>.

Henning, J. (1995a) "Sen:esepera – A Reform of Esperanto". *Model Languages* 1.5.
At URL   <http://www.langmaker.com/ml0105.htm >.

Henning, J. (1995b) *Sen:esepera-English Dictionary*. At URL <http://www.
langmaker.com/ml0105x.htm>.

Henning, J. (1995c) "Meaning". *Model Languages* 1.6, part 1. At URL <http://www. langmaker.com/ml0106a.htm>.

Henning, J. (1995d) "Sidebar: Relative Terms for Relatives". *Model Languages* 1.6, part 2. At URL <http://www.langmaker. com /ml0106b.htm>.

Henning, J.[2] (no date a) *Aiola*. Formerly available at URL <www.langmaker.com/db/ Aiola>.

Henning, J. (no date b) *Farlingo*. Formerly available at URL <www.langmaker.com/db/ Farlingo>

Hietala, J.[3] (2006a) *Gramatiko de Snifferanto 27.10.2006*. At URL <http://pp.kpnet.fi/ jhii/sablo/gramatiko.html>.

Hietala, J. (2006b) *Lernolibro de Snifferanto 31.10.2006*. At URL <http://pp.kpnet.fi/ jhii/ lernolibro/>.

Holmes, N. (2008) "The European Union and the Semantic Web". *Computer* 40.8: 96-5.

Holmes, N. (no date a) *E-speranto: An Introduction to the Language*. At URL <ftp:// ftp.comp.utas.edu.au/pub/nholmes/esprnt/esprnt0.htm>.

Holmes (no date b) *The Orthography of E-speranto*. At URL <ftp://ftp.comp. utas.edu.au /pub/nholmes/esprnt/esprnt1.htm>.

Holmes (no date c) *The Sounds of E-speranto*. At URL <ftp://ftp.comp.utas.edu.au /pub/ nholmes/esprnt/esprnt2.htm>.

Hoover, G.[4] (no date) "Inter-esperanto". At URL <http://divinitychurch.tripod.com/ interesperanto/>.

Horváth, R. (no date) *Perilo*. Available at URL <http://www.posxto.com/perilo/ index.html>.

Jackson, E. L. (1918) *Gregg Shorthand Adapted to Esperanto*. The Gregg Publishing Company, New York.

Janton, P. (1993) *Esperanto* (edited by H. Tonkin, translated by H. Tonkin, J. Edwards, and K. Johnson-Weiner). State University of New York Press, Albany.

Jaque, R. S. (1944) *One Language*. J. F. Rowney Press, Santa Barbara, CA.

---

[2] This and the following webpage do not give an author's name. One might think that Henning is the author since he was the creator of the Langmaker website in which they appear.

[3] This and the following reference are anonymous, but it appears that Hietalo is the author of them.

[4] Hoover is not stated to be the author of this page, but I assume that he is the person who created it.

Jespersen, O. (1918/1921) "Artificial Languages after the World-War". In O. Jespersen (1921) *Two Papers on International Language in English and Ido* (2nd edition) (Danish to Ido translation G. Mönster, Ido to English translation G. H. Richardson), J. Warren Baxter, London, pp. 24-40.

Jordan, D. K. (1987) "Esperanto and Esperantism". *Language Problems & Language Planning* 11.2: 104-125.

Kellerman, K. F. (1909) "The Advance of International Language". *Science* New Series Vol. 30, No. 780:843-4.

Künzli, A. (2001) "René de Saussure (1868-1943) - Tragika sed grava esperantologo kaj interlingvisto el Svislando". At URL <http://esperantic.org/librejo/dbstudoj/35_Kuenzli.htm>. (*In Studio pri Interlingvistiko*, S. Fiedler and L. Haitao, eds., at URL <http://esperantic.org/librejo/dbstudoj/>.)

Lahago, T. (no date) *"Moderna Esperanto"*: *The International Scientific Language*. Heiermann, Amsterdam.

Lalov, B. (no date) *Zamenhof Would Have Approved Mondlango*. At URL <http://www.mondlango.com/ english/Lalov.htm>.

Large, A. (1985) *The Artificial Language Movement*. Basil Blackwell, Oxford.

Libert, A. R. (2000) *A Priori Artificial Languages*. Lincom Europa, Munich.

Liu, H. (2006) "Neutrality of International Languages". *Journal of Universal Language* 7:37-64.

May, R. (2006) *Texperanto*. At URL <http://www.geocities.com/ceqli/Texperanto.html>.

Medrano, V. (2002) *Mondezo: An Esperanto Dialect?*. At URL <http://web.archive.org/ web/20030216174715/planetvix.tripod.com/mondezo/>.

Medrano, V. (2007) *A Story of a Tonguesmith*. At URL <http://www.geocities.com/vixcafe/glossopoeisis.html?200723>. (link broken when checked on 24 April 2008)

Mifsud, O. (no date a) *Why Mondlango?* At URL <http://www.mondlango.com /english/ whymondlango.htm>.

Mifsud, O. (no date b) *Word-building in Mondlango*. At URL <http://www.mondlango.com/english/wordbuilding.htm>.

Monnerot-Dumaine, M. (1960) *Precis d'interlinguistique general et speciale*. Paris: Maloine.

Morales, M. (2008a)[5] *English-Romániço* [Dictionary]. At URL <http://www. romaniczo.com/en_dicionario.html>.

Morales, M. (2008b) *Dicionario di Romániço*. At URL <http://www.romaniczo.com/ dicionario.html>.

Morales, M. (no date a) *Bringing Medieval Back*. At URL <http://www.romaniczo.com/en_ indiczo.html>.

Morales, M. (no date b) *Romániço Frequently Asked Questions*. At URL <http://www. romaniczo.com/en_cuestionos.html>.

Morales, M. (no date c) *Prepositions*. At URL <http://www.romaniczo.com/ gramatico/en_ gramatico_10.html>.

Morales, M. (no date d) *Word Order*. At URL <http://www.romaniczo.com/ gramatico/en_ gramatico_15.html>.

Morales, M. (no date e) *Questions*. At URL <http://www.romaniczo.com/ gramatico/en_ gramatico_ 09.html>.

Morales, M. (no date f) *Useful Romániço Phrases*. At URL < http://www.romaniczo. com/ en _ frasos.html>.

Morales, M. (no date g) *Pronouns*. At URL <http://www.romaniczo.com/ gramatico/en_ gramatico_06.html>.

Morales, M. (no date h) *Adjectives*. At URL <http://www.romaniczo.com/ gramatico/en_ gramatico_07.html>.

Morales, M. (no date i) *Alphabet and Pronunciation*. At URL <http://www. romaniczo.com/gramatico/en_gramatico_02.html>.

Morales, M. (no date j) *Romániço Articles*. At URL <http://www.romaniczo.com/ gramatico/ en_gramatico_03.html>.

Morales, M. (no date k) *Nouns*. At URL <http://www.romaniczo.com/gramatico/en_ gramatico_04.html>.

Morales, M. (no date l) *Affixes*. At URL <http://www.romaniczo.com/gramatico/en_ gramatico_13.html >.

Morales, M. (no date m) *Adverbs*. At URL < http://www.romaniczo.com/gramatico/ en_ gramatico_08.html.

---

[5] Morales' name does not actually appear in this reference or in the other references attributed to him here, but through correspondence with him I learned that he was responsible them.

Morales, M. (no date n) *Verbs*. At URL < http://www.romaniczo.com/gramatico/ en_gramatico_11.html >.

Pankhurst, E. S. (1927) *Delphos*. Kegen Paul, Trench, Trubner & Co., London.

Sabarís, M. F.[6] (2003) *The UTL Language*. At URL <http://www.xente.mundo-r.com/utl/ UTLlang.htm>

Sabarís, M. F, J. L. R. Alonso, C. Dafonte, and B. Arcay (2001) "Multilingual Authoring through an Artificial Language". Paper given at the Eighth Machine Translation Summit, Santiago de Compostela, Spain, available at URL <http://www.eamt.org/summitVIII/ papers/franco.pdf >.

Schubert, K. (1986) Untitled "Package" of Two Documents about the DLT Intermediate Language (both dated 1986 and apparently sent as an e-mail message in 1987). At URL <http://www.geocities.com/raredata/dlt.txt>

Schubert, K. (1992) "Esperanto as an Intermediate Language for Machine Translation". In J. Newton (ed.) *Computers in Translation*, Routledge, London, pp. 78-95.

Selva, I. (2006) *Bonvenu al la reteyo de lingvo internacia* NOV-ESPERANTO *nomata anke Idiomo Mondiala*. At URL <http://espigor.w.interia.pl/Nov-Esperanto/index.html>

Sulky, L. (no date) Esperanto *by Hindsight: a Smug Redesign*. At URL <http:// members.fortunecity. com /lsulky/sulkyfamily/esperloja.html >.

Svendsen, M. (no date) *Neo – et volapükisert esperanto*. At URL <http://home.no.net/ babels/eo.html>

Talmey, M. (1938) "The Auxiliary Language Question". *The Modern Language Journal* 23.3:172-186.

Thompson, M. (2007a) *Intero*. At URL <http://www.gayvegangenius.com/languages/ intero/index.html>.

Thompson, M. (2007b) *Intero: Sample Text*. <http://www.gayvegangenius.com/ languages/ intero/babel.html>.

Vitek, L.[7] (no date a) *Bonveno al le pageni di ARLIPO!* At URL <http://www.arlipo. info/>.

Vitek, L. (no date b) *Konciza gramatiko*. At URL <http://www.arlipo.info/konciza. htm>.

---

[6] The name given on this web page is Marcos Franco, but apparently the author's full name is Marcos Franco Sabarís, as this is the name given in the following reference.

[7] I assume that Vitek is the author of this and the following two references, though no author is listed for them.

Vitek, L. (no date c) *Esprimi kaj frazi*. At URL <http://www.arlipo.info/esprimi.htm>.

Wallace, A. F. C. and J. Atkins (1960) "The Meaning of Kinship Terms". *American Anthropologist*. New Series 62.1:58-80.

Wells, J. C. (1969) *Esperanto Dictionary*. Hodder and Stoughton, Sevenoaks, Kent.

Wennergren, B. (2005) *Plena Manlibro de Esperanta Gramatiko*. At URL <http://bertilow.com /pmeg/elshutebla/pmeg_14.0.pdf>.

Winkelhofer, D. (2007a) *Virgoranto*. At URL <http://pauker.at/VIP/Andoromeda/kate_de/ 6003>.

Winkelhofer, D. (2007b) *Virgoranto in English*. At URL <http://pauker.at/VIP/Andoromeda/kate_de/6196>.

Winkelhofer, D. (2007c) Virgoranto Texte. At URL <http://pauker.at/VIP/Andoromeda/kate_de /6530 >.

Winkelhofer, D. (2008a) *Wörterbuch Deutsch-Virgoranto*. At URL <http://pauker.at/VIP/Andoromeda/ kate_de/6006>.

Winkelhofer, D. (2008b) *Wörterbuch Virgoranto-Deutsch*. At URL <http://pauker.at/VIP/Andoromeda/kate_de/6004>.

# Languages of the World

In this series: